THE TANAHILL STORY

The Carolina Years

ROBERT S. LOTT

The Tanahill Story

This book is dedicated to my beautiful wife Rebecca.
Thank you for always being there for me.

To my editor Carol Jones, whose hard work
and skill brought this book to fruition.
Thank you.

Robert S. Lott

CHAPTER ONE

SAM TANAHILL FELT COMPLETE DREAD THE MOMENT HE'D accepted Spence Rayburn's invitation to the Meyers' cotillion. His loaned suit of clothes, despite their perfect fit, does nothing to ease the displeasure he feels about the whole ridiculous affair. Sam has no ambition of becoming a southern gentleman and refuses to hold with slavery or any of its trappings. Nonetheless, growing up in the Carolinas has left him with one of two positions on the issue—agree with the practice of one man owning another or remain silent. Neither option sets well with Sam, but out of respect for his father, Owen Tanahill, Sam holds his tongue pretty well on most days.

Owen Tanahill hauls freight and sells horses and mules to most of the plantations in the Carolinas, a business that provides a decent living for Owen and Sam both. In fact, Sam fell into his current situation because he'd delivered a blooded racehorse to Spence Rayburn, one of his father's customers. Upon seeing the powerfully built bay stallion, Spence couldn't quit thanking Sam and insisted he stay and attend the Meyers' cotillion with his family.

Taking a deep breath, Sam tries to enjoy the carriage ride and the cool spring morning as he and the Rayburns set off for the Meyers' plantation. The matching set of gray horses is in an easy trot, causing a silent trance to fall over all aboard. Sam is grateful for the silence, having been thoroughly questioned by Bess, Spence's matchmaking wife, on a range of topics including the one of most interest to her—Sam's marital status. The Rayburn's two somewhat plain and overweight daughters, Newella, twenty, and Sistell, eighteen, are always at the front of Bess's mind. Their lack of suitors has become an embarrassment and something Bess has vowed to remedy.

Sitting across from Sam, the Rayburn girls peer over their fans, taking stock of everything from his collar-length black hair and dark-tanned skin, to his tall, lanky frame. Their roving eyes miss nothing and lend to Sam's discomfort. He glances over at Spence who in his fat, jovial way seems to be disconnected from everything except the oversized cigar he is chewing and smoking.

The driver slows the team as he turns onto a red cobblestone drive, passing under a massive wrought iron arch that reads, "Shannon Hill."

Spence points with his silver-knobbed cane. "Ever been here, Mr. Tanahill?"

"Yes, sir, but only hauling freight from the warehouses out on Slick Fork Creek."

"The Meyers family owns more coloreds than you can count and more land than that," Spence continues. "Some say the real decisions in South Carolina politics are made over whiskey and cigars right here on the verandas at Shannon Hill."

Bess smiles a little at Spence's statement and says, "I never knew *Mrs. Meyers* to smoke or partake."

Spence chuckles a fat man's laugh. "No doubt, Jessica Meyers does have an influence, my dear."

The red cobblestone driveway winds off through a small stand of densely overgrown hickory and magnolia trees then straightens out into a wide, tree-lined lane. The fresh plowed fields on either side of the road stretch further than the eyes can see. Sam scans the distant horizon and daydreams. The one thing the planters have that he envies with all his heart is land. Sam longs for the day when he has saved enough money to go west, where there's still land—land that hasn't felt the iron shank of a plow or the sharp tooth of a saw.

Removing the cigar from the creased corner of his mouth, Spence spits over the side of the polished carriage. "Mr. Tanahill?"

The giggling of the women brings Sam back to the present.

"Sir?" Sam replies, embarrassed.

Spence waves his cane in a wide ark. "We have arrived."

Sam surveys his surroundings as he stands to get out of the carriage. The Meyers' mansion stands on a gentle rise of ground surrounded by ancient live oaks and exquisite gardens. The trees' huge limbs are laden with long beards of Spanish moss that nearly touch the perfectly manicured lawn. The mansion's tall, white columns and wide verandas are social copies of European architecture and unspoken statements of wealth.

The red brick horse barn beyond the trees catches Sam's attention. Picketed around the barn are thirty or so of the finest matched carriage teams in all of South Carolina. Sam's father, Owen, has sold many of these very horses to the planters who own them.

Sam feels Spence give him an irritating tap on the leg with his cane, urging him to hurry. An old slave, neatly dressed in a black suit with tails and white gloves, is holding open the carriage door. Sam steps down easily and turns back to the carriage.

"Ladies." Extending his hand, Sam helps each one down from the carriage.

Mrs. Rayburn and the girls move to one side, straightening their gloves and wide-brimmed sun hats as they step down from the carriage. Nodding to Sam, Spence pauses beside Bess and extends his arm. She slides her white-gloved hand through the crook of his arm and smiles.

Bess turns to her daughters and says, "Remember, stay where you can be seen. And Mr. Tanahill, you are not going to the gallows. This is a party; you may smile."

Sam smiles. "Yes ma'am."

"Your mother should be proud of you sir. You are quite the gentleman."

"Thank you, ma'am. I'm sure she'd be glad to know that."

"Well then, Mr. Rayburn, shall we?"

Mrs. Rayburn's unexpected compliment makes it a little easier for Sam to climb the winding, red brick steps to the massive front doors of the mansion. With every step though, the lump in Sam's throat swells like rawhide. If he can just get by the introductions at the front door, perhaps he can find that place where Mrs. Rayburn didn't want her daughters standing.

The tall, lace-curtained windows of the mansion stand open allowing the breeze to carry the sounds of a lively party. The Rayburn girls giggle and whisper with their heads together as though they are children with a secret. As they reach the front door, Mrs. Rayburn clears her throat. Spence drops the cigar in a spittoon on the porch, removes his white straw hat, and the girls fall in line like little chicks behind an old hen.

The brassbound Mahogany door glides open to reveal a sight far-removed from Sam's social experiences of church picnics and barn dances. The smell of money and power drifts across the room. Even a young muleskinner from the hills of North Carolina knows when he's looking at a fixed game.

A broad-shouldered, red-complexioned slave holds the door open, his eyes cast down.

Sam speaks to the doorman, "Sorrel."

Sorrel speaks without looking up, "Mister Tanahill."

Sam senses the tension in Sorrel's voice.

Spence, under his breath, asks as they walk in, "And how do you know that red nigga?"

"He's the gang boss out at the warehouses. Loads my wagons."

The Meyers leave their guests and meet the Rayburns at the foyer.

The Rayburns are handing their gloves, hats, and Spence's cane to an elderly black maid as the Meyers walk up. The maid steps back and remains standing in the foyer with her eyes cast down.

Jessica Meyers speaks in a dismissive tone. "That's all Hattie."

“Yes ma’am.“ Hattie turns and walks into the coatroom.

Sam holds his focus to the business at hand as he stands back a little, listening to the greetings between the Rayburns and their hosts, Jessica and Cordell Meyers. He can feel the inquiring looks, not only from the Meyers, but the guests at the party also. Sam’s curiosity about the rich planters that he hauls freight for pales in comparison to their curiosity about him. But his father’s voice rings clear in his mind. “Stepping back from a decision is like crowding a mule, son. It’ll get you kicked every time.” Sam decides he will not be kicked this evening as he confidently takes stock of the Meyers.

For a woman past forty, the stories of Jessica Meyers’ beauty have not done her justice. Her flawless, bone-white complexion, set out by a mane of sandy blonde ringlets, lends to the hypnotic vision she creates. Her voice, ever so proper as required by southern breeding, lulls Sam into feeling he is welcomed. Her angelic vision, however, takes a darker turn when he looks into her steel gray eyes. The look of determination and power in her eyes cannot be mistaken. The daughter of a poverty-stricken aristocratic family in Charleston, South Carolina, Jessica Meyers vowed early in life to change her station. Standing at her husband’s right hand, she is anything but a supporting character.

Cordell‘s family has two hundred years of American soil on their boots. The legacy of each generation of Meyers men has been to leave more than was left to them, and Cordell has certainly done more than his share. Cordell has acquired more before the age of fifty than all the Meyers men before him; but then again, they weren’t married to the socially driven, Mrs. Meyers. From his plantation to his import-export business, the Meyers’ holdings stretch from Charleston to New Orleans. A man of medium stature and working class looks, he casts a long shadow in southern circles. Fair but driven, some wonder if his nature comes from being pushed by the blonde tigress on his arm.

Jessica smiles graciously at the Rayburns, successfully hiding her displeasure at their choice of guests. "Bess, how good of you and your family to come. My my, your girls get lovelier by the year. Don't you agree Mister Meyers?"

"I do indeed."

Cordell turns to Spence and extends his hand. "Spence, welcome. I heard you were looking for a new racehorse. You figure to win your stable boy back?"

Spence grabs Cordell's hand firmly and says, "I do. I've been lost without that boy. But it just may be different at Charleston this fall. I bought me a promising bay stallion out of Virginia. I think he'll give your gray a run for his money."

"That gray has sent more than a few home lighter than they came, including you."

Jessica interrupts the conversation. "Now, now gentlemen, this is a party, not the track." She turns ever so ladylike to Sam with a mischievous half smile and pointed directness. "And who is this striking young man?"

"This is Sam Tanahill," answers Spence. "You know his father, Owen Tanahill. He has hauled freight and sold stock to most everyone here today. In fact, I bought the bay from Owen."

Cordell replies matter-of-factly. "Ah yes, a good man. My overseer, Mr. Murphy, has done quite a bit of business with your father. He speaks highly of him."

Sam steps up to Cordell in a thoroughly gentlemanly way and extends his hand. "Thank you, sir."

Cordell's smile and nod soothes over an awkward moment as he shakes Sam's hand. Bess and Spence exchange a look of relief. Jessica's social rule for her cotillions is to never bring a guest that is not an immediate family member. In this case, Bess thought it was appropriate to replace her absentee son, Ryland, with a prospective son-in-law. Bess' intention is far better understood by all present than she realizes.

Sam's thoughts drift to his parents as he reads Cordell's approval of him as a man. His mother, Mary Beth, the daughter of a Blue Ridge mountain storekeeper-preacher, sternly demanded social etiquette of Sam. She knew her sums and verses, but she wanted more for her only child. When Sam was growing up, reading was equal to chores on a daily basis.

Under Mary Beth's watchful eye, Sam sat at the kitchen table and studied everything from math and science to the Bible and classical literature. Her attention to Sam's formal education was equally matched by Owens' desire to raise a young man of character who could survive a life of hard work.

The Tanahill name and their inclination towards hard work had stretched back to the earliest days of colonial existence. Back to the days when men took an ax, their rifle, and family, and carved out a life in the backcountry wilderness. The Tanahill clan had always been long on self-reliance, especially when the Crown of England decided to take a hand in controlling a misguided group of ignorant backwoodsmen. The rebellion swept over the colonies and the Tanahill men needed little firebrand debate to step to formation. Their belief in freedom and General Washington saw them through to the final days of battle with Nathaniel Green at Yorktown.

Shortly after the British surrender, Owen's father, Henry, broke and longing for peace and a home, settled down in the Blue Ridge Mountains of North Carolina. He opened a ramshackle trading post on the headwaters of the Yadkin River, traded horses, and studied to become a Free Mason.

"Sam, welcome. I hope that bay you delivered is just a nose slower than my gray. I could use another stable boy," Cordell says laughing at his own good humor.

Jessica moves the greetings to a skillful close. "That's just what we need is another Negro to feed. Y'all stop the horseracing gentlemen, and let's join the party. Sistell, if you would, please escort Mr. Tanahill and make the proper introductions."

Sistell smiles and takes hold of Sam's arm. "Yes ma'am. Mr. Tanahill, shall we?"

CHAPTER TWO

CORDELL AND SPENCE WALK TO THE BAR WHERE POLITICAL wisdom and sour mash whiskey are flowing in equal portions. A group of young girls wave to Newella, and she hurries off to join them.

Jessica takes hold of Bess' hand as Sam and Sistell walk off. "My goodness, what a lovely couple. Things always work better with a little help. Don't you think so?"

Bess, puzzled by Jessica's insight, smiles and asks, "How did you know which girl?"

Jessica leans closer to Bess like two sisters with a sweet secret and says, "Infatuations. Young girls struggle to hide their desires."

Smiling, Jessica motions toward the party. "Shall we?"

She moves back through her guests, holding court as several women crowd around Bess, smiling and talking.

Sistell is literally in heaven, with every woman present stealing glances as she begins to introduce Sam to the other guests. Bess talks with the other women but never takes her eyes off Sam and Sistell. She holds her breath and prays that one of her daughters may at last have a suitor.

After several hours of small talk, shaking hands, and trying to avoid prying questions, Sam needs a refuge. He spies a small, columned doorway at the back of the huge ballroom, and he begins to ever so gently guide Sistell in that direction. Reaching the doorway, Sam stops and takes a deep breath.

Sistell becomes impatient and fans herself as if on fire, pouting like the privileged belle that she is.

Sam looks to Sistell then back to the party. He can feel her displeasure.

"Miss Rayburn, is there some sin I have committed through ignorance?"

"You walk straight to the garden door and just... stop! With everyone in the room watching!"

When Sam turns and looks through the open doorway, embarrassment takes him by storm. There in the flower gardens are several young couples, talking and holding hands.

Sam turns immediately to Sistell and says, "Miss Rayburn, I never meant to deceive. I was only looking for a place to be out of the way. Please forgive me."

Sistell smiles an unexpected smile from behind her fan. "I think I shall save both our reputations and go to the powder room." She curtsies and walks off, flirting with Sam over her fan.

Sam breathes a sigh of relief and leans up against the marble column as the orchestra begins to play a lively quadrille. The couples take the floor and playfully dance around the polished marble floor. The women in their diamond jewelry sparkle and light up the room as they pass in front of Sam. His eyes wander from the extravagant show of wealth to the slaves serving everyone's needs from the kitchen to the ladies' powder room. He has no doubts about his desire to become a man of means one day, but never at the cost of forced labor.

A little tired, Sam looks down at the floor as he shifts his weight from one foot to the other. When he looks back up, he is totally speechless. The most beautiful young woman he has ever seen stands before him. He has never seen eyes so blue or full of life. She radiates a smile that Sam finds contagious as he stares and smiles in return. Her long, strawberry blonde hair encases her thin, freckled shoulders.

With a teasing smile she speaks. "Do all the young men in North Carolina just smile, or can they speak?"

"Uh, yes ma'am. I am...uh..."

Spence walks up by Sam and seeing his obvious distress interjects, "Excuse me. May I present Mr. Sam Tanahill? Mr. Tanahill, this is Miss Helen Meyers, our hostess's daughter."

The moment is lost to silence as Sam and Helen look into each other's eyes.

Helen, ever so catty, says, "Nice to meet you Mr. Tanahill. When you find yourself, please come and dance with us." A dapper young man in a ruffled shirt and a high-collared coat walks up behind Helen. The moment of silence returns as Spence and the young man patiently wait.

As Helen turns to walk away, her flirty, little-girl smile takes on a directness as she nods to Sam. "Mr. Tanahill." The parting look leaves him even more spellbound as the young man offers his hand to Helen, and they join the dance.

Spence, with a controlled belly laugh, slaps Sam on the back. "Mr. Tanahill, you should quit staring, or folks will think you a slow wit." Spence shakes his head side-to-side and snorts a laugh under his breath then starts to walk away when Sam suddenly catches his arm.

Sam, without taking his eyes off of Helen as she dances with the young man, asks, "Sir, who is she?"

Spence is a little perplexed and repeats himself. "Son I just told you who she is. She's Miss Helen Meyers." He snorts his belly laugh under his breath again and looks at Sam as if he *is* a slow wit.

Still holding his arm, Sam turns to look Spence in the eyes, and then releases his grip.

Spence, regaining himself, says, "Oh... who *is* she? Let's see. Where should I start? The favorite daughter of the richest planter in all of South Carolina, the heiress to the Tigress's throne of society, a beauty with looks and grace surpassing Aphrodite, but of course you know that first hand. Ah yes! The most important little point I forgot. The Blonde Tigress and the Blonde Tigress alone will eventually decide who has her hand. So I suggest, sir, you only stare like all the rest of us; it's the safest choice." Spence chokes back his belly laugh as he walks away.

Sam has turned his attention back to Helen as the dance finishes.

She continues to exchange glances with Sam as she raises her fan under her eyes.

The dapper young man leans in and whispers in Helen's ear as they walk off the floor. "Well cousin Helen, you seem to have won the heart and admiration of a dashing young wagon driver. What a conquest!"

Without losing eye contact with Sam, she replies, "Mind your manners Justin Terrebonne, or I shall make known your conquests, including the darker ones."

"I meant no insinuations in the word conquest."

"But I did. Now, what else do you know about him?"

"He is a wagon driver from the hills of North Carolina. What else is required to know? Your mother... "

"My mother what? Would not approve?"

Justin smiles at Helen and slightly bows taking his leave. "I think I shall step away from this plot before I am hanged as an innocent."

She does not acknowledge Justin leaving as she intensely surveys the room. Her attention comes to rest on a gangly young man sitting at the end of the room by himself. His misery shows on every feature of his face. Helen smiles as she starts toward the young man. When he notices her coming his way, he rises and smiles an unsure smile.

"Miss Meyers."

Helen lights up with a sweet smile and taps him on the shoulder with her fan. "Why Ira Paul Hansen, you and I baited too many hooks together as kids for me to be Miss Meyers."

"Yes ma'am," he stutters, "I mean Helen."

Helen takes him by the coat sleeve and leads him out of earshot of the other guests.

"Can you still keep a secret, Ira Paul?"

"I suppose. What is it?"

"You and the Tomkins boys still coon hunting together?"

"You want to talk about coon hunting?"

"No, about dogs."

"Dogs?" Ira Paul is more confused than ever at this point, but then again, he never was too quick in understanding the ways of women.

Helen continues. "Sorrel's Plot hound, Jill, had a litter of pups a few weeks back. How would you like to have the pick of that litter?"

"That ain't possible. Them pups been spoken for, for awhile."

"You help me with a little matter today, and first pick will be yours."

"Must be some little matter."

"You know Sistell Rayburn?" Helen asks.

"There ain't nothing little about her except the space between her eyes."

"You want that pup or not?" Helen snaps.

"You know I do."

"Then listen. I want you to occupy every minute of her time today, plus invite her to the Robinson social next week."

"Gosh almighty Helen, that ain't a fair trade."

"Ira Paul, who in this room can you depend on more than me?"

"No one."

"Then don't make a bad decision here and lose a friend plus a hound."

"Do I have to dance," he asks, trying to negotiate a better deal.

"Dance, talk, walk in the gardens! You just be at her elbow everywhere except the ladies' powder room until she walks out of my front door."

"All day and the social. I get it."

"Cheap price for a hound like that."

"This is a dog deal in more ways than one."

Helen laughs and says, "Now Mr. Hansen, smile and come dance with me, before everyone thinks we're conspiring."

Helen leads him by the hand to the dance floor. After several missteps and some guidance from Helen, they begin to move with the flow of the other couples. As they circle the floor, Sistell returns to Sam's side. Sam watches Helen dance as Sistell continues talking as if Sam hangs on her every word. The dance comes to an end and Helen and Ira Paul walk off of the floor.

Helen says to Ira Paul, "Remember Mr. Hansen, failure is not acceptable. Be persistent!"

Ira Paul reaches out and puts his hand on Helen's arm. "First pick?"

"Absolutely."

Ira Paul begins to work his way around to where Sam and Sistell are standing.

Helen accepts an offer from another young man to dance as she watches her plan unfold. She smiles as Ira Paul and Sistell take the floor. As Helen turns her attention back to Sam, she finds his slight nod and smirk amusing. She doesn't acknowledge the nod and gives the young man she's dancing with her charming attention.

When the dance is over, the young man thanks Helen and departs. She smugly opens her fan and begins to fan herself as she walks around the dance floor toward Sam. When she feels a tap on her shoulder from behind, Helen turns around and comes face-to-face with Jessica.

Helen, smiling, says, "Well Mother, I've hardly seen you all day."

"I can believe that. You have been distracted ever since the Rayburns arrived." Gesturing toward Sam, Jessica says, "Looks like Mr. Tanahill has lost his escort."

"It does now, doesn't it?"

"Why would Sistell leave a handsome young man like Mr. Tanahill for the rumpled Mr. Hansen?"

Helen replies without playing her mother's game. "It does seem a poor choice."

"That's something we should all try not to do," Jessica says pointedly.

Helen with a touch of arrogance replies, "Make a poor choice, Mother?"

"Exactly."

Jessica walks away as Helen turns her attention to the couples dancing. She stares off in thought for several moments, and then she abruptly closes the fan, turns, and walks straight to Sam.

"Mr. Tanahill, I hope you're enjoying the party."

"I am now. Thank you."

There is a pause and an awkward moment, then the orchestra begins to play Strauss's "Little Doves Waltz."

"Mr. Tanahill, would you... would you like to dance?"

Without speaking, Sam offers his hand. Helen, looking relieved, smiles and accepts. They walk out on the floor, turn, and face each other. Sam takes her in his arms and in one easy move they are in motion. Helen looks surprised.

"Not only can we speak in North Carolina, but we can also dance."

Helen smiles and becomes lost in Sam's dark eyes.

Jessica has watched Helen's manipulation of Sistell with a combination of approval and panic. The intense looks passing between Sam and Helen as they dance become more than Jessica can bear. She cannot idly stand by and watch any longer. She coolly goes in search of Cordell and finds him discussing horses, as usual, with Spence and several other men.

"I hate to interrupt, gentlemen. But if you would be so kind as to loan me my husband, I shall return him momentarily."

The men, almost in unison, answer, "Yes ma'am."

Cordell follows Jessica out of sight of the guests. She stops, takes a deep breath, and turns to face Cordell.

Cordell can sense the coming drama, but keeps his voice cool and disinterested as he says simply, "Jessica?"

Jessica gathers herself and then speaks, "Your daughter walked right up to him and asked him to dance, in front of God and everyone, and to a waltz no less!"

"Jessica, settle down. Who did she ask to dance?"

"That Tanahill boy that came with the Rayburns. Now she's dancing with him, and he can't take his eyes off of her."

Cordell almost laughs. "My dear, all the young men stare at Helen, even the old men do. So what's so different about this young man?"

Jessica wrings her lace handkerchief and begins to pace. "It's the way she's looking back. She's looking at him the way they stare at her." Jessica, distraught, persists. "Cordell, she's making a spectacle of herself. His family is a bunch of horse traders for Christ's sake!"

"Jessica wait a minute. You're making way too much out of a little flirting."

Jessica continues to pace. "Flirting? Believe me she's not flirting."

"Jessica is there something else here I should know?"

Jessica stops and turns to face Cordell squarely. "Yes, he'll be back. You mark my word."

Cordell becomes even more impatient with Jessica's theatrics and snaps a reply, "Be back? He lives in Charlotte for God's sake. That's three days ride on a good horse. Besides, who's given him permission to call on Helen? You?"

Jessica, shaking her head in disgust, answers, "She has."

Cordell's face turns a flush red with anger. "Hold on! She invited him to call on her, here at my house, without asking my permission? She told you that?"

"No, she didn't."

"If she didn't tell you that! Then who did?"

"No one! It's her looks that say it."

Cordell's anger turns to aggravation. "I think you're drawing conclusions without facts."

"The fact is, Mr. Meyers, you're too old to remember when I gave you that same look. You came back, and he'll come back."

Cordell works to become civil. "Fine. There is nothing I can do about this at the moment. If and when he does return, I'll deal with it then. In the meantime, let's return to our guests and enjoy the rest of the day."

"Cordell, this needs to be dealt with today!"

"Jessica, Helen has always had a mind of her own. Be patient! She knows who she is. But if you continue to meddle, you'll get the very results you don't want."

Jessica continues to pace and becomes more agitated with each step. Cordell sees that his advice has had little effect on her mood or her resolve.

He catches her by the arm and stops her. "Jessica, I want you to let this go. He is a guest in our home!"

Jessica's posture becomes rigid. "I suggest, sir, you give this equal attention with your horseracing, because there is far more at stake here than a stable boy."

Jessica looks down at his hand. After an eternity of several seconds, Cordell releases her arm.

"Jessica, I am very aware of what is at stake. Now the party is almost over. We will finish this discussion later."

Jessica answers him with a condescending tone. "As you wish sir."

Cordell watches her walk away knowing she has no intention of letting the matter go. When Jessica doesn't get her way, her wrath surpasses the wrath of God. Experience has taught him that, to be sure. The last two years in the Meyers' household have been anything but pleasant, not only for Cordell, but for the entire house staff as well. Jessica has personally arranged all of the marriages of the Meyers' children and is determined to have the final say in Helen's also. But Helen most certainly disagrees on the matter.

The undercurrent of stress between Helen and Jessica started when Helen began to blossom from a lanky, pigtailed, all arms and legs creature, into a beauty, blessed by nature. Without Helen's approval, Jessica began to invite eligible young bachelors from surrounding plantations to Sunday dinners, an action that generated many hot debates between the two women, with neither willing to comprise.

Helen is respectful of her mother, but she will not be intimidated like her sisters were, nor will she be forced to marry someone she doesn't love. And even though Jessica understands Helen's dreams of passion and romance, she has no room for such ignorance when it comes to marrying below one's social status. Jessica is adamant that her children will not suffer the humiliation of poverty the way she had to do.

Before Jessica returns to the main ballroom, she masks her aggravation at Cordell with a gracious smile and an air of elegance. She knows there are only two things in his life that get full attention—race horses and making money—everything else he leaves to her.

Jessica's housemistress, Bell, is overseeing the serving of guests when Jessica walks into the room. Bell is dark of color and thin of frame, with a commanding presence. The entire wait staff, both men and women, takes her every cue as they serve.

Bell was purchased by Cordell when she was a young girl and given to Jessica as a wedding gift. As the relationship grew between the two women, Bell eventually took over the management of the house staff for Jessica. She is precise and orderly in everything under her hand and knows well the boundaries of a slave. All the Negros on Shannon Hill love, fear, and respect Mama Bell.

Jessica summons Bell with a look from across the room. There is a shared bond of respect between the women. They both rule their social order.

Bell walks over. "Yes ma'am?"

Jessica quietly leans in and speaks. "When our guests leave tonight, you know what's required. I want the house put back in order. Everything cleaned from the chamber pots to the crystal. Oh, and anything personal that the ladies left in the powder room, make sure it goes out with the chamber pots. I swear I think every woman here is having her time."

"Yes ma'am. And ma'am, could I be keepin' Sorrel? I could use that strong back to move some heavy stuff back in place."

"Keep him as long as you need, Bell. But you make sure the furniture is the only thing he puts his hands on. I don't need any more of my house girls screaming their heads off trying to have one of his half-grown, red babies, you hear?"

"I told him, ma'am, when he came up to be at the door, that there would be nothing but hardship if he didn't mind hisself," Bell replies.

"Well you tell him again. But for now we need to light the lamps. Folks won't start to leave the party until the moon comes up full, and they can see to go home."

"Yes ma'am."

"And Bell, the young man that came with the Rayburns, has he danced with anyone?"

Bell smiles and answers, "Other than Miss Helen? No ma'am, but it's just cause he ain't asked."

Jessica looks over at Helen. "That's the problem. He didn't have to."

"There's a problem, ma'am?"

Jessica turns her attention back to Bell. "Not with you Bell. Now remember, I don't want any laziness on the cleaning. And you tend to Sorrel. I don't want that boy busying himself with any of my girls."

"Yes ma'am."

Bell lowers her eyes and walks away.

Jessica watches Helen as she dances an occasional dance, smiles, and charms everyone around her. Her smile and elegance captivate the room just as strongly as her eyes are captivated by Mr. Tanahill.

Jessica has finally had enough of Mr. Tanahill. She intends to find out if there is a man behind those rugged good looks or just a backwoods wagon driver.

Sam sees Jessica out of the corner of his eye as she starts his way. He has felt her disapproval all day, especially when he danced with Helen. Sam figured he would have seen her eye-to-eye long before now. But she's nothing new; he has seen plenty of her kind while hauling freight in the Carolinas. They always mean to have the road, even if they have to run you off of it. He knows she will make clear who owns the road today.

Sam takes a deep breath and squares his chin up as she walks up to him. He remains facing the dance and Helen.

"Ma'am." Sam nods ever so slightly to her.

"Mr. Tanahill." She turns and stands by his side as her focus comes to rest on Helen.

Helen gives her mother a curt smile from across the room.

"It's far removed from a barn dance, wouldn't you say Mr. Tanahill?"

"Music and folks, it's all about the same," he replies without as much as a hint of emotion or a glance her way.

"I would hardly think you would hear Chopin in a barn."

Sam pauses for a moment. Jessica takes delight in the game as she returns Helen's curt little look. The women are staring at each other when Sam abruptly turns to Jessica.

"Mrs. Meyers, would you care to dance?"

Jessica experiences a rare moment of being caught socially off balance.

Helen doesn't know what Sam said to her mother, but she can see he has the advantage. Her heart jumps to her throat.

Jessica regains herself instantly and the mischievous little smile Sam saw at the door earlier in the day returns.

He extends his hand with all the polish of a southern gentleman.

Jessica curtsies, takes his hand, and they walk side-by-side to the dance floor. When she stops and turns to Sam, he steps up to her at the proper distance, and in that same easy motion as with Helen, he sweeps her onto the dance floor. Jessica is only momentarily impressed.

"Mr. Tanahill, I think it obvious that you are taken with my daughter."

"Ma'am, everyone in the room knows the obvious."

Sam dances Jessica around the floor in a firm and commanding way, occasionally looking into her piercing gray eyes. With every step, he lets her know that for these few minutes, she is not in control. His unflinching silence unnerves Jessica and pushes her social graces to the limit.

"Well then I hope we've reached an understanding, Mr. Tanahill."

The dance comes to an end and Sam escorts Jessica off the floor.

"With all due respect ma'am, I have felt your disdain. Today was not my choice, nor will it ever be again."

"I think disdain is a little harsh."

"Thank you for the dance, ma'am." He bows ever so slightly and turns to walk away.

"Mr. Tanahill. I... "

Sam pauses and turns back to Jessica. "That wasn't Chopin by the way; it was the Sussex Waltz by Turner, though Mozart's influence in the piece is certainly notable."

Sam turns and walks out of the ballroom into the gardens. He stands gazing up into the early evening sky as Spence walks out behind him smoking a cigar.

"I don't know what you said to her in there, but she looked like someone pulled her corset too tight. Don't think I can ever remember seeing that."

Sam ignores Spence's observation and comments, "You ever wonder what's out there?"

"Out where? In the sky?"

"No," Sam replies, deep in his own thoughts, "Out West."

"Well I know what's not out there son, clean sheets and decent liquor."

Sam, still completely lost in his thoughts, continues. "They say you can ride a horse for days on end and never see a soul."

"Son, your paw does well. I can't see the reason to wonder off somewhere and get killed just to be wondering around."

Sam turns to Spence. "It's land, Mr. Rayburn. If you have it, you never think about it; and if you don't... well it makes a man start to look."

"Son, looking is about the only thing a man can do these days. Hell, Old Hickory's Specie Circular of 36 stopped lots of folks from buying anything. Caused nothing but grief and now Van Buren holds to the same stupid policy."

"With all due respect sir, I don't care who is President. Somebody is going to own that land out there, and I figure it had just as well be me."

Sam continues to look off into the night sky as Spence looks over at Sam and smiles.

"I admire you for that. I really do, son." Spence turns and stares off into the sky with Sam smoking his cigar.

A full, golden moon begins to rise in the east, streaking ghostly gray rays of light through the majestic oaks that surround the mansion and horse barns. The sounds of a harmonica and banjo carry in the cool night as the drivers play some lively tunes around several campfires by the stables. Their teams are brushed, fed, and harnessed to their carriages ready for the night trip home.

After a while, Spence takes notice of the music coming from down at the horse barns.

"Do me a favor Sam. Walk down to the barn and tell my driver, Teddy, to bring the carriage up. We'll be leaving soon."

"Yes sir," Sam replies.

Spence, pointing with his cigar, says, "Go on through the gardens like you're going to the outhouse, except stay straight on the cobblestone. It goes to the barn."

"Yes sir."

Sam walks down the path and passes several men returning from the outhouse.

"Evening," he says as he passes the men.

One of the men recognizes Sam and calls him by name. "Mr. Tanahill."

Sam stops and turns around. The man walks closer to Sam.

"Mr. Tanahill, may I have a moment?"

Sam, unsure of who the man is, inquires, "How can I help you?"

"Justin Terrebonne, we met earlier this evening," he says as he cordially extends his hand. With an equal amount of caution, Sam shakes the young man's hand.

"I was actually thinking, Mr. Tanahill, that I may help you."

Sam repeats, "Help me?"

"My cousin, Helen, seems to have placed you in favor."

Sam grins and says, "I think you assume too much."

"I understand your caution sir, as well as your merriment. I would not be this bold if it were not for the sour mash. I witnessed your encounter with my aunt, and I must say you did better than most of us who know her. In fact, there were many silent cheers when you turned and walked away in there. Especially from Miss Meyers."

"And what did Miss Meyers tell you?"

"Mr. Tanahill, you have the unfortunate luck of finding yourself on the field of battle today."

"Not to be rude, Mr. Terrebonne, but the point please."

"The point is simple. If you find favor with one, you find disfavor with the other. Helen and my aunt can't agree on the weather, much less men. So sir, do not be dissuaded from your ambitions. Because you did tonight what many would like to do, but can't. You did not bend to Jessica Meyers' will."

"I understand, Mr. Terrebonne, but I assure you my ambitions do not include any of this. And rudeness should never be given quarter. Now if you will excuse me."

Sam follows the moonlit path through the shadowy oaks and thinks about Justin's comment concerning Helen.

His words keep turning in Sam's mind. "Do not be dissuaded from your ambitions."

Sam's first thought was that the sour mash had given Justin's tongue the courage to make such a statement. Then reality hits Sam with the force of a mule's kick. Justin wouldn't chance Jessica's scorn for his own advancement, much less a stranger of no consequence. The reason comes clear to Sam as he walks on and smiles to himself. The message was from Helen.

His smile soon fades as Sam walks up on the drivers sitting around the campfires playing music. When he walks out of the dark, they immediately quit playing and all stand up, removing their hats. The men wait on Sam to give an order or make a request, bringing clarity to Sam's mind as to where he is.

The silence of the moment is finally broken as the house orchestra begins to play a waltz. The music is soothing, yet pronounced, and defines the moment. Sam looks back to the two-story mansion shimmering in the light and feels his resolve strengthened. No matter his ambitions or where they may lead, he will never be found with his hat in his hand.

An old, gray-haired driver breaks Sam's train of thought. "Evenin' boss."

"Evening. The Rayburn's driver, Teddy. Is he here?"

Teddy walks out from around the corner of the stable. "Mr. Tanahill."

"Mr. Rayburn is ready for you."

"Yes sir. I was just checking my hosses."

Sam walks around the stable to the carriage, followed by Teddy. He never breaks stride as he steps on the wheel of the carriage and climbs up to the driver's seat. Teddy stands looking up at Sam not knowing what to do. Sam takes the lines in his hands and easily lets the team know he is there.

"Untie 'em Teddy and get up here. I just want to see if these grays feel as smooth in the bit as they look."

Teddy hurriedly unties the team and climbs up beside Sam. "They smooth, Mr. Sam. Never no trouble, no sir."

Sam releases his easy hold on the bit, brushes the team across their hips with the lines, and the grays step into the harness. The carriage glides behind the grays as they move with an even, measured stride.

Teddy watches Sam drive the team. "You gots the touch, Mr. Sam."

Sam drives the team up to the house, swings them around the circle drive, and stops in front of the steps.

Sam hands the lines to Teddy. "You've done a good job keepin' 'em soft in the bit, Teddy."

"Thank you sir."

Sam gets down from the carriage and walks up the steps to the front door of the mansion. He takes hold of the polished brass door handle and pauses. He knows that his exit will be a lot more interesting than his entrance. Justin's comment will not leave Sam's mind, nor will Helen's radiant smile. He has to see those eyes and that smile up close one more time before he leaves.

Sam opens the door and walks in to find Sorrel and Hattie standing in the foyer waiting on the guests to leave. He proceeds on like a man with a divine purpose.

Sam speaks to Sorrel as he walks by. "Sorrel. Mr. Rayburn's carriage is outside, should he ask."

"Yes sir, Mr. Tanahill, sir."

Sam boldly walks into the ballroom and pauses to look for Helen. As usual, she is the center of attention talking with a group of young couples. Sam walks straight by Jessica and gives her no recognition on his way to Helen. She has her back to Sam as he walks up to the group. Helen becomes uneasy as her friends suddenly quit talking and all wear a sheepish grin. A tall, thin, young man of bearing breaks the moment and acknowledges Sam.

"Mr. Tanahill." The young man extends his hand. "George Robinson."

"Nice to meet you."

Then Sam smiles and realizes his boldness, as does everyone else. He turns to Helen and speaks.

"Miss Meyers, may I have this next dance?"

Helen pauses, then graciously smiles and extends her hand. "I would be delighted."

With a nod to her group she says, "If you will excuse us."

She walks away followed by Sam.

"I thought asking you to dance made you think me a forward woman."

Sam smiles and feels an easiness for some odd reason as he looks over at Helen as they walk to the dance floor.

"But then you danced with no one else all day except my mother. I suspect you share your attentions somewhere else."

"Your mother is an extraordinary woman."

Helen speaks with a mischievous tone. "Extraordinary, I think so, but that's probably not the term used by most."

"Would that term be driven?" Sam asks.

Helen laughs and says, "It comes to mind. I guess I must be forward again if I am to get an answer."

"It seems that beauty is not the only quality you share with your mother."

Jessica walks out in front of the orchestra as the orchestra leader taps his baton to draw everyone's attention.

"Ladies and gentlemen this will be the final dance of the evening. I would like to thank Mr. Arthur Milinski and his wonderful orchestra for a day of beautiful music. They must leave, but the party is not over."

Jessica begins to clap along with everyone in the room. She turns to the orchestra and motions for them to stand and take a bow.

The applause dies away, and the orchestra members take their seats.

Jessica nods to Mr. Milinski, "Gentlemen, if you will."

The music begins and Jessica walks over to Cordell who has been in horseracing debates all day.

"Mr. Meyers. I believe this is our dance."

Jessica walks to the floor, followed by Cordell, with her gaze fixed on Helen and Sam as they dance.

Cordell reaches and takes hold of Jessica's hand from behind and turns her around.

"If this is our dance, then that is my expectation."

Jessica starts to say something when she catches the sternness of Cordell's eyes and holds her comment. Cordell offers his hand. She takes it, and they join the dance.

Sam and Helen dance in silence with no thoughts of their different lives beyond the moment. The common bond they share, unknown to both, is the desire to have a life far removed from where society has placed them.

The waltz ends, and they remain on the floor for a second longer than everyone else. They smile and walk off together.

Sam speaks. "That's not the reason I haven't danced."

"Excuse me?" Helen smiles.

"My attention is not given somewhere else."

They are walking toward the garden door when Helen stops and turns to Sam.

"Mr. Tanahill. I would be flattered if... "

Helen is cut off in mid-sentence, and is totally shocked to hear her mother's voice.

"Mr. Tanahill. Mr. Rayburn and his family are about to leave."

Jessica waits in silence as if she is required to escort Sam to the front door. Helen and Sam exchange a look.

"Mother," Helen says, challenging Jessica with her eyes, "If you would give us a moment."

Jessica replies, "I think not."

Helen's eyes flash anger as she turns on Jessica, "How dare..."

Sam steps between the two with a quickness that surprises both women.

He turns to Helen and looks into her eyes.

In an easy tone he speaks. "Thank you for the dance and a very memorable day."

Sam turns to Jessica, and they stand face-to-face. "And thank you, Mrs. Meyers, for your generous hospitality. The Rayburns were correct when they said it would be an unforgettable experience."

Sam slightly bows and acknowledges both women. "Good evening."

He is followed to the front door by both women, each with a definite and distinctly different agenda.

The Rayburns are already at the front door waiting on Sam. Spence and Cordell are talking while Bess and Newella put on their gloves and hats. Ira Paul and Sistell stand just out of hearing talking in hushed tones.

Spence addresses Sam. "Ah, Mr. Tanahill, right on time."

Sam nods. "Didn't mean to keep everyone waiting."

He turns to Cordell and says, "Mr. Meyers, thank you for the day, sir."

"Glad you could be with us. Give your father my regards."

"I will sir."

Sam shakes Cordell's hand, then walks over and stands by Sorrell at the front door.

Sorrell grins and speaks under his breath, "You a sight Mr. Sam. Made folks take notice."

Sam smiles and returns, "Don't know if that's a good thing or bad Sorrell. Making folks take notice."

The Meyers and the Rayburns finish saying good night, and Sorrell opens the front door. Sam is the last to walk out when he glances back for one fleeting look at Helen. Helen and Jessica are standing side-by-side, both intense in their looks. Sam smiles when he looks from one woman to the other. Helen's dazzling eyes are a sharp contrast to Jessica's cold, piercing stare. Sam walks out the door with a mix of thoughts and emotions. This day was nothing like he had envisioned.

The old slave holds open the carriage door for the Rayburns as they get in. With everyone seated, Spence taps on the back of the driver's seat with his cane. "Watch the road Teddy, lots of folks out tonight."

"Yes sir, Mr. Rayburn."

Teddy slacks the reins and clucks to the team. The grays, well-broken and seasoned to the harness, move the carriage into the moonlit night. The lamps on each side of the driver's seat cast a dull light on all aboard as they get comfortable for the long ride home. The clicking of the horses' shod hooves on the cobblestone seems to hold everyone silent for the moment. It's clear to Sam, though, that the night will not pass this peacefully. When the carriage reaches the plantation entrance and turns on to the dirt road, the dam of silence is broken.

Bess speaks first. "Mr. Tanahill, I think you were a pleasant surprise for a certain young lady today."

Sistell follows quickly. "Fact is, Ira Paul told me she was quite taken with you."

Newella rolls her eyes at her sister and says, "I would say she's not the only one taken with someone. Ira Paul looked like your shadow today. You two going coon hunting next?"

Sistell answers her sister's veiled innuendo, "Oh, he did invite me somewhere. The Robinson social next week. And who invited you?"

Newella enjoys toying with her sister and says, "Maybe Mr. Tanahill would like to be my escort. Can you just imagine the grief that would cause? We would probably all have to leave the state, Mr. Tanahill."

"Newella, mind yourself," Spence cautions his oldest daughter.

Sam laughs at Newella and says, "You figure she'd take that personal?"

"If you mean Mrs. Meyers, Mr. Tanahill, she is not that way," replies Bess.

Newella answers. "Well I know this. Anyone who crosses the Tigress usually disappears socially."

"Newella, that is by far enough," her father replies sharply.

Sam's sudden smile and laugh catches everyone by surprise.

Newella protests unconvincingly, "Mr. Tanahill, I was not making light of her at all. It's the truth."

"Miss Rayburn, that is my exact solution for her. To completely remove her from my social calendar."

Sam's statement makes everyone pause and reflect for a moment. Then all at once, the Rayburns burst out into uproarious laughter.

Spence, laughing, groans out, "Oh my God, son. If there were just more like you."

The carriage continues into the night followed by the echo of laughter for many miles.

CHAPTER THREE

SORRELL CLOSES THE DOOR BEHIND THE LAST GUESTS AND looks over at the grandfather clock in the foyer just as the chimes are striking ten. Bell informed him only minutes before that he was to report to her when the guests had left. Sorrell walks into the kitchen as Bell is giving out cleaning assignments to the house girls. She stops talking and turns to Sorrell.

"You mind yo'self nigga. If I catch a problem over you, you gonna feel the whip on yo' ass."

Sorrell looks squarely at Bell and says, "I know my place. I don't need no walking on."

Several of the girls smile at Sorrell while Bell has her back turned, giving instructions to the rest of her girls. One in particular is Helen's personal servant, Petal. She was a present from Cordell and Jessica on Helen's sixteenth birthday. Petal was born in the Caribbean somewhere and sold to a Georgia planter at the Charleston slave auction when she was a little girl. Cordell acquired her when she was fourteen, from a horse trader who was a hundred dollars short in paying him for a yearling stud colt. She was too thin to work the fields, so he assigned her to housework under Bell.

Petal constantly wears a smile that is full of pearly white teeth. Her yel low color and love of bright colored clothes makes her stand out from the other women. She's had a strong yearning to spend time with Sorrell, but Jessica has stopped it from happening. Jessica decides whom her girls give their favors to and most of her girls are off limits to Sorrell. His company is confined to the bigger women who've had at least one child and work in the fields.

Bell knew why Sorrell offered to come up to the main house and be the doorman. There isn't a nigger gang boss on the place that would offer to do that unless there was a reason.

Bell turns back to her girls. "Nobody gonna lay they head down till we done. So no piddlin'. One of you show Sorrell what to move. Not you, Petal. You go see if Miss Helen be's ready for bed. She be on the veranda out back, talking to her folks."

Petal answers softly with a slight edge of disappointment in her voice. "Yes ma'am."

Sorrell can't take his eyes off of Petal as she walks off.

Bell's voice breaks his concentration. "Damn it nigga, you got more of that stuff than you can get to. I done told you that Calico dress gonna bring you hardship the Lord can't fix. Now get on with you."

Sorrell follows the women out of the kitchen and catches a glimpse of Petal at the veranda door. She stands at the door listening. Jessica and Helen are in a heated argument as Cordell sits in a high back bamboo chair smoking a cigar. She gently opens the door, steps out, and closes it quietly. The women continue as if Petal is not present.

"I will tell you again! Your father and I will decide who calls on you, and it will not be a damned backwoods horse trader!"

"You don't own me, Mother! It's my life, not yours, and I can live it as I choose."

"Helen, you are a Meyers and you will live accordingly."

"Live like Z, you mean? Every time Miles put his hands on her he reeks of whiskey and shows her no respect. Is that how a Meyers is supposed to live?"

"Your sister and Miles are married! They will work things out like we all do."

"You call being put on her back with force, working things out?"

"Z and her marriage have nothing to do with what we are discussing."

"It has everything to do with it, Mother!" Helen points to Petal. "You've treated Z and Liz just like you do Petal and all the house girls. You have selectively bred them all, and I will not be next."

Cordell stands up from his chair. "Stop this right now! I've had enough! Young lady, you will be respectful of your language in this house."

Helen is silent for a moment as she collects herself. "I love you, Father, with all my heart, but this is not about Sam Tanahill."

Jessica counters. "I assure you that will not be the gossip if this goes any further."

Cordell snaps, "Jessica please!" He turns to Helen and says, "Look, it's been a long day, and tempers are short. Let your mother and I talk. You take Petal and get ready for bed."

Helen hugs Cordell and kisses him on the cheek. "I love you, Daddy." She turns to Jessica and lightly kisses her cheek. "Mother."

Helen walks back into the house followed by Petal.

"Go on up, Petal, and turn my covers back. I'll be up shortly."

"Yes ma'am."

Jessica stands at the veranda door watching Helen through the glass.

Cordell sits back down in the bamboo chair. "Somehow, I want some peace in this house. Today was too much."

"I agree, Cordell, but we can't give in now. She will settle and marry before long, and this will be behind us."

"Jessica, have one of your girls cook me some bacon and eggs and then turn my bed back. Oh, and shut the door there when you go in."

Jessica, curt and cold, replies, "Would you like that served out here?"

"I would. And have Jolene bring it out."

"Jolene. Well, if there is anything else you require this evening, please feel free to take that up with her as well."

Jessica stares through the veranda glass, momentarily lost in thought. Then the distinct aroma of Cordell's cigar brings her back to business.

"Cordell, I will compromise on the Jolene's, but not on the father of my grandchildren."

Jessica opens the door, then pauses. "Good night sir." She closes the door behind her and proceeds into the kitchen to find Bell.

Sam rides in silent thought, staring out into the early morning night, while all the Rayburns sleep, and Teddy guides the grays toward home. Sam has courted several prominent young women in North Carolina, but never a planter's daughter, and he had no real thoughts of courting Helen. That is, not until that last waltz. When they danced in silence, staring into each other's eyes, suddenly everything Sam had dreamed of in life was replaced by what he held in his arms.

Even though he knew what Helen was going to say when Jessica interrupted, Sam wished he could have heard her say it. On the other hand, he knew he wasn't going to wait on an invitation to call on Helen Meyers.

Sam feels Teddy rein the team up as the carriage comes to a stop in front of the Rayburn's mansion.

"Mr. Spence, we's home sir."

Spence curses under his breath as he tries to sit up straight. "Damn, it's hard being old and fat."

Sam opens the carriage door and steps down. The women wake up and gather their hats and gloves.

Old Jeb and the Rayburn's two house girls come out to help the women as they wearily climb down from the carriage. Bess and the girls trudge off to the house while Sam stretches and waits on Spence to get out.

Spence slowly steps down from the carriage. "Go on in Sam, Old Jeb and the girls will get you some breakfast. Then we'll get some rest."

"Mr. Rayburn, I appreciate the offer, but I have to go. I am late for home now. My paw will have a rider looking for me if I don't get on."

Spence rubs his lower back and says, "I understand."

"I am going to change my clothes and hook up."

Spence looks to Teddy and says, "Teddy, catch Mr. Tanahill's team and help him get 'em harnessed."

"Yes sir."

Sam goes in the house and changes clothes. When he comes out, Spence is sitting on the porch in a rocker.

Sam casts a worried glance. "Can I get you anything?"

"Naw, son, I'm alright. Those long carriage rides get me down some. Go on and get your wagon."

"All right. I'll stop back when I get hooked up."

Spence, hesitating before he speaks, "Sam, you have a moment?"

Sam detects a tone in Spence's voice. "Yes sir."

Spence fumbles for a cigar in his coat pocket. He retrieves it and sits staring at the cigar in his hand as if not sure of his next words.

He regains himself and begins. "I had an offer for you Sam. Given a reason one way or the other, I thought you might entertain it. But then standing there in the garden, I heard an all too familiar dream and saw a look that won't rest. My son had that look before he left. He never saw what was under his boots, no matter the possibilities."

Spence smiles with a little envy and points with the cigar. "His eyes were always out there, on a distant horizon. And when the sun set late in the day, it brought him full misery. It was like he was being left behind one more time. Then, there he was late one evening, sitting on a horse at my front gate. Hell, I didn't hardly recognize him. He was grown past my thinking. I guess he just couldn't bear the sun headed west one more day without him. Rode off down that road 627 days ago."

Spence wipes at the corner of his eye, looks away from Sam, and laughs his fat, jovial laugh. "Sam, I don't think you can ignore the sun any more than Ryland could. But if ever you do, I've plenty of land. Land that could use a tough young man with dreams."

"I appreciate the respect and the offer sir. But you're right; I can't ignore that sunset."

Sam nods slightly and starts off of the porch when Spence raises his cigar.

"Sam, when your day comes to leave, don't forget to step down off your horse and say your goodbyes proper like."

It's a day Sam has long thought about, and so have his parents, Mary Beth and Owen. He walks off the porch and out to the barn.

Teddy has the mules caught and tied at Sam's wagon when he walks up.

"Don't believe I ever seen me no mules that big, Mr. Sam. If they hadn't put they head down, I'd never got a bit on' em."

"They had good mamas, Teddy, Belgian mares. Don't treat 'em any different than your grays, and they'll take the harness gentle."

Sam and Teddy start with the collars and dress each mule out. Sam works with an eye for detail, making sure that every piece of the harness is in its proper place. He has five hard days of travel to get home barring any problems. The weather and muddy roads in the spring are hard on a team that is sound. If one or more of his mules get sore, it can add days to his travel.

An hour later Sam walks around the team checking the harnesses one last time before he starts off into the early morning darkness. Satisfied that his team is ready, he climbs the tall front wheel up to the wagon seat.

"Teddy, thanks for your help. Take care of your grays; a man doesn't find many like them."

"Yes sir, Mr. Sam, I sho' will."

Sam picks up the leather reins, whistles to the team, and speaks to the lead pair. "Little Bill, Henry, step up."

The mules all lay into their collars at once, and as the harness comes tight, the wide-rimmed Conestoga wagon lurches forward. Sam whistles again and pulls the left reins tight, swinging the big wagon away from the barn and onto the road.

Approaching the house, Sam can see Mrs. Rayburn standing by the lamp on the porch. He reins the team up as she walks down the front steps, carrying something wrapped in cloth. Sam crawls down from the wagon.

Bess hands Sam the bundle. "Some sweet potatoes and ham for your trip."

"Thank you, ma'am. Mr. Rayburn feeling poorly?"

"He is. I had to put him to bed. He said to tell you goodnight and thank you."

“I appreciate everything, Mrs. Rayburn. Hope Mr. Rayburn is up before long.”

Bess hugs Sam. “My Ryland’s been gone near two years now. Seeing you in his clothes tonight somehow renewed my hope.”

She turns Sam loose and steps back, wiping tears from her eyes.

“Maybe the Lord will hear me one day, but no matter. You come back any time, Sam Tanahill.”

“Thank you, ma’am.”

Bess turns and walks toward the house.

Sam climbs back up on the wagon and takes the reins in his hands. He looks back at the house and sees Bess standing on the porch. She waves as Sam whistles to the team.

The big mules fall into a long stride that neither hurries nor slacks. The even pull on the wagon never requires Sam to do much more than decide which turn to take at a crossroads.

CHAPTER FOUR

THE DAY IS BREAKING LIGHT AS SAM REACHES THE GREAT Wagon Road at Beeches Crossing. He pulls the team to a stop in the middle of the crossroads and sits staring off to the south, toward Shannon Hill. He daydreams about what Helen looks like in the early morning. Her strawberry blonde hair scattered across a white linen pillow as her freckled bosom rises and falls to an easy rhythm. Of all his dreams, nothing could ever compare to lying next to her and seeing those blue eyes open first thing in the morning. He doesn't know when, but he does know he will be back. There has never been anything in Sam's life he was so sure of.

The mules become impatient and rock the wagon, jarring Sam back to business. He smiles and swings the team north, toward Charlotte and home. He whistles to the lead pair and brushes the mules with the lines, urging them to step a little quicker.

The last six a.m. chime of the grandfather clock fades through the house as Helen lies in bed, listening and looking up at the ceiling. Bell has the full kitchen staff up making preparations for the day. Helen eases out of bed and starts down the stairs in her bare feet and nightgown to find Petal. She stops half way to the kitchen when Bell walks out of the door.

"Miss Helen, what's you doin' up so early? You jest laid down."

Helen walks forward and motions for Bell to be quiet.

"Shhhh. Where's Petal?"

"She's fetchin' me eggs. Child, you gonna catch your death on this cold floor. Where's your shoes?"

"Tell her to go to the barn and have Rabbit saddle the stud. I am going for a ride. And Bell, please avoid telling anyone where I went for as long as you can."

"Yes ma'am. Now go on, get off this floor."

Helen leans in and kisses Bell on the cheek.

Bell laughs. "Go on with that child. You know you ain't supposed to be kissing me like dat."

Helen turns and dashes up the stairs to get dressed before anyone gets up. Bell returns to the kitchen, smiling, and meets Petal coming in the back door.

"Right on time girl. Miss Helen wants you to run down and have Rabbit saddle Mr. Cordell's stud. She goin' for a ride."

Petal leans close to Bell's ear and says, "I think she got a stud picked out she wants to ride, but he ain't gray."

Bell turns on Petal. "You tend Miss Helen and watch yo' mouth. Folks don't take to busy niggers. Now you get on, hear."

"Yes ma'am."

A little while later, Helen walks back into the kitchen in a pair of tall, old leather boots and a pair of men's pants that she has gathered at the waist with an even older leather belt. The homespun jacket is straight from the slave quarters.

The kitchen help all pause at once upon Helen's entrance. Bell walks over and gently leads Helen back out of the kitchen.

"Child! What you thinkin' dressed like that? You a lady now."

Helen starts walking to the garden door followed by Bell. "My grandma'am Meyers use to say a lady makes the lady, and nothing else."

"Well your grandma'am never went gallivantin' around on a race stud dressed like a stable hand neither."

"No, but I would say that her cigars and taste for sour mash are more than equal."

Bell stops at the garden door as Helen goes out. "Lord, child, yo' mama is gonna have another frightful day."

Bell walks back into the kitchen as Jolene comes walking in, still half asleep.

Jolene is a light-skinned house wench that has comfort girl written all over her. She is tall and thin, with a walk and look that every plantation owner in the South would fight to own. Cordell bought her and her worn-out mother for an outrageous amount of money at an Atlanta slave auction.

Bell walks over to her. "You late, Jolene. I done told you about bein' late."

Jolene speaks slowly and without much concern for Bell's frustration. "Ain't my doin'. Master had me up most of the night."

"Listen to me girl," Bell says, "What you got between yo' legs don't get you no special privilege around here. No matter how good you think it is. You gonna be workin' under me longer than you gonna be workin' under him. So you better do yo' thinkin' with what's between yo' ears and not yo' legs."

All the other girls in the kitchen start giggling.

Bell gives them all a look. "Hush now. Y'all tend yo' business. Jolene, go fetch a bucket of water, you got floors to scrub. A little bit more time on yo' hands and knees shouldn't bother you. Go on girl."

Helen no sooner walks out of the garden room door then she meets Petal returning from the barn.

"Rabbit got the stud saddled like you asked, Miss Helen."

"I have one other thing Petal. And I don't want it discussed in the kitchen either. Understand?"

"Yes ma'am?"

"I want you to bake me a pecan pie, and put it up. Then late tonight, after the quarters settle down, I want you to clean yourself up, put on a fresh dress, and take that pie down to Sorrel."

Petal instantly begins to smile. "Yes ma'am."

"Now along about midnight, you be out of his bed, or we'll both be in trouble."

"Oh yes ma'am."

"And Petal, one last thing. Under no circumstances are you to ever see Sorrel without my permission. Understand? Under no circumstances."

Petal is all smiles as she answers. "Never Miss Helen, I won't ever. I promise."

"Good. I'm glad we understand each other."

Helen walks on to the stable.

"Thank you ma'am."

Rabbit sees Helen coming and walks briskly back into the barn to get the stud. When he leads the stud out, Helen begins pulling the girt tight and checking the stirrups while Rabbit holds the bridle reins.

"He's ready ma'am. He's more'n ready. Yes ma'am, this boy stays ready. Careful, Miss Helen, on lettin' him out, though. He start runnin', you be in another county before lunch. Oh and I changed to a bit he respects more, but that ain't no sign he won't run. No ma'am and..."

Helen finishes the saddle inspection, then takes the reins from Rabbit. "Rabbit! Enough! Now give me a leg up."

Helen raises her left boot off the ground. Rabbit hesitates, then grabs her ankle, and lifts her up on the stud's back. Helen takes a firm but gentle hold of the bit as she holds the stud in place until she finds both stirrups. In control, she lets the stud walk off easy.

Rabbit watches nervously as Helen rides off. "What do I tell Master Cordell, Miss Helen?"

Helen yells over her shoulder, "The truth!"

Rabbit walks back into the barn. "Lord Jesus, I wish there was something other than the truth. I'd be the first man to tell it today. The first man."

Helen lets the stud find an easy lope as she heads to the warehouses out on Slick Fork Creek to see Sorrel. The men in the plowing crews hardly look up as Helen takes a short cut through a mile of fresh plowed fields to reach the tree-lined warehouse road. The Shannon Hill overseers scattered along the way merely tip the brim of their hats as she rides by.

Reaching the road, she passes several places where the slave women and their children are setting up wagon camps for the men's noonday meal. Three miles on, and the warehouses come into view.

Sorrel and his crew are repairing some boards on the warehouse dock when Helen rides up. Sorrell stops working, removes his hat, and wipes the sweat from his face with a ragged sleeve. His crew continues working and never looks up.

"Mornin' Miss Helen."

She rides by the crew toward the far end of the dock.

"Sorrell, could you walk down here? I need you to look at a shoe on the stud. He seems to be favoring his front left."

"Yes ma'am."

Sorrell walks down the dock steps as Helen slides off the stud. She holds the reins as Sorrell approaches and places his hand on the horse's left shoulder. He starts his hand down the shoulder to the foreleg and ankle.

Sorrell, bending down, speaks soothingly. "Easy now."

Helen whispers, "There's nothing wrong with him."

Sorrell, kneeling looks up at Helen. "Beg your pardon ma'am?"

"Just keep looking at the horse while we talk."

Sorrell looks back down. "Yes ma'am."

"I need to make a trade Sorrell."

"A trade Miss Helen?"

"Yes. A trade with you."

Sorrell smiles slightly. "Well, yes ma'am. But what for?"

"For the first pick of old Jill's pups."

Sorrell stands ups humbly. "Ma'am them..."

A gruff voice booms from the docks on the other side of the stud. "Sorrell!! What the hell you doin' nigger?"

Helen steps out from behind the stud. "Mr. Henry is there a problem?"

Pate Henry is an overseer at the Slick Fork warehouses. He's a fat, squatty young man with ill-fitting clothes from boots to hat. Pate is standing at the edge of the dock holding a large bullwhip in one hand. Upon seeing Helen he almost goes into convulsions.

"Gosh almighty. I never saw you Miss Meyers. I mean the... the boots. When I saw the boots under the horse, I..."

"It's understandable, Mr. Henry. Go on and tend your crew. I just wanted Sorrell to check a shoe for me. We're about done."

Helen speaks softly to Sorrell. "Walk off with me and keep looking at his leg."

Helen leads the stud away from the dock as Pate pretends to busy himself while straining to listen in. Some distance away she stops, and Sorrell kneels to re-examine the stud's ankle and shoe once more.

"On them pups, Miss. I jest..."

Helen interrupts. "Sorrell. What do you think about calico dresses?"

"Uh, well ma'am, I uh," Sorrel stammers.

"How about this? You give Ira Paul Hansen the pick of old Jill's litter, and along about dark, I'll send Petal down to visit with a hot pecan pie."

"Ma'am that's puttin' old Sorrell slap in the middle. Somebody don't get a dog, plus there's Bell. Dat's full trouble."

"You sort your pups, and I'll take care of Bell."

Helen puts the reins over the stud's neck and raises her left ankle for Sorrell to lift her up. He reaches down with one massive hand and effortlessly lifts Helen to the stud's back.

Helen looks down at Sorrell. "She's baking that pie this morning."

Sorrell looks off, takes a deep breath, and nods his head yes without looking up at Helen.

Helen smiles, touches the stud with her boot heels, and lopes away as Sorrell turns to find Pate standing on the dock staring holes through him.

Pate, snarling and shaking out his whip yells, "Get your burrhead ass back to work. You get to thinkin' you something special, and I'll peel your black ass."

Sorrell, ducking his head as he walks back up on the dock, smiles to himself and answers, "Yes boss."

Pate stands staring at Helen as she rides out of sight.

After a long ride through the plantation, Helen arrives back at the horse barn just before lunch. Rabbit walks out looking like a man about to be eaten alive by an imaginary monster. Helen stops the stud in front of the stable and slides off as Rabbit takes hold of the bridle reins.

"Wash him down good before you put him up, Rabbit. He's covered in dry sweat."

"Yes ma'am. And ma'am, master came by lookin' for you, soon after you rode off."

"And what did you tell him?"

"The truth ma'am, just like you told me. Was that right ma'am? I mean..."

"Rabbit. You did the right thing. Now bathe the stud."

Rabbit turns and leads the stud into the barn, talking to himself. "Just need to be careful ma'am. You know how the master is about this here gray hoss."

Helen pulls off her coat and shakes out her hair as she walks toward the main house.

Cordell and Jessica are having lunch on the veranda when Helen walks through the garden door. Upon seeing Helen's wardrobe, Jessica bristles, puts her coffee cup down, and stands up. Helen pauses. She knows better than to avoid the royal invitation. She walks straight for the veranda door, opens it, and steps outside. Cordell continues reading his newspaper.

Jessica coolly looks Helen over before speaking, "Morning."

Helen works to cover a smile that only further infuriates her mother. "Good morning, Mother. Father."

Jessica gestures toward a chair at the table. "Please, sit down. I think your father has something to discuss with you. I know I do." Helen remains standing looking eye-to-eye with her mother.

The determination of both women causes a blizzard of cold, iron wills.

Jessica looks down at Cordell. "Cordell?"

Cordell half closes his newspaper and looks Helen up and down with a twinkle of a smile in his eyes. "What do you have to say for yourself?"

Helen looks down at her boots and clothes. "I just wanted to be comfortable."

He shakes his head. "No not the clothes—the horse."

Jessica erupts. "Yes! The damn clothes!! What on God's earth would possess you to be seen this way! People will..."

Cordell slams the paper down on the table and half rises out of his chair. "Damn it Jessica, sit down!" He points at Helen. "You too!"

Cordell sits back down at the table and pauses for a moment, waiting until both women are seated. He literally despises being caught in the middle of this never ending war between Helen and her mother.

"Now back to the stud," he says firmly. "In the future, I would prefer you select another mount. Of the fifty or so other horses on this place, I am sure you can find something that will suit you."

"Yes sir, but there's none like the stud. He's the best."

Jessica cannot stand it that Cordell is not concerned about her attire. "If you were trying for the best, then why would you dress this way? Do you not know what people say about women who wear men's clothes?"

"My grandma'am smoked cigars right here on this veranda and never cared what people thought."

Cordell smiles.

"Yes and she was totally..." Jessica halts mid-sentence and looks over at Cordell who gives her an unflinching stare.

Jessica takes a deep breath. "She was eighty, and you're eighteen. Rich, eligible young men aren't looking for a wife who rides and dresses like a man."

"Maybe I am not looking for rich, Mother! Maybe I am looking for a wagon driver that needs a woman who can work!"

Jessica gets up and begins to pace. "Is there never an end with you? Cordell please!"

"Helen..." Cordell starts.

"Father! I understand about the stud, but the clothes are comfortable."

Cordell pauses. "I'll allow the clothes, but on one condition."

Helen lights up "Anything."

Jessica grits her teeth and looks off.

"You only wear them for riding when we have no guests."

"Yes sir. Absolutely." Looking over at her mother, she asks, "May I go now?"

Cordell looks over to Jessica, who only raises an eyebrow.

Cordell answers, "You may."

Helen politely addresses her mother as she gets up and walks into the house. "I need a bath and a dress."

Jessica stands, fuming, until Helen closes the veranda door. "Will you please take a hand with her before the gossip ruins her?"

Cordell goes back to his paper. "Me take a hand? You should have done that long before she was grown. It always seemed to slip your mind that you had three daughters, not two, and now you're paying the price."

Helen walks to the foot of the stairway, stops, and looks up the stairway then back to the kitchen.

"Petal? Petal where are you girl?"

Petal walks out of the kitchen wiping her hands on her apron. "Right cher, Miss Helen."

"Draw me up a hot bath Petal, there at the back of the kitchen. Call me when you're done. I am going to lie down."

"Yes ma'am."

Helen leaves the room, smiling at her momentary victory in today's war of words with her mother.

The late evening light casts a spring green hue over the neat rolling hills around Charlotte as Sam approaches town on the Great Wagon Road from the south. When he turns west toward home on State Street, he can hear the distant clanging of a bell. He knows exactly who's ringing it; his mother, Mary Beth, is calling his father to supper. The old bell has a lame sound that seems to get cleaner and more tolerable to the ear on the fading echo. Sam urges the bone-weary mules up and over a small rise as the Tanahill home comes into view on a distant hill.

The warehouse, barns, and pens sit across the red dirt road from a picturesque two-story house with a well thought out garden and yard. The house, barns, and surrounding pastures are all enclosed by rail fences that could not be built any straighter or more uniform. Normally, the sight of home fills Sam with anticipation of Mary Beth's cooking. But after five hard days of muddy roads, cold food, and rain-drenched campsites, Sam can still only think of one thing—the day that he can return to Shannon Hill and ask Cordell's permission to call on Helen.

Owen walks out on the warehouse dock and waves as Sam swings the team around in the road and reins them up next to the other parked wagons at the end of the warehouse.

Owen walks down the warehouse dock steps and says, "Another day, and I was going to head a rider south."

Sam climbs down from the wagon and shakes hands with Owen. "Got hung up at the Rayburns, Paw. Between Ms. Rayburn's matchmaking and the stud, I had to slip off in the dark."

Sam unhooks the trace chains on the lead team and walks them over to the harness shed.

Owen unhooks the second pair. "Tillet and the men just left. I'll help you get 'em put up."

"Thanks Paw, but I got 'em. Maw's waiting supper; tell her I'll be up directly."

Owen watches Sam as he goes about hanging up the harness. He doesn't seem like a man that's been on the road for near three weeks. Owen lights a couple of lanterns and hangs them on a slide wire above the mules at the hitching rack.

"Figured Bess Rayburn would've married them girls off by now," Owen says.

"Well, Sistell finally caught the eye of some fella at the party."

"The Rayburns had a party?"

Owen and Sam continue hanging up harnesses.

Sam answers. "No sir, the Meyers."

"How do you know that?"

Sam answers matter-of-factly. "Seen it with my own eyes."

"You went to a party at the Meyers? The Meyers at Shannon Hill?"

"Yes sir. Why?"

Owen walks out of the shed, stopping at the door.

"Well they're not exactly your choice of social circles. And you're pretty casual with that answer."

"Wasn't any choice of mine. Spence used the stud as an excuse, but Mrs. Rayburn was just trying to match me off with Sistell. So they insisted I stay and go to the party. And the only reason I didn't say no was Spence paying you five hundred for the..."

Sam stops work and stares off.

"You taken the chills son?"

Sam clinches his jaw and turns to face Owen. "I forgot to get the money for the stud."

Owen holds Sam's look for a moment.

"Any particular reason why?"

Sam turns his attention back to the mules. "I'll leave horseback as soon as I'm done. This is mine to sort."

"No need in a special trip, son. I'll have Tillet pick it up next month on his way to Charleston."

"If it's all the same to you, Paw, I'll take care of this."

"Is there something I need to know here? Because it doesn't seem to be the money."

Sam pauses. "No sir. Just something I need to put to rest."

"Fair enough. When should I look for you?"

"Ah, a week or so."

"I'll tell your maw that you're not staying."

Owen turns to walk off, stops, and turns back to Sam.

"I traded for a smutty dun gelding; I call him Slick. He's over there in the back pens. Looks like a wrung out cur, but you can't kill him. He'll get you there and back."

Owen turns and walks toward the house. "Come up and see your maw before you strike out."

Owen walks up onto the back porch of the house, takes off his hat, and washes his hands and face in a large ceramic bowl. He is drying off when Mary Beth comes to the back door.

She asks, "Sam about finished?"

"Yeah, but he's not staying."

"He just got home. Where's he going?"

Owen walks into the house followed by Mary Beth.

Owen sits down at the kitchen table. "Back to the Rayburns. He forgot to collect for the stud. I told him Tillet could pick it up next month, but he wouldn't hear of it."

Mary Beth starts setting the table. "Old Spence will drink and gamble with the best of 'em, but he's no cheat. Don't figure Sam worrying that hard."

Owen nods his head and says, "You're right, but you know how Sam is about settin' things right."

"I suppose," Mary Beth says, "but it still don't figure."

Mary Beth is setting the table when Sam walks into the kitchen.

Without stopping her work, she says, "Don't reckon I heard you wash up."

"All the same Maw, I need to go."

Without a look up she replies, "Near three days ride to the Rayburn place. Sitting down for a meal won't make you late."

"Not much hungry; besides, I'm gonna ride most of the night."

Owen looks over at Sam and says, "You stop somewhere, tie them hobbles tight. Old Slick will leave you afoot."

Sam fidgets with his hat and struggles with his guilt. He stood right there on the porch talking to Spence and business never crossed his mind.

"I reckon you best go on, so's you can get back. Couple of weeks, I got lots of freight to move. I'll need you."

Sam answers with resolve. "I'll be here." He turns toward Mary Beth and says, "Maw."

Mary Beth stops her work and turns to Sam. "You mind your raisin', Sam Tanahill."

Sam and his mother share a look for a moment. "Yes ma'am." He nods to Owen, "Paw."

Sam turns and walks out, steps up on the dun gelding, and lopes off.

Mary Beth sits down at the table and passes Owen the roast and potatoes.

Owen takes the bowl. "I hope whatever's causing that boy grief, he gets it settled."

In a matter-of-fact tone Mary Beth surprises Owen. "I'd say it's a woman."

Owen pauses. "A woman?"

Mary Beth takes the bowl back and continues, "And my guess would be a low-country woman at that. I just hope he don't come to grief trying to settle it either. That bunch down there has their ways."

She reaches across the table and takes hold of Owens' hands, and they both bow their heads.

Owen prays, "Almighty God, we ask that you continue to lead, guide, and direct our lives as we go forward. In Jesus name we pray, amen."

"Amen," Mary Beth says in agreement.

"You may be right. He went to the Meyers's cotillion with the Rayburns."

Mary Beth smiles. "There's an odd thought—Sam and a rich, low-country belle."

"Well, given his view of things, I'd say that would be a little farfetched."

Mary Beth laughs knowingly and says, "Not farfetched at all, if it's the right woman."

She passes Owen the bread.

"Thank you," he says, taking the basket. "I thought he took a shine to... what's the girl's name that lives over in the Shenandoah?"

"You thinkin' of Dancy Higgins?"

"Yeah, the lanky German girl."

"Don't think so. Dancy never gave him that look he's a carryin' now."

"Look or not, I need him to get it sorted. A man don't need to let his personal matters get him outta balance."

"Well, that's never been his problem before, and I doubt it will be now."

Owen smiles. "Doubt all you want, but he just rode away from your roast and potatoes. I would say that's outta balance."

CHAPTER FIVE

THE SCATTERED DRIZZLE GIVES THE EAST WIND A CHILLING bite as Sam once again sits in the middle of the road at Beeches Crossing. After three hard days, Old Slick needs little encouragement to stand still while Sam stares off to the south at Shannon Hill. The evening darkness is rapidly settling in, leaving the roads a mere black mark through the timber. Remembering the real cause of the trip, Sam turns the dun gelding west and strikes a lope for the Rayburn's. Cordell will have to wait one more day.

Several hours later, the lights of the Rayburn place shine through the woods, accompanied by the soft sound of a piano and the mournful balling of a hound. Sam pulls the gelding up and lets him walk on in easy. He steps down from the mount and ties him by the picket fence gate, then walks up onto the porch and knocks. The piano playing stops and so does all sound in the house. The hound falls silent as Sam listens, then catches the movement of a curtain out of the corner of his eye. The front door slowly opens. Sam watches cautiously, and then Ira Paul steps from behind the door.

Sam speaks first. "Ira Paul, evening."

Ira Paul, looking more than a little relieved, "Evening Sam."

"I didn't quite expect to run into you tonight. Mr. Rayburn home?"

Ira Paul relaxes. "Naw. Ms. Rayburn took him to see the doctor down in Charleston. We're thinking they'll be home tomorrow or the next day. Come in Sam."

Sam removes his hat and steps through the door. His attention is drawn to a Colt pistol lying on a small table behind the door.

"Ira Paul, between your fretting and that Colt, is there something going on around here?"

Sistell walks into the room followed by Newella.

Newella answers Sam's question. "Only niggers' killin' white folks. I'd say that he has reason for both."

Sistell corrects her sister. "It was only one nigger, Newella. You make it sound like a war."

Sam turns to Ira Paul. "Here?"

"Naw, two places over at the Palmore's. Last week a field hand took a trace chain to an overseer."

Sam pauses then says, "I take it they didn't catch him."

"Nope, he's a runnin', but they will. Shannon Hill's overseer, Ike Murphy, sent his man, Paxton Henry, through here a few days ago. I 'spect that spook's a hangin' in a tree by now."

Sam says, almost to himself, “Long way to ride to catch one man.”

“Ike don’t see it that way when it comes to catchin’ niggers. Especially one that’s done harm.”

Newella reminds them, “Folks haven’t forgotten The Nat Turner Rebellion, and rightly so. Lots of women and children died under that nigger’s hand. Ike and some others just mean to see it doesn’t happen again. Not in South Carolina, anyway.”

Sistell cuts in on Newella. “So what is it that brings you all this way, Mr. Tanahill?”

Newella talks over Sistell, “And what do you have to say to that, Mr. Tanahill?”

Sam speaks first to Sistell. “I have business with your father.” Then he turns to Newella and says, “I say that is none of my business, and I intend to keep it that way.”

Sistell motions toward the dining room. “Gentlemen, shall we?”

Newella persists. “I think you’re wrong Mr. Tanahill. Niggers like that are everyone’s business.”

Sam ignores Newella as he and Ira Paul follow Sistell into the dining room with Newella close behind.

Sistell tries to move the conversation. “You look wet and hungry, Mr. Tanahill. I think we can do something about both. Newella, go to Ryland’s room and bring Mr. Tanahill a dry change of clothes.”

Newella snaps at her sister. “I beg your pardon. I’m not a house girl.”

“Given the circumstances, dear sister, I would say you’re well on your way.”

Sam interrupts their sibling spat. "If you will excuse me for a moment, my horse is twice as wet and hungry. I would like to see to him first."

Sistell stops by the dining room table. "Nonsense." She turns toward the kitchen and says, "Jeb, come out here."

Jeb walks into the room. "Yes ma'am."

"Take Mr. Tanahill's horse down to the barn, and tell Teddy to see to him."

"Yes ma'am."

"Thank you, ma'am. Uh Jeb, I'll be leaving soon so don't turn him out."

"Yes sir."

Jeb walks out of the room.

"Evidently," says Newella, "Mr. Tanahill has other business in these parts."

Sistell gives her sister a sharp look. "That is not our concern, Newella."

"Then where on Earth would a man be going on a night like this?"

Sam stares at Newella.

"I guess we all just got our answer. According to Ira Paul, they've been expecting you."

Sam looks over at Ira Paul. "Have they now?"

"They have Sam. You made an impression on everyone."

"Mr. Tanahill," says Sistell, "Stay the night with us and rest. I am afraid your present condition may change that good impression you worked so hard on."

Sam catches sight of himself in the large mirror behind the dining room table. The wet clothes and days without a bath never crossed Sam's mind until now.

Sam looks to Sistell and replies, "Thank you, ma'am. That would be kindly of you."

Sistell gestures toward the liquor cabinet. "Good, then that's settled. Newella, make yourself useful and pour everyone a glass of wine. I'll have the girls draw Mr. Tanahill a bath and fetch him some supper. And I'll get the clothes, Miss Busy Body!"

Sam and Ira Paul sit down at the table while Newella pours the wine.

"That your hound I heard ridin' up?" Sam asks Ira Paul.

"Yep, got three of 'em there in the dog yard. Old Trashy is the only one that hates a piano."

"So you working for Mr. Spence now?"

Ira Paul looks a little sheepish. "Well, I am not right sure so far. You see, I uh..."

Newella smirks. "Not right sure! Hell, everyone around here has been giving him liberties like he owns the place, including Sistell."

The house girl is setting Sam's supper on the table when Sistell walks back into the room with the clothes and boots.

"Careful, Newella, you may just slip and fall again." Turning to Sam and Ira Paul she says, "My apologies, wine is in fashion with my sister of late."

Sistell places the clothes and tall boots next to Sam. She sits down close to Ira Paul and sips her wine while Newella drinks and gives her a glaring stare.

After supper and a hot bath, Sam walks back into the dining room dressed, once again, in Ryland's clothes. The room is empty and the house is quiet, except for the sounds of muffled conversations in the kitchen between the house girls and Old Jeb. Sam walks through the house and out onto the porch looking for Ira Paul and the girls. He finds Ira Paul sitting in a rocker on the dimly lit porch.

"The girls are gone to bed. I was waiting on Jeb to finish cleaning up for the night. He'll show you to your room in a bit. In the meantime, sit a spell."

Sam walks down the porch and sits down in a rocker next to Ira Paul.

"How do you know they're expecting me?"

"Well I'm kinda, sorta family in a way."

"You kin to the Meyers?"

"No, no. My paw was an overseer on and off for Mr. Cordell, and my maw... well, she died when I was four or so. Anyway, Bell kept me up at the big house to play with Helen while my paw was in the fields."

"You grew up with Helen?"

"I did, and we had a time together."

"Who is Bell?"

Ira Paul smiles. “Mama Bell. She runs most everything at Shannon Hill, from the big house to the quarters. You saw her at the party, skinny little nigger woman, blacker than pitch night.”

Sam acknowledges Ira Paul’s description. “I did notice her. She stood there by the kitchen door most of the day.”

“That’s her. And if you aim to court Helen, you best find favor with Mama Bell.”

“I am a little confused here. Is Bell a slave, or free, or what?”

“She’s a slave alright, but she’s Helen’s mama in everything except name.”

“Wait a minute. Start from the front of this story and shed a little light on it. I feel like I’m in a thicket here.”

“Well, it ain’t a short story. You got time?”

Sam stares holes through Ira Paul.

“Course you do. Dumb question.”

Sam impatiently pushes Ira Paul on. “The story.”

Ira Paul smiles and looks off. “My old pap was a man of the Book, and he always said the Lord had his ways.”

“I don’t follow you.”

Ira Paul takes a deep breath and continues, “Well, let me start from the beginning. You’ll follow soon enough. You see, there was a big calamity about...”

The front door opening distracts Ira Paul. Sistell stands half out the door in her nightgown.

"Ira Paul, you coming to bed?"

Ira Paul turns a crimson red as he glances over at Sam.

Ira Paul looks away from Sistell and answers, "Directly. We're near done. Go on in."

Sistell quietly shuts the door, and Ira Paul sits in guilty silence. Sam clears his throat, and Ira Paul fidgets.

Ira Paul looks over to Sam. "Well dang, what's a fellow supposed to do? I ain't got 'no' in me when it comes to such things."

Sam smiles. "You were saying there was a big calamity."

Ira Paul avoids eye contact with Sam and tries to regain himself.

"Yes sir, and lots of bad blood over it."

"Between who?"

"Mostly between Helen and her maw."

"That's easy enough to see. So what caused it?"

"Well it all started when Helen's sisters, Z and Liz, were 10 or 11 years old."

"How old was Helen during all this?"

Ira Paul answers. "Wasn't born yet. That was the calamity. Miss Jessica was all through with children when Mr. Cordell came home one night, all liquored up, and had his way with her."

"And that's when Jessica got pregnant with Helen?"

"Yes sir, but she wasn't happy, no way. When Helen was born, Miss Jessica gave her to Bell, and that was that."

"What do you mean 'that was that?' Lots of children are raised by nannies."

"That's true enough," says Ira Paul, "but as Helen got older, Jessica never done none of the raisin'. She was too busy travelin' or goin' to parties."

Sam rocks and stares off into the night. "I understand now."

Ira Paul and Sam sit quiet for a moment.

"Yes sir, I figure God knew. That's what scares Jessica about you. You're the only kind Helen ever took a second look at. "

Sam smiles easy. "And what's my kind?"

Ira Paul gets up and walks to the door to go inside.

He looks back at Sam and answers, "A man that won't take no for an answer. Oh, and if you don't mind, I'll ride over with you in the mornin'. Gotta hound pup to pick up."

Sam nods as he stares off into the night, thinking.

"When you've a mind to, your bed's ready. Second door down the hall on your left. What time you want up?"

"Four'll do."

Ira Paul walks into the house. "I'll tell Jeb."

The next morning, long before daylight, Sam is saddling the gelding when Ira Paul walks into the barn.

"Old Jeb said he was getting you up half hour ago. Guess you got tangled in the sheets."

Ira Paul ignores Sam's remark and begins to hurriedly saddle his horse. Sam steps up on the gelding and rides out of the barn.

He is riding back by the house when Ira Paul lopes up beside him and slows his horse to a walk. Ira Paul waves to Sistell, who is standing on the porch wrapped in a blanket.

Sam nudges the gelding into an easy lope and disappears into the early morning darkness, followed by Ira Paul.

They ride through the Shannon Hill archway as the mid-day sun shines bright through the sentinel oaks that line the red cobblestone drive. Ira Paul fidgets and frets as the gleaming white mansion comes into view at the end of the tunnel of oaks. He reins his horse up with a nervous jerk. Sam turns around and rides back to Ira Paul, who still fidgets.

"Go get your pup," Sam says, "I'll see you at the Rayburns."

"I'll be here a'waitin'. We can ride back together."

Sam nods and rides on. The mansion gets closer, and Sam's resolve stiffens. His eyes scan the mansion as if it were Kanetuck Indian country. He boldly rides up the circle drive and dismounts at the hitching post with Mary Beth's words fresh in his mind. "Mind your raisin', Sam Tanahill."

Sam takes the front steps almost two at a time, reaches the giant mahogany door, and knocks without hesitation. Time ticks away as Sam waits and waits, and a dry stillness washes over him. After several callous minutes, the door begins to open. Sam removes his hat as Bell steps from behind the door. The two stand looking at each other for a moment.

Sam nods. "Bell."

Bell stands erect with her eyes forward. "How can I help you sir?"

"Is Mr. Myers home?"

"Yes sir. Come in." She motions toward the foyer. "Wait here sir. I'll tell Mr. Myers you're here." She turns to walk away.

"My name is Sam Tanahill, ma'am."

Bell turns back with her eyes cast down. "I am not a ma'am, sir. I am Bell, and we all know who you is, sir."

Bell glances up at Sam and gently smiles, then walks away.

The eleventh chime of the grandfather clock begins to fade away when Sam hears boot steps on the marble floor. He turns to see Cordell walking toward the foyer with the bearing of a king on official business. Sam reads the situation and comes to attention. He full well understands that Jessica's message at the party is about to be delivered. Cordell stops in front of Sam as if to answer a challenge.

Sam respectfully extends his hand, "Mr. Myers. Sam Tanahill."

Cordell is direct and formal in his handshake.

Cordell pointedly asks, "Mr. Tanahill. How may I help?"

"I am here sir to request your permission to call on Miss Myers."

Cordell's answer is quick and to the point. "You may not, Mr. Tanahill, call on my daughter, and that is final, sir!"

Cordell's sharp disrespectful tone is met by a cold stare from Sam, a stare that only lasts for a moment, until he begins to smile. The momentary silence and Sam's continued smile only heightens Cordell's irritation. Without turning around, he knows Helen is standing behind him.

"Mr. Tanahill! Is there anything else?" Cordell asks.

Sam is lost in her radiant beauty as she stands on the spiral staircase. He nods in a gentlemanly fashion as he says her name, "Miss Myers."

Helen says his name in a soft whisper, "Mr. Tanahill."

Cordell turns to Helen. "Go upstairs. Now!"

Helen turns and gradually walks up the stairs without taking her eyes off of Sam. She knows that if she is to ever see Sam again, she has to do as Cordell requests. Her father is and always has been her only ally.

Cordell turns back to Sam. "Sir. You have your answer. I expect you, as a gentleman, to honor that decision."

Sam turns to Cordell. "I would hope, sir, that the final decision would be hers."

"Mr. Tanahill, I am the final decision on all things in this house and a lot of other far reaching places. Am I clear, sir?"

Cordell abruptly turns and walks away. "Good day, Mr. Tanahill. Bell! See the gentleman to the door."

Sam glances back to the stairs to see Helen standing at the top. She points to herself, then writes an imaginary note in her hand, and then points to Sam. Sam smiles and goes out the door and down the steps to his horse. He mounts the dun gelding and sits looking at the grand mansion for a moment. He tips the brim of his hat to all the eyes that are hidden from view, turns, and rides away easy.

In the far distance, at the end of the cobblestone road, Sam sees a rider sitting in the shadows of the giant oaks. Drawing closer, he sees it's not Ira Paul, but Ike Murphy, the main overseer for Shannon Hill. Ike rides out into the middle of the road and stops, facing Sam.

Ike Murphy is twenty years Sam's senior, with a polished hardness that lives in every corner of Ike's being. He rules the field help at Shannon Hill, both slave and white, with pain that could only come straight from hell. His brand of evil is known and feared far and wide.

Sam knows he isn't here by accident. He rides straight up to Ike, stops his horse, and the two men sit staring for a moment.

"I'll get to the point Tanahill. You're not to call at that house. Ever again!"

Sam gets a crazy look in his eyes, kicks the gelding, and starts by Ike. Ike catches the gelding's reins and stops him. The men are looking eye-to-eye.

Sam says in a painfully measured tone of voice, "Careful what you take hold of."

"I know your grit, Tanahill, but this is not about me and you. It's about your father."

"My father?"

"You do as that man asks," Ike points to Shannon Hill, "And your father's business prospers. You defy him... and well, you're not stupid."

Ike turns the reins loose and rides away.

Sam sits in a silent, blind rage staring down the road until he hears his name.

"Sam?"

Sam looks up to see Ira Paul riding up.

"He told me to sit down by the woods—that y'all had business. I didn't know what to say or do. Ike's crazy."

Sam smiles easy. "No worry, Ira Paul. We got it all straight."

Sam nudges a heel to the dun as Ira Paul falls in beside him. The two ride off in silence. Ira Paul is just about to burst at the seams with a sack of questions, but clearly sees that now is better suited for silence. Sam rides, staring down the road with a grinding anger that numbs him through and through.

Ira Paul breaks the silence between them. "I know it don't give comfort, but you ain't the first to get the two-barrel treatment."

Sam looks over to Ira Paul with a cold, offhand grin. "You figure I got the two-barrel treatment?"

"Well. What I figure was, you sure weren't up at the house long. And then Ike waitin' on you down here. Yes sir. That's what I'd say."

"Tell me," Sam says, "Why did he send Ike?"

"Oh Mr. Cordell didn't send him. That's Miss Jessica."

"Is that a fact?" Sam asks.

"Yes sir. Mr. Cordell will look you in the eye and tell it like it is. Now Miss Jessica, she'll tell it like she wants it to be, and then move half of hell makin' it so."

Sam repeats to himself, "Half of hell." Turning to Ira Paul, he asks, "Being you've seen this before. Is it all bark, or will she bite?"

"Nare no idleness to her. If Ike said it, she'll make it happen. And you can rest on that."

Sam grits his teeth and thinks about Helen. The West is really no place for a woman, especially one raised up never knowing hardship. Besides, even if he weren't going west, he could never do anything that would harm Owen. Sam turns his mind to a thousand thoughts, but Helen's radiant smile and dazzling blue eyes have his heart and soul conquered.

He leans forward and taps the dun with both boot heels, pushing the gelding into an easy lope. He intends to collect for the stud and get on home as soon as possible. With the break of spring, Owen will need every driver. Ira Paul yanks the puppy out of the sack and cradles him in one arm as he lopes after Sam.

The fading light of the warm spring day begins turning cool as darkness settles over the Rayburn farm. Spence, Bess, and Sistell are sitting on the porch with Old Jeb standing close at hand, holding a quart of whiskey. Sistell rocks easy and softly hums, longing for Ira Paul to be home. She glances over at her mother, who is in a world of her own, reading passages from the worn family Bible. Spence winks at Sistell and taps a large whiskey glass on the arm of the hickory rocker. Old Jeb uncorks the bottle and pours two fingers in the glass.

Spence laughs a raspy-throated belly laugh, "Jeb. That needs to be two fingers up and down, not sideways."

He holds the glass up, and Jeb fills it to the brim. Recorking the bottle, Jeb's attention is drawn toward the dark road leading up to the house.

"Riders coming boss," Jeb says.

Sistell is up and out of the rocker with a quickness that slightly startles Bess.

"Sistell, mind yourself," Bess says.

When Sam and Ira Paul ride into the lamplight at the gate, Sistell lets out a sharp sigh and starts for the gate. Ira Paul's boot barely touches the ground when Sistell has her arms around him.

Sam nods to Spence and Bess. "Evenin'."

"Evenin' Sam," says Bess. "Jeb, tend their horses."

Ira Paul and Sistell are talking in hushed tones.

Ira Paul turns to the Rayburns. "Evenin' folks. I got the horses, ma'am. I need to put my pup up down at the barn."

Bess acknowledges Ira Paul and says, "Come on up, Sam. I'll have the girls get y'all supper."

Sam hands Ira Paul his reins. "Tend to' em, but don't turn' em out. I am riding on."

Ira Paul asks, "Tonight?"

"Tonight," Sam answers as he walks toward the door.

Ira Paul leads the horses off toward the barn, hand-in-hand with Sistell.

Sam walks up onto the porch and takes off his hat.

"Ma'am... Mr. Rayburn."

Sam extends his hand.

Spence goes to put a cigar in his mouth when Bess catches his hand gently.

"Mr. Rayburn. That wasn't our agreement."

Spence relinquishes the cigar to Bess and shakes Sam's hand.

In a low, gravelly voice he says to Bess, "How could I forget?"

"Jeb," Spence redirects his attention, "Fetch Mr. Tanahill a glass. I am sure he could use a cool drink after visiting the bowels of hell."

Bess gets up abruptly and says, "Mr. Rayburn, that's not Christian." Then to Sam she says, "Have a seat, Sam, and rest a spell."

"Thank you ma'am."

"Yeah, sit down Sam. We'll drink to treacherous minds and Christian hearts," Spence says, amusing himself at Bess's expense.

Bess turns to Spence, less than amused, and says, "More listening than talking now. That was also our agreement."

Spence nods as she walks off. Jeb returns and hands Sam the glass.

"Pour Mr. Tanahill a drink Jeb. Two fingers down."

Jeb pours the glass full. "Yes sir."

Spence holds his glass up in a salute. "It ain't the answer, but it helps while you're lookin' for one."

Sam returns the salute and takes a deep drink.

"I have the answer, Mr. Rayburn, I just can't make it ride well."

"Saw that in your eyes." And then raising his glass again, he says, "Well here's to Christians. God bless their sorry souls."

Sam hesitates a moment, then empties the glass. The whiskey burns in his guts, but not near as hot as Ike's threat. Sam's mood darkens with the reality that some things can never be changed. He holds the glass up for Jeb to refill it. When he finishes filling the glass, Sam empties it in one long drink.

Spence reaches over and puts his hand on Sam's arm. "Easy son. There ain't no answers in that stuff. If there were, I'd be a genius."

Sam sits the glass on the porch by his rocking chair. He takes a deep breath, grabs the rocker by both arm rests, and stands up. His heart damaged, but his dreams unbroken, his thoughts turn to Owen and home. It's time he had that talk with his father about the West. By Sam's reasons, everyone would be better served if he lived in other parts.

"I'll be gathering my belongings and heading on, sir."

"Before we let the matter get looked over again, Bess'll pay you for the stud."

"Appreciate it."

"Sam, I hope that stud gives us both a little satisfaction."

"In what way, sir?"

"Cordell sent a match invitation the day after the party."

"For when?" Sam asks.

"The second Saturday after Easter, over at the Robinson place. It's the big spring horse race they have every year."

"Yeah, I've heard about it," Sam replies.

"Seeing Journey beat that gray would be... well... Cordell handing me money would be a prayer answered."

"Journey," Sam says thoughtfully. "Kind of an odd name."

"Well, it's been a long hard road trying to beat Cordell. I hope the bay is the end of that journey."

"I wish I could be there, but Paw's got too much work a'coming. Send me word, win or lose."

"I will. Go on in now; supper's probably gettin' cold."

Sam walks on into the house as Ira Paul and Sistell walk back up from the barn.

"Come sit, Mr. Hansen, and tell me of the spring plowing and my race horse."

He refills his glass and hands the bottle to Ira Paul. "Old Jeb says you're no slacker. Up before the sun and in after dark."

Ira Paul fiddles with the bottle. "My paw would have never tolerated less."

"Son. A better man I never knew. He'd stay hooked and finish any job he started, no matter how difficult. Now tell me about the stud."

"We been breezin' him just like you laid out. Gosh amighty, I never rode such power."

"Can he get the gray?" Spence inquires.

"The gray's fast, but I don't think he has a heart like Journey."

Spence smiles and leans back in the rocker. "Give that bottle to Jeb there, and get yourself to the table."

"Yes sir."

He gets up and starts for the door, stops, and turns back to Spence.

"I just want you to know... I'll stay hooked sir. Never give that a thought."

Spence sits in silence while Ira Paul waits.

Finally he breaks the silence. "Never crossed my mind, son."

Later that night, Old Jeb is holding a lantern up in the hallway of the stable while Sam saddles the dun gelding. He's tying his slicker and bedroll on the saddle when Ira Paul walks in, carrying table scraps for his dogs.

There is an awkward silence between the two men as Sam finishes checking the saddle.

"I guess Mrs. Rayburn told you about his cancer," Ira Paul says to Sam.

"She did. Said the doc down in Charleston didn't give him long."

"Hard way for a man to die. My Uncle T had it. You could hear him screaming for miles. Aunt May finally shot him in the ear."

Sam steps up on the gelding and extends his hand to Ira Paul.

"I hope it don't come to that."

"I ain't wantin' to pry, Mr. Tanahill, but you coming back this way?"

Sam sits in silence staring at Ira Paul.

Ira Paul looks off and shakes his head kinda crazy. "She's gonna ask."

Sam smiles. "Take care, Ira Paul."

He rides out of the stable, headed home.

CHAPTER SIX

HELEN SITS IN THE GARDEN ON A BENCH BENEATH A MASSIVE live oak, which is surrounded by an array of spring flowers. The sounds of the quarters carry up through the surrounding oaks while dusk settles over the plantation. She sits, thinking how far removed the day has made her feel about everything that has been her life. When she saw Ike stop Sam in the road today, she decided then and there that she would live life as an old maid before she submits to her parents' choices of men in her life.

Cordell walks out into the garden. "Bell said you asked to be excused from supper. I would prefer you join us."

Helen stands up and turns her back to Cordell. "I haven't an appetite, thank you."

Cordell, in a tone bordering on an apology, says, "I know you don't agree with my decision, but sometimes..."

Helen turns on him suddenly, with a sweet smile. "But I do agree with your decision father. This is your house, and you are entitled."

Jessica walks up and hears Helen's comment. "I would hope that is heartfelt, and not anger. Your father and I are only thinking of you, and what's best."

Helen, stepping around her father to face Jessica, squares off. "That man came to call on me. He rode a long way to see me!"

Cordell, stepping between the women, intervenes. "This will not evolve into a shouting match. Do I make myself clear?"

Helen turns and walks a few steps away.

Jessica, savoring a moment of victory, answers, "There'll come a time when you will see the blessings in your father's decision."

Helen, turning to her mother, replies, "You call treating someone so callously a blessing? It wasn't enough to dismiss him like a field hand. You had to send Ike to reinforce the message, with kindness and dignity I'm sure."

"What would you have us do? Allow anyone who knocks on the door to come marching in? Your mother and I have our differences, but on one thing we agree."

Helen, with tears coming to her eyes snaps. "I don't want to hear it!"

Pointing at her father, she asks, "How would you like it if I told you what horse to race, what whiskey to drink, who you could talk to, or how to dress? And worst of all, who you'll share your bed with? The only difference between me and the girls in the quarters is the table I sit at."

Jessica responds. "There is a substantial difference, my dear. But I warn you. With callers like Mr. Tanahill, the gap will narrow beyond repair."

Cordell takes a deep breath. "There are some choices that are rightfully yours. But men like Mr. Tanahill are my decision, and my decision alone."

Helen ignores Cordell and speaks to Jessica. "The difference you speak of, I came to terms with today, and it gives me great relief. I finally faced the truth in myself concerning the Meyers name and money. Because if it only yields what you have, I don't want that kind of misery. EVER!"

Jessica lashes out, almost blind with rage. "By God in heaven, you have never lived without either, and you're not tough enough to do so!"

"There you're mistaken, Mother."

Cordell, raising his voice, "Goddammit, enough!!"

Cordell paces and runs his hands through his unruly wavy hair, wishing he had a drink.

"My decision on Mr. Tanahill is final," he says.

"And my decision on anyone you invite here to call on me is final!"

Cordell turns to Helen. "What exactly are you saying?"

Helen looks straight at her father, then to Jessica. "I'll treat them with the same genteel kindness and hospitality that you've shown Mr. Tanahill."

Cordell's sandy complexion turns bright red. "Is that a threat?"

Jessica starts, "For God's sakes, what…"

"Shut up Jessica!" Cordell interrupts. "Helen, I am waiting."

"I veil nothing I've said as a threat, Father. You said yourself that some choices are rightfully mine and mine alone. So, I will retain control over whom I will receive and whom I will not. Mr. Tanahill will not be welcome by you, but all others will not be welcome by me."

Jessica's eyes blaze and she demands, "Cordell! You can't."

Cordell holds up his hand for Jessica to be quiet.

"I've lived with this war long enough. Helen, we're in agreement for the time being."

Jessica storms into the house.

Cordell, with a whole new respect for his daughter, takes a deep breath, nods his head with a twinkle in his eye, then turns and walks away.

Helen leans back in the large white porcelain bathtub and reflects on the day. She hopes that somehow, someday, Sam will sit on that bench with her in the garden.

Petal pours another bucket of warm water into the tub at the far end. Helen closes her eyes and relaxes, humming softly.

"Petal," Helen asks, "Which one of the girls in the quarters is keeping Ike company these days?"

"Gosh almighty Miss, dat could be anyone. Was my friend, Switch, she da one dat heps Big Polly cook."

"What's her name?"

"We calls her Switch. Dat cause she be skinny like a switch."

"Can you trust her, Petal?"

"Oh yes ma'am. With anything, Missy."

"You remember the day Mr. Tanahill came calling?"

"Oh... Yes ma'am."

"Mr. Tanahill passed Ike on the road leaving. I sure wish I knew what they stopped and talked about. Probably be worth some time at Sorrels if you could find that out."

"Dat may be hard. Most times, Mr. Ike don't allow her to talk while he visiting."

"Well ask around, Petal. Ike drinks and brags. Somebody's heard the story."

Petal pours more warm water into the tub and answers, "Yes ma'am."

"Go turn my bed back and set out pen and paper. I want to send a letter over to the Rayburn place."

Yes ma'am, Miss Helen.

Later that night, Helen sits at her desk in her bedroom, silently reading a letter she has just finished writing. Petal sits nearby in Helen's rocker, sound asleep. Her long slender hands lying in her lap with a candle flickering nearby gives Petal's face an angelic pose. The soft light falls across her smooth tan face, highlighted by the colorful scarf she wears bound around her wavy black hair.

"Petal, wake up."

Petal slowly rubs her face.

"Come on girl, open your eyes. I have something important for you to do."

Petal raises both arms above her head and stretches, moaning softly. "Yes ma'am?"

"I want you to take this letter down to Sorrel's tomorrow night and give it to him, and make sure nobody sees you carrying it. It's for Mister Ira Paul. You tell him to give it to Ira Paul when they go coon huntin' next week. And Petal… tell him don't let a soul see the letter or know he's carrying it either. Understand? Now tell me, what did I just tell you?"

"Give it to Mr. Ira Paul and don't let a soul see it or knows he's carryin' it."

"That's right, Petal. Now, you can visit Sorrel for a spell. But you be back in your bed long before Mama Bell stirs the next morning. You hear me?"

Petal smiles. "Yes ma'am, before Mama Bell stirs."

Helen hands her the letter. "Now get off to bed with you."

The dun gelding takes every step forward as if on a mountain ledge, while the rain blows sideways, stinging both horse and rider. Sam turns up the west road in Charlotte, barely able to see from under the brim of his hat. He holds his slicker tight around his neck and rides the gelding on a loose rein, allowing the horse to pick his own path through the deep ruts that cut the road from side to side. Sam knows there is no need to crowd the horse when they both know that home is just over the hill.

Sam briefly glances up when the house comes into view. He is a little puzzled to see that there isn't one wagon parked by the warehouse—not even his. Riding on by the warehouse to the barn door, he can hear the ringing of a hammer over in the blacksmith shop. He rides into the barn, dismounts, and ties the gelding up in front of the saddle room. He pulls his slicker off and begins to unsaddle the worn out horse.

Owen walks in wearing a blacksmith's apron. He is covered in sweat, with his sleeves rolled up. Seeing the condition of the horse, he remarks, "Don't look like he'll run off any more."

Sam is surprised to see his father working in the blacksmith shop.

"I doubt he had another mile in him," Sam replies, putting the horse in a stall. He looks around and asks, "Where is everybody?"

"They're all on the road. Shine and Little Jim took your rig to pick up some whiskey for Peach's store over in the Shenandoah."

"You shoeing something in there?"

"Naw. Just making a set of shoes for your team. Shine's goin' to shoe 'em when they get back. Figured I'd get the iron ready."

Sam's matter-of-fact way catches Owen's attention. Sam rode off almost two weeks ago barely knowing the day of the week, and now he rides back in with the presence of a man long past his years. Whatever happened in those few days, he's sure Sam will discuss it when he's ready.

Sam hangs the horse's bridle up and starts for the blacksmith shop.

"Where you going, Son?"

"To help you."

"You're soaked plum through. Go to the house and change first."

Sam walks on toward the shop. "I'll dry soon enough at the forge. Let's finish."

Sam walks into the blacksmith shop, grabs a leather apron from a bench, and puts it on without saying a word. He pulls the red-hot iron bar from the forge and begins to pound it flat on the anvil. Sam swings the hammer with a force that Owen knows is anger-driven. The two men work at a grinding hot pace until Mary Beth breaks the silence with the noonday dinner bell. Sam swings the hammer one last time and stands motionless, looking down at the anvil.

Owen begins taking his apron off, and Sam can feel the question about the money long before Owen says anything.

Owen turns to walk out of the blacksmith shop and says, "Let's eat. Your maw will want to see you."

Sam hasn't moved from the anvil. "I am going to pay you for the stud."

Owen turns around and says, "What?"

Sam looks up. "I said I am going to pay you for the bay that you sold Spence."

Owen can see the trouble in his son's eyes. "Why would you do that Sam?"

"Long story."

"Son, we've always talked. Sit down and talk to me; your mother will wait."

Sam takes a deep breath. "Well, there's two reasons. Spence has cancer and won't live till summer."

Owen, almost to himself, "Cancer."

"Yes sir, of the throat. He was sitting on the porch drinking when I rode up. We talked a minute, then he sent me into the house to see Mrs. Rayburn about the money. When I said something to her about it, she took me out on the back porch and started crying. Well the short is, he's dying, and they're broke. So I told her to keep the money, that I'd pay you, and after... Well, I'd come and fetch the horse. He'd be mine and nobody had to know till then."

The two men sit in silence for a moment. Owen knows his son well enough to know that something else is causing his anger.

"You said there were two reasons for buying the horse?"

Sam struggles with his decision. He knows that his next words will break his father's heart.

"Well, sir, I'm going west. I need a blooded stud to raise some horses with."

Owen ducks his head and smiles, then looks up at Sam.

"Son. That's not a new revelation."

Owen pauses. "Tell me what's driving all this. You come in here wet and wore out. You pick up a hammer and beat horseshoes for almost three hours. That takes a powerful lot of anger to drive a man like that. Wouldn't you say?"

"Don't take this wrong, Paw, but there's nothing here for me. I want to go where a man has a chance. Where there's land. Land as far as the eye can see. Can you understand that?"

"I do. More than you know. But going west is not the answer to whatever made you angry. And whatever it was has had a powerful effect on you. Want to tell me about that?"

"No sir. It's of no concern. Just something that made me think."

"Nothing wrong with thinking. It keeps a man moving forward."

Sam takes a deep breath. "Yes sir."

Owen smiles. "Well, we'll finish loading your wagon this afternoon while Shine shoes your team. Tomorrow I need you to head to the Shenandoah with a load of whiskey and farm equipment. Oh, and about the West. Leave your mother be about you leaving just yet."

Owen puts his arm around Sam's shoulder. "Come on, let's eat."

Mary Beth is standing on the back porch wiping her hands on her apron and watching Owen and Sam walk toward the house. Her prayers were answered this morning when she saw him riding up the road in the driving rain, and her heart is full as she sees them both walking up onto the back porch.

"Off with them muddy boots. I just mopped this morning."

Sam smiles and hugs his mother. "Yes ma'am."

Mary Beth looks him up and down and says, "Y'all wash up and come in. Your paw and Tillet butchered a bar hog last week. I've some fresh pork chops and potatoes smothered in onions on the table."

Owen leans over and kisses her on the cheek. "Those pots and pans sure know their favorite."

"Since when did you ever go hungry around here?"

Mary Beth is setting the food on the table when Owen and Sam walk in and sit down.

Owen says, “Let us pray. Dear heavenly Father, we give thee thanks today for all of our bountiful blessings. Lead, guide, and direct us all the days of our lives. Amen.”

Sam feels his anger ease up for the first time since that day on the road at Shannon Hill. He never before in his life felt such an overwhelming urge toward violence, an urge that bordered on being uncontrollable, as he sat there on his horse looking at Ike. After Ike rode away, he realized for the first time, with a clarity of mind and soul, that his future lay in an undiscovered distant land.

When Sam moved the horse forward that day on the road, he knew it was his first step on his journey west. He had momentarily held a dream of a completely different life as he danced that last dance with Helen in his arms. Now, as he sits across from his mother and father, he is finally at peace with his decision.

The high-pitched whistle carries off into the dim morning light like the crowing of a 6:00 a.m. rooster. It definitely isn't a wakeup call for the Tanahill place, but it absolutely is a command for Sam's six-mule team to go to work. Upon hearing the piercing whistle, the mules all lean into their collars at once and the trace chains come tight to the wagon. The heavily laden Conestoga wagon rocks in place for a moment, and then easily swings away from the loading docks at the warehouse. The dun gelding tied to the back of the wagon trots along as the wagon moves off down the road.

Sam smiles and waves to his mother and father who are sitting across the road on the side porch of the house. Owen rocks and smokes his pipe, while Mary Beth reads her morning passage from her page-worn Bible. Owen stares off into the hazy morning sunlight until the white canvas cover of the wagon disappears over the hill to the east. Mary Beth closes her Bible and pulls it to her chest, softly humming an old spiritual.

Mary Beth speaks her thoughts aloud. "Odd thing. That boy left here some weeks back, I'd say a woman owned his heart and mind outright. Now it seems he has both of 'em back."

"He is a different Sam, that's for sure."

"That he is."

"Yesterday at the forge, I've never seen a man so angry. I pried a little, but he avoided the question. Then this morning harnessing the team, he's in the best mood ever. Don't figure."

"Well good mood or bad, he sure ain't got courting on his mind. Cause you send him off to the Shenandoah for four or five weeks with Little Jim, and he don't say a word. Fact is, I'd say he was happy to go."

Owen pauses. "I don't know if he's happy. But I know he told me he came to a hard decision ridin' back home."

"A decision on what?" Mary Beth asks. "Leavin'?"

"He tell you that, did he?"

"Didn't have to. He's young and restless like all of 'em his age. All they talk about is the West. The only thing that's been holding him here has been us. But he'll go sooner or later, like all the bold ones do."

Mary Beth stands up and walks over behind Owen and touches his shoulder softly. "We'll let the Lord take care of it. He knows best."

Owen sits, silent, and feels the reality of what he's always known settle over him. He always hoped that Sam would be one of the ones that talked of the West, but never found the time or money to go. He takes a deep breath, fully realizing his son is leaving.

Sam's long, high-pitched whistle carries back to Owen along with a lively tune that Little Jim has struck up on his harmonica. Owen smiles and shakes his head as he gets up to go into the house. He doesn't know what would be worse, all that time on the road with Little Jim's harmonica, or Sam's moody ways

Sam and Little Jim reach the Great Wagon Road on the edge of Charlotte where they swing the team north. They head toward Big Lick, where they'll cross the Blue Ridge Mountains through the pass and turn south down the Wilderness Road into the Shenandoah Valley.

Little Jim sits next to Sam on the wagon seat with his feet propped up on the front of the wagon as he continues to play the lively tune. While he plays, he taps and shuffles his boots like he's dancing to the music. Little Jim's Irish father taught him to play the harmonica during their long trips across the Alleghany Mountains hunting, trapping, and living off the land. His mother, now deceased, was a breed being some mixture of Indian, African, and Anglo. She died from the fever when Jim was a small boy. Jim's father had originally bought her to work around the hunting camps and keep his bed warm at night. Through their shared hardships, his parents acquired a mutual respect for each other that was based more on survival than any other natural tendencies.

Owen had hired Little Jim several years back because of his extensive knowledge of all of the trading posts scattered through the Alleghany Mountains and further west to the Mississippi.

A coon hunter's full moon is rising bright in the eastern sky when the distant sound of several hounds carries through the heavy timber of the Santee River bottom country. Their bawling momentarily falls silent as the hounds scatter out in search of the coon's scent on the forest floor. Suddenly, one of the hounds strikes the trail and lets out a high-pitched, warbling howl, signaling to the pack that the race is on. The rest of the hounds take up the trail, creating a chorus that makes music to the hunter's ears.

The four hunters hold their lanterns high as they slowly pick their way through the dense river bottom forest. The pack is running hard and singing loud as they go off through the bottom, hot after their prey. The hunters follow along and stop ever so often to listen to the race. They know it's just a matter of time until the coon has to take to a tree to avoid a fight with the pack. Finally the running howl of the pack turns into sharp baying barks, a sure sign that the pack has the coon in a tree.

Sorrel, Ira Paul, Chance Tomkins, and his kid brother, Rip, all step up their pace through the timber, trying to get there before the coon gets too high up in the tree. They need to shine his eyes in their lantern light to be able to shoot him.

Cordell sits in a high-back rocker on the veranda of the mansion, listening to the hounds running in the far off distance toward the river. He sips on a glass of sour mash whiskey, smokes a cigar, and thinks of his youth spent hunting coons down in the Santee bottoms.

Helen walks around the corner. "Mind if I sit and listen with you?"

Cordell is momentarily caught off guard daydreaming.

He stands up and smiles. "I'd be delighted."

Helen sits down, looks over to her father, and smiles as he sits back down.

"Hear that lead dog?" he asks. "I'd bet money that's Sorrel's old red jip. What does he call her? Lill?"

"I think it's Jill, Daddy."

"There you go. That's it. Man, old Sorrel has had some good dogs. Really good dogs."

Helen realizes her father is long past drunk.

"When we were young, I guess we were the best ever at night huntin'. The best ever."

"Who is 'we' Daddy?"

"Why, me and Sorrel. That's who."

"Yeah, I figured. Some of the old folks down in the quarters tell wild stories about you and Sorrel growing up."

Cordell looks surprised. "They do? What do they tell? Aw, never you mind, just a bunch of old women gossiping."

"It's all in fun, Daddy. They never mean no harm."

"Truth is, we were like brothers. Yes sir... brothers."

"I know the feeling. That's how I felt about Ira Paul growing up."

Cordell pauses and then says, "Well there's a little difference there than with Sorrel."

Helen looks puzzled. "How do you mean?"

Cordell takes a deep, drunken breath. "Because Sorrel is my brother. Darker mother but same Scotch Irish father."

Helen rocks and says nothing.

Cordell asks, "Well? Are you shocked speechless?"

"A little, maybe," Helen replies.

"I see. So what's a little?"

Helen smiles. "Everybody knows it, Daddy. I just never thought I'd hear you say it."

"Me either girl. Me either." Cordell is near passing out now as he says, "The skin don't count little sister. It's like horses. They come in all colors. It's the blood that binds us."

A gun shot echoes across the bottom country and the dogs fall silent. Cordell and Helen sit quietly, listening for the next race to begin. Helen thinks of the letter she's written Sam, and hopes that Ira Paul goes on and gets it delivered. The horse races at George Robinson's are less than a month away, and she hopes he'll meet her there. She has agreed not to invite Sam to Shannon Hill, but she never agreed not to talk to him if they were to bump into one another somewhere socially.

Helen says, "Daddy, you better..."

Helen looks over to her father who's leaning back in the rocker, passed out. The cigar lies on the floor burning where he dropped it, and the whiskey glass is still in the grip of his left hand.

The dogs strike another hot scent and let out a mournful chorus that carries through the timber. Helen closes her eyes for a moment and lets her memory take her to that last dance with Sam, his strong hand in the middle of her back, guiding her around the floor. Her imagination is drifting away when she is startled by a noise from the dark end of the veranda. Helen stands up, straining to see who's standing there.

Jolene clears her throat and walks to the dim edge of the light.

"Jolene?"

"Yes ma'am, Miss Helen."

"Step up into the light. What are you doing standing there girl?"

"I didn't mean no harm, ma'am. Master said I's to wait on 'im. So I been sittin' and waitin'."

"Well, help me get him up so I can take him in. Then you best be getting on."

"Yes ma'am, Miss Helen."

CHAPTER SEVEN

FROM THE HILLTOP WHERE SAM AND LITTLE JIM ARE CAMPED, the lush green Shenandoah Valley stretches out to the south as far as the eye can see. The Sun is breaking clear and cool with radiant light pushing up from behind the hazy Blue Ridge Mountains to the east. Sam pauses from checking the harnesses on the mules and stands looking out across the fertile valley. No matter how many times he has camped on this very spot, the view is always inspiring. It makes him wonder how many valleys in the West are left to be settled.

Little Jim loads the last few items on the wagon. “You ready boss?”

Sam continues checking the harnesses and says, “Yeah. Just one last quick check.”

Little Jim walks around to the other side of the wagon and comes back leading the dun gelding. The horse is saddled, with a slicker and bedroll tied behind the saddle. Little Jim steps up on the gelding while Sam gets some papers out of the side box on the wagon.

Sam hands the papers up to Little Jim. "Here's your pass in case someone stops you, and a list of what I want to buy. The two main things I need are ten to fifteen sides of leather and buckhorns for knife handles. Go to old man Benson's place first; he should have the leather and the horns."

Little Jim puts the papers in his coat pocket and asks, "If he's outta sides, what do I do?"

Sam answers, "You know most folks in these parts; just keep riding and make the rounds."

"Jest in the valley or across the Cumberland Gap too?"

"Stay in the valley, Little Jim. I'll be down to Sapling Grove in a week or so, after I unload at Peaches' store. You tell folks to meet me there if they have anything to trade."

"Yes sir, boss. Sapling Grove in a week. I got it."

"If I don't get what I need here in the valley, then we'll cross over the Cumberland together"

"Yes sir," answers Jim.

"Little Jim, don't be idle with your time. We need to get loaded and get on back home. Oh, and they don't call that dun, Old Slick, for nothing. He'll leave you afoot if you don't pay attention to how you hobble him."

Little Jim kicks the dun and rides off yelling, "I know hobblin' boss. Hobbled my pap's pack string 'fore I's tall as a game rooster."

Sam says to himself as Little Jim rides off, "Mind them hobbles or you'll be a walkin' game rooster."

Little Jim rides off down the road and the harmonica strikes a lively tune.

Two days after unloading at Peaches' store, Sam swings the team off the road and into a stand of white oaks on the edge of Sapling Grove. The road coming south had caught some heavy evening showers and had turned into a knee-deep hog waller in places. Sam parks the wagon, pulls the harnesses off of the team, and works to get them fed and picketed before he loses the light. With the team taken care of, he builds a warm fire and begins to clean the mud from the leather harnesses before it can dry. His mind is not on the work at hand, but on Little Jim, when he hears a voice from the dark.

"Hello in the camp."

Sam turns his head slightly, trying to see into the dark, and slowly slides his hand to the pistol in his belt. The voice was definitely a woman, which makes him all the more suspicious.

"Sam."

Sam remains silent with reflexes coiled. On the dim edge of the campfire light a human figure appears to move, then hesitate.

Sam replies, "Show yourself."

A beautiful young woman eases into the light.

Sam, standing up, smiles and says, "Well as I live and breathe. Dancy Higgins."

Dancy returns Sam's smile and replies, "Edgy as you are, I was wonderin' about my breathing there for a minute."

"A man hears a woman call his name out in the dark, makes him edgy."

Dancy walks toward the fire, pulling her shawl around her shoulders. Her loose fitting cotton dress highlights her thin, lanky frame and her every move. She stops across the fire from Sam and smiles. He had forgotten how beautiful she was. Her faded blonde hair is plaited down each side of her head and hanging loose on her back. Her blue eyes sparkle and smile long before her lips ever move. She seems different, but Sam doesn't know exactly what is different about her.

Dancy breaks the silence. "Little Jim said you were coming by."

Sam wonders where Little Jim could have seen Dancy, so he asks, "Where did you see Little Jim?"

"He stayed a night at our place, here in town."

"Your place?"

Dancy's whole expression changes just for an instant, then the smile returns. Sam can sense she's having difficulty holding something back.

She answers, "Maw and I own the big brown house right there on the edge of town. We call it the Higgins House. Lots of clean rooms and hot meals. We, uh… run a boarding house and tavern."

Sam senses that's not all of the story. "What about your paw, and the farm?"

"Paw died a-plowin' early last fall. Wasn't any of my brothers left to help us, so we sold the farm and moved to town. Jacob and Stancil went across the Cumberland going west last summer, and Patch left the month before Paw passed. Maw said seeing them boys ride off was more than he could take."

"I am sorry for your loss, Dancy. Your paw was a good man."

"Thanks," she says, nervously wiping her palms down the front of her skirt. "But enough of that. I didn't come down here looking for sympathy. Maw and I want to invite you to supper and a room for the night, plus a bath if you've so a mind."

"Supper and a bath I can use, but I'll pass on the room. I can't leave the mules and wagon. Besides, the wagon's empty, and I've been sleeping in it."

"Well come on then, Mr. Tanahill. The table is set and waiting."

Sam goes to the wagon for a change of clothes.

"You think I could get that bath first? I am a little too rank to be at your table."

"Sure. I'll help Maw do the serving and clean up. Then we'll have supper together, if you don't mind waiting?"

They walk off into the pitch-black darkness toward town.

"I don't mind waiting. It's my lucky night, a hot bath and your maw's cooking."

Dancy laughs. "You ain't changed none. Seems you always came to the farm a-courtin' right at supper."

"I see that razor tongue is still sharp as ever girl."

"It never bothered you when you kissed me. Course that's been near forever since that happened."

Sam smiles playfully. "Near forever huh? How long is that exactly?"

"This coming spring, be two years."

Sam walks along with his mind on going west, like Dancy's brothers. "Where were your brothers headed when they left?"

"Not sure. They talked about up the Missouri River, wherever that is."

Sam walks on in silence. Dancy can feel the tension in Sam's voice when he asks about her brothers. It seems to her that her answer makes him withdraw into his own world of thought.

"I see you're still a touch moody."

"I'm sorry, Dancy. Just tired and hungry."

"Truthfully, I thought you'd be like my brothers. Long gone 'fore now."

"I imagine I will be before the year's out."

She says the phrase over in her mind, "Before the year's out." It's the last thing she wanted to hear come out of Sam Tanahill's mouth. She smiles and thinks it's a long time till then, telling herself, "He's here tonight."

Dancy stops in front of a large two-story house with a neat, white picket fence and a sign at the gate that reads, "Higgins House." The aroma of home cooking hangs in the cool evening air and the voices of a lively crowd carry into the night from the house.

Dancy runs her arm around Sam's and pulls him close, smiling. "Come on now. Maw'll be glad to see you. She always said you was the best looking man that ever walked this valley."

Sam laughs, "Now that ain't so and you know it, Dancy Higgins."

"Well you can think it ain't so, but you can go ahead and turn a pretty shade of red, cause when we walk through that front door, she's goin' to embarrass you."

Sam, still smiling, thinks of all the nights he and Dancy went for walks when he was courting her. Back then, she was a girl with an unsure giggly laugh that came and went for no real reason. Now, she carries herself with a directness and a look in her eyes that reflects a hard-lived life.

"If that's the price for a bath and a meal, I'll pay double."

"Your memory's short. She never had an audience before, but tonight she has a packed house. You're going to pay past double."

Sam, squeezing Dancy's arm says, "Then lead on."

Arm-in-arm, Sam and Dancy walk up onto the front porch. Sam totally dreads being the center of attention, but he takes great comfort in knowing he's walking through a door where he's welcome like family.

They reach the door and Sam stops. He smiles, looks over at Dancy, winks, and opens the door for her. She leads him by the hand into a large dining room where twenty men and women are eating supper.

Maw Higgins is serving the guests when Sam follows Dancy into the dining room. When she sees Sam, her worn, tired face breaks into a smile that covers the room. She brushes a long lock of gray hair behind her ear and wipes her large calloused hands on her apron as she approaches Sam. She has a larger-than-life presence that is driven by the force of her gentle heart.

"You better quit standing there looking all lost and give me a hug, Sam Tanahill. These women were expecting a mountain man that looked like Jesus. Not a preacher caught with a choir girl. Come on now."

Sam smiles and Maw gives him a stout bear hug. Turning around, she introduces Sam to her table of boarders.

"Folks, this is Mr. Sam Tanahill." Looking over to Dancy, she says, "And no, he's not married yet, ladies."

Maw starts to shepherd Sam to a seat at the table against his will.

"Mother, Sam would..."

"Get 'im a plate Dancy. He can sit right down there between Aunt Ida and Mr. Bill."

Sam's balking protests are having little effect on Maw as she moves him around the long table to the far end. He finally stops and turns around to face her.

"Ma'am I am hungry to starvation, but I can't sit at your table."

"Why in creation not?"

"Ma'am, I need a bath. Real bad."

Maw holds up a hand laughing. "Lord Jesus! More 'an half of everyone in here needs that."

"No ma'am. I've been longer than normal."

"Suit yourself. The bath's out back. Show him where, Dancy, then come on back and give me a hand."

"Yes ma'am."

"Sam, you better not be long with that bath. This bunch'll be licking the plates shortly."

"Yes ma'am."

Sam follows Dancy through the kitchen, out to a small bathhouse on the back porch. Sam puts his change of clothes on a bench.

"I'll put some water on to heat."

"No need. Just give me a bucket and show me the well."

"A cold bath?" Dancy asks.

"She said hurry."

"There's plenty. You fetch the water, and I'll heat it."

"You sure?" Sam inquires. He surely doesn't want to miss a home-cooked meal.

"I am sure, Sam Tanahill. Now go. The bucket's settin' on the back steps."

Sam walks out the back door and picks up the water bucket.

Later that night, Sam and Dancy are sitting at the dining room table finishing dinner. Maw is rattling around out in the kitchen cleaning up, when she hollers at Dancy.

"Dancy, finish up, and come give me a hand. I need to get on to the bar and help Addie and Mr. Bill. Sam, you can go wait in the bar. She'll be done directly."

"Thank you, ma'am, but I'll be going."

Dancy mumbles to herself, "Damn, you would think one night." She hollers back at her mother. "Yes ma'am." To Sam she says, "It won't take me long to be done. If you don't want to go to the bar, you can wait on the porch swing. I'll be just a minute."

Sam stands up. "I can't Dancy. There's no one down at the camp, and I been gone long enough."

"Then after I finish I'll walk down, and we'll visit. If that's okay?"

Sam grins and says, "Sure. That'll give me time to check my mules and get things put up."

Dancy smiles, gets up, and gathers up her and Sam's plates, then heads to the kitchen.

"Maw. Sam's a-leavin'."

Maw starts talking before she clears the kitchen door. "Sam Tanahill, I expect you at my table every night while you're here. And don't give me no bull excuses. You hear me?"

Sam knows better than to say much more than, "Yes ma'am," as she gives him a big hug.

"Oh yes ma'am. Nothing I'd like better, and thanks for everything tonight."

Maw turns and walks back toward the kitchen, passing Dancy on her way.

"Walk him to the door, Dancy, and let's get busy. Night Sam."

Sam tips his hat and says, "Good night ma'am."

The moon is in its last quarter, making the night pitch black and the walking a mite tricky. Sam takes his time, stopping occasionally to listen to the hoot owls calling to each other off in the deep timber. When he reaches camp, he walks on to the picket line where his mules are tied. He pauses a few steps from the team and speaks the lead pair's name. It's a good practice not to surprise a 1400-pound mule, especially in the dark.

"Easy now. Henry... Little Bill... whoa now. I just need to check your shoulders."

Sam speaks softly to the team as he rubs the shoulders of each mule, checking for collar soreness. Satisfied that all they need is a few days' rest, he heads for the wagon to get things put up for the night. He pokes the campfire to life, then picks up the harnesses and lays them in a neat order on the tongue of the wagon. He washes the mud from his hands and pours himself a drink of sour mash.

The fire begins to catch just as Sam makes himself a comfortable place to sit and enjoy the drink while he waits on Dancy. He leans back, sips the whiskey, and stares up into the crystal clear night. The stars shine with a special brightness that fills the sky from horizon to horizon.

Dancy's voice breaks the silence. "I hope that far-off stare doesn't have a name."

Sam gets up and makes Dancy a place to sit by him. "Didn't hear you walk up."

Dancy pulls her shawl around her shoulders and sits down. "I know. Well, does she?"

Sam sits down and raises the cup to drink. "Does she what?"

Dancy reaches for Sam's cup. "What are we drinking?"

Sam moves the cup out of her reach. "We?"

She stares into Sam's eyes and gives him a mischievous, catty look that stops him dead still.

Dancy slowly reaches and takes the cup out of Sam's hand. "A name. Does she have a name?"

Sam, still watching Dancy's every move, sidesteps the real answer and says, "Her name is the West, and it's sour mash."

Dancy smiles. "Good."

She takes a long drink of the whiskey and coughs slightly. She hands Sam the empty cup.

Sam doesn't know what to think. "Well that's a little different. I didn't know you drank."

Dancy reaches down and goes to unlacing her shoes. "I don't."

Sam is a bit bewildered by her behavior. "That drink burning you all the way down to your feet, is it?"

Dancy looks over to the wagon. "There room for two in that wagon?"

Sam comes back to life as the seriousness of both her look and her question settles over him. He sits still, watching her unlace her shoes.

"Dancy, let me ask you a question."

Dancy looks up as she finishes unlacing her shoes. "I don't think so, Sam. Not now. Cause I might change my mind. Now you give me a few minutes and you come to bed."

Sam watches her walk off and thinks of all the nights in her daddy's hay barn when she kissed him so hot and passionately, but never gave in. He never got a feel, much less touched a button on her dress. And now, without laying a hand on her, she's in his bed, waiting.

Sam sits looking into the fire, lost in thought. For some odd reason, Helen flashes through his mind, then Jessica, Ike, and Cordell. He comes to his decision; that was the past, but the anger still burns his soul. He stands up, looking to the heavens, and tells himself it's time to move on.

"Sam?" Dancy calls from inside the wagon.

Sam walks to the wagon, climbs the front wheel, and steps over into the wagon bed. He sits down on a box and pulls his boots off, and then he slips off his shirt. He kneels down and reaches for the edge of the quilt that she is covered up with.

Dancy grabs the quilt and stops Sam from pulling it back. "I want you to have me with all my heart, but ..."

Looking softly into his eyes, she touches his hand. "Could you just come to bed and hold me?"

Sam pulls his pants off and slides in next to Dancy, taking her in his arms. When he pulls her close, she puts her head on his chest and begins to tremble.

"You okay?"

Ever so gently, she nods yes without moving.

Sam rolls her over on her back, pushes her hair out of her eyes, and kisses her softly. When he moves his hand down her side to her leg, she jumps and takes in a quick breath. He sees a tear come to her eye when she rolls over on her side facing away from him, trembling.

Lost and confused, Sam lies back on the bed.

“I am sorry. I didn’t, I don’t...”

Dancy says in a quiet, soft voice, “You didn’t do anything wrong. It’s just been a hard year. All the men in my life left me, including you. And then I...”

She begins to cry when Sam touches her shoulder. In the dim light, there are some dark spots on her back that catch Sam’s attention. He raises up and pulls the canvas flap back, letting the campfire light fall across her. The deep bruises on her lower back and buttocks are still a faded purple.

Sam drops the canvas flap and lies back down next to her. He stares at the top of the wagon cover.

“Who did that to you, Dancy?”

“Doesn’t matter, it’s done. I went for a walk one night with a young man that dragged me into the barn. He beat me and had his way with me until I passed out.”

“You tell your maw?”

“No. He said he would kill both of us if I ever told.”

She rolls over into Sam’s arms and begins to cry uncontrollably. “I’m sorry Sam. I am so sorry. I really wanted to ... I thought I could ...”

“Hey, it’s okay to cry. But you have nothing to be sorry for.”

He pulls the covers up and gets her comfortable on his arm. “Come on. Let’s get some sleep.”

“Sam I ...”

"Shhhh, it's okay."

Sam strokes her hair, and Dancy finally settles down as they fall off to sleep in each other's arms.

Early the next morning, Sam feels something lightly touching him. He awakens to find Dancy softly kissing his chest as she rubs the rippled muscles of his stomach. Her hand gently follows the thin black line of hair down the middle of his torso until she gently wraps her hand around him. Sam closes his eyes, takes a deep breath, and stretches. Her soft stroking touch makes his wide chest rise and fall in short breaths. He reaches and pulls her up into his arms, stopping her lips within inches of his. She closes her eyes as he leans in to kiss her. When his lips touch hers, she kisses him passionately and rolls over on her back, taking him with her. He runs his hand down the inside of her leg and gently pulls her legs apart.

"Be easy," is all Dancy says, and those are the only words spoken between the two of them.

They lose themselves for a time making love, laughing, and talking, until Sam realizes it's long into the day. He gets up, pulls his pants and boots on, and grabs his shirt. He kneels down and gives Dancy a kiss.

Sam teasingly pulls on the edge of the quilt she is rolled up in. "You can't lay around here naked all day, woman. Come on. Get up and get dressed."

She laughs and says, "That's not what you were saying a little while ago."

"Come on. I've got to see to my team. Let's go. Maw 'll be down here looking for you."

Sam steps down off of the wagon, walks around to the feed box on the other side, and starts measuring out the grain for each of his mules.

"Don't worry about Maw. I told 'er I was spending the night and not to bother me."

Sam finishes and closes the lid on the feed box. "That a fact?"

"Fact is, I told her I was staying here every night you'd let me."

Sam stands at the box, staring at the side of the wagon.

"You hear me?"

Sam answers slowly. "I did."

"Well?"

"Is this a yes or no question?"

"Sam!"

Sam gathers up his feed bags, then turns and walks off smiling. "Give me a bit to ponder on that."

Dancy rolls over on her back, pulls the quilt tight to her chest, and closes her eyes. Her long, shaggy blond hair is unplaited and scattered about her head and shoulders. In the last year, there has not been one day of happiness in Dancy's life, until today. She thinks about the morning and smiles. When she hears Sam back around the camp, she kicks the covers off and stretches; it feels good to be naked in bed.

"You up?"

Sam steps up onto the wagon wheel and sticks his head around the wagon cover to see Dancy lying on the bed, stretching. Seeing Sam, she props up on one elbow and makes no effort to hide her body. A loose tendril of her hair falls across her pretty, upright breast.

"You think I might help you with your pondering?"

"You know the answer. Now get moving before I crawl in there."

Sam hears the sound of riders and steps down from the wagon. Coming up the road from the south are two riders that appear to be heavily armed. He feels for the pistol in his belt while he walks to where his rifle is propped up on the rear wheel of the wagon. Picking up the rifle, he cradles it in his arms and walks a few steps toward the road. Sam's jaw locks when he recognizes the lead rider. It's Ike's right-hand man, Paxton Henry, and his kid brother, Pate.

Paxton is an animal of a human who is Ike's enforcer among the white overseers, and among the tougher black slaves that work at Shannon Hill. The only thing more treacherous than Paxton's six-foot frame of oversized, twisted muscles is his undersized twisted mind. His small, fat, ignorant brother, Pate, lives and survives only because Paxton enforces that also.

The two men ride with a cocky arrogance that gives any man reason to be cautious. When they get close, they turn off the road and ride toward Sam. He grits his teeth and returns their stoic gaze. Paxton rides his horse within a disrespectful distance of Sam, but Sam doesn't give any ground.

"Tanahill."

Sam stands there staring at Paxton, thinking about his encounter with Ike at Shannon Hill. The anger rises to his eyes, and he stares holes through Paxton.

"Paxton."

Dancy, not knowing what's going on outside, sticks her head out of the wagon and calls to Sam.

"Sam."

Paxton breaks out in a big smile, looking over at Dancy. "My, my." He laughs an evil noise and looks back to Sam. "You're a hound, Tanahill. You got 'em treed all over the country." He raises his voice so Dancy can hear him. "She looks real special, just like the other one."

Sam speaks coldly, "State your business, Paxton."

Paxton cocks his head sideways and looks at Sam with one crazy eye from under the brim of his floppy hat. He grins, then spits and says, "Got none today."

Sam doesn't change one thing, not the way he stands, or the force in his voice. "Then you take care."

Time ticks away for a moment as the men stare at each other.

"You too, Tanahill."

They turn to ride off, and Paxton nods to Dancy. "Ma'am." He stops and turns in the saddle. "Oh, by the way. I passed your nigger walking this morning. Looked like he got bucked off."

Sam doesn't move or respond.

Paxton makes that evil noise of a laugh, then yells over his shoulder, "Just trying to be neighborly," as he turns and rides off.

Sam's rage holds him in place until the two men ride out of sight. The cold and edgy exchange with Paxton only confirms his long held suspicions—that his problem with Ike is far from being over. When Sam told Ike to "be careful of what he took hold of," on the Shannon Hill road that day, it was a challenge that Ike couldn't answer at the moment, but Sam knew without a doubt that an answer would be coming.

Dancy walks up behind Sam and touches his shoulder. "You okay?"

Sam doesn't turn around or respond for a while. "Yeah, I am okay."

Dancy can hear and feel the anger in his words. She turns around and walks back to the wagon, climbing in to get her shawl. Sam walks up, leans his rifle against the wagon, and helps her down. She can see that he is still moody, but his anger is passing.

Dancy smiles, feeling protected and proud of Sam. "I am going up to help Maw. You coming up for dinner tonight?"

"I am."

Dancy smiles and gives him a soft kiss. "Good."

She turns to walk off.

"You coming back tonight?"

Dancy turns back around and asks, "Why wouldn't I?"

"What he said today and all."

"You mean about another woman?" She pauses, then says, "I knew that yesterday."

Sam stares into Dancy's eyes.

"Well?" he says, "Are you coming back?"

Dancy gives Sam a mischievous look of devilment, turns, and walks off. "I thought that got settled this morning in bed."

As she walks away, Dancy pulls her dress up a few inches so it doesn't get dirty, making the cotton pull tight around her hips. Sam can't help but stare, wondering if he has ever seen a woman with a better ass.

She looks back and catches him staring.

"Do I need to come back down there?"

Sam waves her on. "I got work to do. Go on now."

She smiles, turns around, and continues on. "See ya tonight."

CHAPTER EIGHT

LATER THAT AFTERNOON, SAM IS WALKING HIS LAST PAIR OF mules back from a nearby creek when he sees a wagon coming up from the south. He hopes it carries settlers coming to trade or sell him something. He walks on to the picket line, to tie the mules up, when he hears Little Jim call his name.

"Sam."

He turns around to see the wagon driving off and Little Jim walking toward him. It catches Sam's attention that he's walking all stove up, like Old Slick busted him pretty hard.

Sam smiles and says, "Old Slick stuck it on your ass, did he?"

Sam can hardly contain himself, until Little Jim gets closer. Then Sam's smile quickly fades away when he sees Little Jim's swollen lips and black eyes. He reaches up and turns Little Jim's head to get a better look at his face.

"What the hell happened to you?"

Little Jim starts to wobble and catches hold of Sam's arm.

"Here, sit down. Let me get you some water."

Little Jim hangs his head. "I was ridin' back here, boss, when they rode up all friendly, and then out of nowhere I get this here beaten."

Sam hands him a cup of water and asks, "Who rode up?"

"Them goddamn Henry brothers. I was tryin' to tell 'em who I worked for, when that little fat one calls me a smart mouth nigger and slaps me."

"Did you show 'em the papers?"

"I tried to, boss. When I reached for 'em, that big un hits me right in the eye."

He rubs the side of his head tenderly. "Son of a bitch gotta lick like a mule."

Sam thinks of the crazy smirk on Paxton's face when they were talking. He knew Paxton was enjoying every minute of trying to intimidate him.

"And then I wake up lying in the goddamn mud in the middle of the road, and that sorry ass horse had run off."

Sam helps Little Jim to his feet. "Don't worry about the horse. Come on; get on your feet. Can you walk?"

"Good enough. Where we going to, boss?"

"To town. Them Henrys were by here this morning. I figure they're still in Sapling Grove, drinking and whoring. I am not letting this go."

Sam picks up his rifle when he walks by the wagon and hands it to Little Jim.

"Here, you may need this. Pate's a back shooter, so stay close to him. If you point a gun at him, he won't go for his gun, but if he does, kill him." Sam looks Little Jim straight in the eyes and holds his gaze for moment. "You hear me?"

Little Jim checks the rifle to make sure it's loaded. "Yes sir, boss."

Sam finds the Henrys' horses tied across the street from the Higgins House, at a ramshackle trading post and tavern called Bull's. The place is a clapboard shack with a bloodstained dirt floor and a blanket hung up for a front door. It's owned and run by Axle Bull, a low life character who has two young daughters, barely in their teens, who he sells to his hard case patrons. He drinks all day and brags to his customers how good his daughters are in bed because he broke 'em both in himself.

Sam and Little Jim step just inside of the door and pause to let their eyes adjust to the dim light. Paxton's at a corner table drinking with one of Axle's daughters sitting in his lap. Sam glances around the room for Pate then starts walking toward Paxton, who leans up and whispers something in the girl's ear. She smiles and slides off of his lap, then walks over behind the bar with her father.

"Gents," Axle says, "What'll it be; pussy or whiskey? I got the best of both this side of the Cumberland."

Sam ignores Axle and walks on toward Paxton with a deadly look in his eyes. Axle and his mangy customers sense a killin' is at hand. The customers take their whiskey, ease up, and move out of the way.

"Killings are bad for business, gents. So take it outside. Done had two this week."

Paxton, cold and calculating, speaks first. "They don't allow no niggers in here. Especially ones carrying a gun."

Sam returns, "He's a free man. Goes where he likes."

"That's what I never liked about you Tanahills. Y'all just a little too friendly with niggers for me."

Sam points to Little Jim. "I think the beating you gave him this morning made that point plain enough."

"A beatin'!" Paxton says, "Hell, if I whipped that scrawny nigger, he'd be dead."

Pate walks in from a back room, followed by Axle's other daughter, a short, dowdy girl with a fresh, swollen lip. He stops at the end of the bar, glaring at Little Jim.

Pate's hatred for blacks has never been easy for him to contain. "Maybe you should whip his black ass till he tells you the truth. Would've sure saved you from bothering us."

Sam answers matter-of-factly. "I think it's the other way around. Maybe you need your ass whipped until you tell the truth."

Paxton laughs, "Oh so that's what this is all about. Your nigger gets bucked off, loses your horse, and blames us. Sounds to me like he's feedin' you pure hog shit."

Pate loses his self-control and shouts, "The damn nigger is lying!"

Angrily, Sam snaps, "You're both liars, and you know it."

Paxton gets a crazy look in his eyes, kicks the table away, and stands up. "Tanahill, you best goddamn quit pushin', you hear me?"

Pate starts around the end of the bar. "You son of a..."

Sam growls, "Little Jim!"

Little Jim points the rifle at Pate and cocks it. "Easy boss. I'm one jumpy nigger."

Axle starts to the far end of the bar. "Hold it right there. Girls, y'all get to the back, out of the way. Now!" He walks around the bar toward the men, his hands up in the air. "Damn a'mighty, gents. Y'all go outside. I run a respectable establishment, and I don't need any more killin's in here."

Little Jim speaks in a measured tone. "Keep your hands where I can see 'em, fat boy."

Sam keeps his focus riveted on Paxton. "Back away, barkeep."

The room falls eerily silent, and the tension is rising, with both men staring eye to eye, poised for someone to make a move, either planned or by accident. The air hangs thick with death.

Paxton is overtaken with craziness, but can't bring himself to reach for his gun. "Get to your business, Tanahill, whatever it is."

"Two things. One, you owe me a horse, and two, I owe you an ass whipping."

Paxton, in disbelief, makes an evil noise, laughing, and points to himself. "You're going to fight me straight up? Kid, you just overmatched your ass, but I tell you what I'll do. If you do whip my ass... the horse outside is yours, plus the saddle."

Sam points over his shoulder and says, "Let's go. Outside." Without looking at Little Jim he says to him, "Bring the back shooter with you and keep your eyes on him."

Paxton takes off his gun and knife and lays them down on a table, laughing as he walks to the door.

Little Jim motions to Pate with the rifle. "Your gun and knife. Put 'em on the bar, fat boy."

The thought of taking orders from a nigger sends Pate into a rage. "You ill-bred fuckin' burrhead, I'll..."

Paxton stops half way to the door. "Pate! Let me get finished and the nigger is yours."

Pate puts his gun and knife on the bar and starts for the door. "You're a dead nigger!"

Little Jim doesn't take his eyes off of Pate. "Maybe. But you won't see it. Because if your brother wins, I'm gonna send daylight through your guts."

Pate gets a sick look on his face following Sam and Paxton out the door.

Sam takes off his gun and lays it down on a bench by the door, following Paxton into the street.

Paxton holds his open hands up and begins to circle Sam with a twisted look in his eyes. "Your dance. Fire your best shot."

Axle walks out of the bar with a chair in one hand and a whiskey bottle in the other, followed by all of his high caliber clientele and both of his daughters. He places the chair on the porch and sits down.

All of the months and months of pent up anger in Sam strains his every muscle. From Ike's threats toward Owen to his rude dismissal by Cordell, it all flashes red hot through his mind. He grits his teeth and wades into Paxton with a vicious hatred.

Paxton sidesteps Sam's wild swing and hits him solid on the side of his head, knocking him down hard.

Axle whistles a shrill whistle through his teeth. "Ooo wee. What a lick." Looking around, he says, "I got five dollars on the big un. Any takers?"

Sam stumbles up and shakes his head, trying to clear his mind. He squares back up to Paxton and wades right back into him with the same red-hot anger, and gets the same brutal result. Paxton squats down in the street laughing, not far from Sam, while he rolls around on the ground, struggling to get up. Paxton enjoys making people suffer, and he has every intention of prolonging Sam's suffering.

"Hell," says Axle, "I thought this would be entertaining. Looks like my five dollars is staying home."

Sam gets to his feet, trying to catch his breath. "I got your five dollars, old man."

Axle takes a big drink of whiskey. "Damn a'mighty, there's guts. That's the kind of man you girls need to marry. Yes sir!"

Sam spits the blood from his mouth and takes a deep breath. His left eye and the side of his head are turning black, and his ribs ache. He realizes that his hotheaded anger is only going to get him a terrible beating. He remembers a lesson that Tillet taught him about fighting when he was young. He always preached that you had to inflict pain in a fight, terrible, grinding pain, if you wanted to win.

Sam begins to circle Paxton, who laughs and lets Sam come closer and closer. With lighting speed, Sam fakes a punch and lands a roundhouse kick to the outside of Paxton's left knee. The knee folds in, sending him to the ground, clutching his knee and cussing. Sam follows it up with a drop kick to his short ribs that takes all of his air away. Paxton rolls up onto his hands and one knee, trying to breathe, all the while cussing and swearing revenge.

"Get up! I am not leaving this for another day."

Paxton lets out a deep-throated growl and comes after Sam, tackling him viciously. The two men hammer at each other to near exhaustion, until Sam gets the upper hand and beats Paxton nearly unconscious. He stands over Paxton, beat up and bloody, barely able to keep from falling down. Sam kneels down and grabs Paxton by his bloody shirt and yanks him to his feet. He draws back his fist when Paxton hangs his head and holds up a hand. His right eye is swollen shut, the left is a bloody mess, and his lips are raw meat.

Paxton speaks, barely above a whisper: "Enough. I've... had... enough."

Sam's rage returns, and he jerks Paxton to him hard, trying to wake him up. "Wake up, you son of a bitch; we're not done."

Paxton chokes on his words and gasps, "I am done. No more."

Sam is almost out of control, shaking Paxton. "Listen to me! Can you hear me?"

Paxton nods a weak yes.

"If you, or any of Ike's bunch ever bother me or my family again, so help me God, I'll kill every one of you." Sam violently shakes Paxton by his shirt. "Do you hear?"

Again, Paxton nods a weak yes.

Sam, with rage in his eyes, jerks Paxton hard by his shirt and draws back his fist. "Then answer me you son of a bitch!! Answer me!"

Paxton holds up a hand, and gasping for breath, answers, "Yes."

Sam stands there in a daze for a moment, holding on to Paxton's shirt with his fist drawn back. He finally releases his grip on the shirt, and Paxton falls limp at his feet.

Sam looks down at Paxton, then over to Pate. "Get your brother's bed roll off my horse. Little Jim, bring the horse, and let's go."

"Yes sir, boss." He pokes Pate with the rifle and smiles, "You heard the man. Move, fat boy."

Pate removes the bedroll from behind the saddle while Little Jim picks up Sam's pistol, then unties the horse and walks toward Sam in the street.

Sam tries to walk off, staggers, and almost falls when he feels someone catch him from behind. He stiffly turns his head to see Dancy holding him. He tries to smile, but shooting pain floods his face. He puts his arm around her shoulders, slowly straightens up, and takes a deep breath. He looks down in her apron pocket and sees a pistol.

Dancy looks at the pistol and back at Sam. "I wasn't gonna let him kill you." He looks into Dancy's eyes and nods his approval.

Sam looks over to Axle. "Pay my man here, if you would, barkeep."

Axle gets up and goes into the tavern, drinking whiskey from the bottle and carrying the chair. "My pleasure, son."

Dancy says, "Come on. Let's get you to the house and cleaned up. Maw's got some salve and bandages."

"No," Sam says, "Help me on the horse. I am going down to the camp."

"No Sam! Little Jim can look after everything. You need some doctorin'."

"Dancy. Not by himself. Those two are crazy. Now hold the horse while Little Jim helps me get on. Come on y'all, trade places. Lay the rifle down, Little Jim, and give me a leg up."

Dancy holds the horse by the reins, and Little Jim helps Sam get in the saddle. She hands him the reins while Little Jim picks up the rifle.

Paxton finally gets up, with Pate's help, and lamely hobbles back into the tavern. Pate stops at the tavern door with Paxton's hat in his hand, staring at Sam.

Axle pushes by him at the door carrying a bottle of whiskey. He walks up to Little Jim and hands him the money and the bottle.

Axle, looking up at Sam and pointing to the bottle, says, "It's the good stuff. Just a little extra for taking it outside. Wouldn't have been much left of my place if you hadn't."

"Thanks," Sam says weakly.

Axle turns around and sees everyone is still standing outside watching. He raises both hands above his head. "Jesus! You girls can't make any money out here. Come on! Take these gents back inside and show 'em paradise."

Dancy stands by the horse, staring at Sam with a worried look. She puts her hand on his leg. "I see I can't change your mind, so go on. I'll get the bandages and salve, and bring y'all some dinner."

Sam reaches out and touches her hand. "Don't fret about me; I am okay."

Dancy nods her head. "I know."

She steps away from the horse, and Sam rides off with Little Jim walking by his side.

Riding along to camp, the reality of whipping Paxton Henry begins to settle over Sam. He feels a tremendous sense of newfound pride in himself and in his family as well. That day at Shannon Hill had torn a ragged hole in his self-worth, a hole that filled with unforgiving anger—the kind of unforgiving anger that not only ground Paxton Henry under his boot heel, but Shannon Hill as well. He served notice today that nothing, not even the Meyers' name, will save Ike and his bunch if they ever bring grief to him or his family.

The evening sun has disappeared below the horizon when Sam finally walks back into camp after a cold soaking bath in the creek. He sits down by the fire, laying his pistol down within easy reach, and tries to get comfortable.

Little Jim is closing the lid on the feed box while watching Sam. "Want a drink, boss?"

"Sure."

Little Jim gets Axle's bottle out of the wagon, and a couple of cups. He walks over and sits down by the fire across from Sam, then pulls the cork.

Sam points to the rifle lying nearby. “Don’t get far from that. Just in case they get stupid.”

Little Jim pours a cup of whiskey. “Yes sir.” He hands Sam the cup. “You don’t look near as bad with the blood washed off. A mite black and blue, but better.”

Sam takes a deep drink and closes his eyes. He tries to get comfortable, but the soreness nags at his body from head to toe.

A faint, clanking noise far out in the dark catches the men’s attention. They pick up their guns and quietly back away from the firelight. The noise gets louder, and then Dancy comes into the light, carrying a pot of stew with a rattily lid in one hand, and a sack of bandages and salve in the other.

Dancy stops and looks around. “Sam?”

Sam and Little Jim walk out of the darkness and back up to the fire.

“No need to worry, they’re gone. Pate bought a horse for Paxton and they rode out.”

Sam painfully eases around and sits back down by the fire.

“Which way they headed?”

She hands Little Jim the pot. “Here. Hang this over the fire to warm.” She turns to Sam and answers, “They rode out the back way and headed south about an hour ago.”

Sam looks at the fire and thinks, “South. That figures. They’re headed for Shannon Hill, and Ike.” Looking to Little Jim he asks, “You find everything we needed when you made your rounds?”

"Yes sir. Folks should start showin' up tomorrow or the next day."

Sam, looking back in the fire, says, "Good. I want to finish and get home."

Dancy walks around to Sam and sits down. "Well let's have a look at you. With a bath you look like you might live."

Sam picks up the cup of whiskey and takes a drink. "Looks are deceiving. My body feels like death."

Dancy tugs at his shirttail. "Come on. Off with the shirt. Let me check the ribs."

"Can we eat first? Whatever's in that pot sure smells good."

Dancy smiles. "Sure." She looks to Little Jim and asks, "Will you get us some forks and plates?"

Little Jim is up and moving. "Yes ma'am."

After they finish dinner, Dancy tends Little Jim first, doctoring his minor cuts and his black eyes.

Then she looks over to Sam. "You're next. Come on. Off with the shirt and let me wrap those ribs so you can breathe. I know you're sore, but they'll feel better, believe me."

Sam gives her a look, and struggles to get his shirt over his head. She reaches and gently helps him pull it off. While she wraps his ribs, he sips the whiskey and stares into the fire. She saw a Sam Tanahill today that she never knew existed. The sheer vicious courage that drove him in the fight today was a little scary. She doesn't know who Ike is, or Shannon Hill, but whoever they are, there's a lot of bad blood between them and Sam.

She finishes, and puts the bandages and salve back in the sack. "Few days' rest, you'll be fit and ready."

Sam rubs his ribs and takes a deep breath. "Feels like you pulled the knife outta my ribs. Thanks."

She gets up and starts toward the wagon. "I am turning in. You coming?"

"Not yet. I want to talk to Little Jim."

"Come on when you're ready."

"I will."

He turns to Little Jim. "I am sorry I got you into this. This didn't end in that street today, for either one of us. Especially you. You being black and ordering Pate around, they'll never heal over it. They'll..."

Little Jim cuts him off. "Boss, I got no regrets. Like you said, I am a free man. My maw was a slave, bought and paid for by my paw, who freed her. She taught me from an early age that freedom is only temporary, because no matter what color you are, or where you live, there will always be folks trying to take it from you. I'm free, and you treat me like a man, boss. Those are things I'll fight and die for."

Sam sits there thinking about Little Jim's words, and how they push off into every corner of his being. After his encounter with the Meyers, it drove home the realization that the West was the only equalizer for men like him. The planters' enforced social structure controls all men in the South, both slave and free. Sam understands the social boundaries, but he will not be bullied by the Meyers' political clout or money. They will treat him like a man and never interfere in his life.

Sam finally looks at Little Jim and nods his approval. "Well my friend, I agree. Those are things I'll fight and die for also."

Little Jim picks the rifle up and lays it across his lap and punches the fire up. "Get some rest boss. I'll keep an eye on things."

Sam gets up and walks to the wagon, steps up onto the front wheel and then inside. Dancy has her hair down and is under the covers when Sam sits down on a box.

Sam smiles. "You wouldn't want to help me pull my boots off, would you?"

"Sure."

When she sits up to help Sam with his boots, she is buck naked. She reaches down for his boots, and Sam just stares.

"The boots are a little lower than where you're looking."

Sam shakes his head and smiles while she helps him take his boots off. He slips his pants off and eases under the covers.

"That fight today..." Dancy says.

"What about it?"

"Just never saw that in you. Not ever. Plus, I sure wouldn't want to be Ike or Shannon Hill."

Sam rolls over on his side next to Dancy and brushes her hair back, kissing her softly.

She looks up at him with a smirky, devilish smile and says, "You're not going to talk to me, are you?"

"Not now."

Sam pulls the covers back and softly runs his hand down the long curve of her side while he stares into her eyes. She leans up and gives him a passionate kiss, pulling him down next to her. They hold nothing back from each other, making love and living in the moment. They finally fall off to sleep in each other's arms with no thoughts of the world past the edge of their bed.

Early the next morning, long before daylight, Dancy lies awake in Sam's arms. "Hey," she whispers, "You awake?"

Sam tries to move and groans. "Yeah. Let me have my arm; it's asleep."

Dancy raises up, and Sam pulls his arm out from under her head. He holds his breath and rolls over on his side facing her, trying to find a little comfort.

"You okay?"

Sam breathes shallow, holding his ribs. "Just body sore... Why are you awake?"

"Just thinking."

"What do you want to talk about?"

"Did I say I wanted to talk?"

"You're thinking, and it leads to it. So what's on your mind?"

"I don't mean to pry, but you fought like a man leveled up with hatred yesterday. The kind that comes from being wronged."

Sam rolls over on his back and stares at the top of the wagon cover.

Dancy can sense the change that came over Sam when she asked him about the fight. "I am sorry. That's none of my business."

"No need to be sorry. I asked you what you had on your mind."

Sam lies there a long time, thinking back about the events that led to his confrontation with Ike on the Shannon Hill road.

"The short of the story is a woman."

"That's the woman Paxton referred to in the camp that morning?"

"It is."

"You courtin' her?"

"No. That's where the problem started. I delivered a racehorse to one of my father's customers, and he insisted I attend a cotillion with him and his family. I met a planter's daughter there who invited me to call on her. When I went back to see her, her father dismissed me and told me not to ever come back on the place."

Dancy can't understand how that could generate such vile anger. "I don't understand. You were going to kill that man yesterday. All over that?"

"That's not the reason. When I rode away, the plantation overseer stopped me on the road. He basically said his boss would ruin my father's freight business if I ever called at the house again."

"The overseer, is that Shannon or Ike?"

"Ike Murphy is the overseer, and Shannon Hill is the name of the plantation."

"Oh, I thought that was a man. And Paxton works at Shannon Hill for Ike."

"That's right. He's Ike's slave catcher and enforcer."

Dancy lies next to Sam in the dark, not really wanting to know any more of the story, but she can't bear not knowing the most important part.

"I know you won't like this question, but I think I deserve an answer."

Sam doesn't say a word. He lies there knowing the question, not sure of his feelings for either woman.

"Did you hear me?" Dancy asks.

"I did. So ask."

"Are you in love with her?"

"At one time I was, but I don't know now."

Dancy presses the question. "If her father allowed it, would you call on her again?"

Sam answers a little more directly. "I said I don't know. And I really don't. Besides, after yesterday, there's no more ifs."

"Don't be moody. I haven't asked you for anything, and I am not asking now."

"I am not moody. I just want that whole bunch behind me."

"You are moody, and they're not behind you. You left nothing in that street because you're still in love with her. They're the only thing standing between you and her, and you're mad about it. You're mad to the core, and it shows on you."

"I don't know what to say. Hell. I should have told you about all this before now."

"Don't worry yourself. I took for granted that all the men in my life would be there forever, you included. When I saw you sitting by that fire the other night, I made up my mind not to take another day of my life for granted."

"I have to leave tomorrow or the next day."

Dancy sits up and replies, "I know."

Sam reaches up and touches her shoulder. "I'd like it if you stayed with me until I leave."

Dancy shakes her head yes, wipes the tears from her eyes, and lies back down in Sam's arms.

Several days later, the wagon sits loaded under the white oaks with the mules standing in their harnesses, ready to start home. Little Jim ties Paxton's bay horse to the rear of the wagon and walks around the team for one final check before they start out. Sam and Dancy are walking off through the stand of oaks in awkward silence. They are both struggling with saying goodbye.

Dancy stops walking and turns to Sam. "Look. Let's not make this hard on either of us." She puts her hand on the side of his face and smiles. "No matter what else was going on in your life, when you were with me, you were nowhere else. And for that, I love you."

Sam looks off and is at a loss. "Like I told you. I don't know what to say about all of this."

Dancy smiles and takes him by the hand. "You don't have to say anything. Come on, it's time for you to go."

They walk back toward the wagon in silence, holding hands. When they reach the back of the wagon, Sam takes off his hat, turns to Dancy, and takes her in his arms, kissing her passionately. When he turns her loose, she feels her heart break in a thousand pieces.

With tears in her eyes, she says, "Good-bye, Sam Tanahill."

Sam puts his hat on. "I can't tell you I'll be back."

"I know. It's okay."

They stand looking into each other's eyes, then with one easy motion he steps up onto the wagon wheel and onto the seat beside Little Jim, who is holding the reins.

Little Jim nods to Dancy. "Ma'am."

He shakes the reins and whistles for the mules to step up. The wagon lurches forward, and Sam waves to Dancy as they pull away. She waves, then turns and walks back toward the Higgins House.

Sam looks back at Dancy as she walks away. He watches her until she goes out of sight, with her shawl pulled tight around her shoulders and her dress dragging in the muddy road. She never turns around or looks back.

Sam finally turns around and looks down the road toward home. "Push 'em, Little Jim. I want to get on home."

"Yes sir."

The fight weighs heavy on Sam's mind, and he worries for Owen. He knows the Henrys will be back at Shannon Hill no later than today. He also knows Paxton will lie about the fight, which will only put Ike on the prod. It doesn't make any difference to Sam, because Dancy was right; the anger that drives him is still burning red-hot. If Ike or any of his bunch press the issue, hell will come calling for 'em all.

CHAPTER NINE

THE NEXT MORNING THE BREAKING DAWN STIRS SHANNON Hill to life, from the wagons headed to the fields to the kitchen at the main house. There are dozens of men, women, and children of all ages going about their assigned tasks. The overseers ride through the quarters, checking to make sure that all of the slaves are getting to work. The distant crack of bullwhips sends echoes that split the still morning air.

Jessica sits on the back veranda drinking her morning tea and working on an invitation list. Jolene opens the door and walks out on the veranda carrying a tray with breakfast and coffee. She sits the tray on the table and steps back, waiting.

Jessica, without looking up from her list, says, "Take your clothes off."

Jolene stands there, not sure of what she heard. "Ma'am?"

Jessica doesn't look up. "You heard me, or has my husband fucked your brains out? Take—off—your—clothes. Now!"

Jolene fumbles with the buttons and finally drops the dress to the floor. She stands there trembling, trying to cover herself with her hands, while tears roll down her cheeks.

Jessica glances up. "Stand up straight and put your hands by your side."

Jessica goes back to her list and leaves Jolene standing there naked for several minutes.

Finally, she turns to Jolene and begins to slowly look her up and down.

"Dry the tears up, bitch. You like to be naked." Motioning with her hand, she says, "Now turn around."

Jolene turns around and faces the door.

Jessica goes back to writing and leaves Jolene standing there for several more minutes.

She finally pauses, picks up her cup of tea, and stares off into the gardens. "I guess with enough sour mash, even a cow looks inviting."

Jessica sets the cup down and goes back to writing, just as Cordell walks through the door. When he sees Jolene standing at attention naked, and Jessica writing, he is consumed in rage in a matter of seconds.

"What in the hell is going on? Jolene! Put your dress on and get back to the kitchen."

Jolene grabs the dress up off of the floor and runs naked for the door and for Bell.

Cordell calmly walks around the table and sits down across from Jessica. His bright red face is the only indicator of his level of anger. He pours himself a cup of coffee while Jessica continues to write, ignoring him.

Jessica finally looks up from her list. "Do you think we should invite Bess, now that Spence is dead?"

"What was all of that?" Cordell asks.

"All of what?"

"Stripping her down. You know what."

Jessica goes back to her invitation list. "I'll invite her and her family. It's really the Christian thing to do. Don't you think?"

Cordell pauses for a moment to maintain his self-control. "You will never again strip one of my niggers for any reason. Do you understand?"

Jessica is still occupied with her project. "I do understand. That is obviously your privilege sir. Yours and yours alone. My only complaint is that you strip that one on a regular schedule."

Cordell takes a drink of the coffee and tries to refrain from thoughts of violence.

Jessica lays her quill down and looks up at Cordell with a sweet smile. "Your daughter will be down shortly. I want you to inform her of the Henrys' story concerning the wagon driver."

At that moment, Helen walks out onto the veranda, half asleep, and inquires, "What wagon driver?"

Cordell sets the cup down roughly, gets up, and looks at Jessica. "I'll leave that to you. You're having fun in the dirt this morning."

Cordell walks around the table to Helen, stops and gives her a kiss on the forehead, and asks, "Are you still going riding with me this morning?"

Helen looks at her mother, then back to her father, whose face is still bright red. "I am. Just let me get dressed."

"Good. I'll meet you at the stable."

Cordell turns and walks off without speaking to Jessica.

Helen walks around the table and sits down in Cordell's chair. "What wagon driver were y'all talking about?"

Jessica pours Helen a cup of tea. "The wagon driver that you thought was such a gentleman."

"Are you referring to Sam Tanahill?"

"You'll be interested to know that the assessment of the young man's character by your father and me was closer to correct than yours."

"Mother, please. Just get to the point."

"The Mister Tanahill that you were so head over heels taken with... well it seems the Henrys saw him over in the valley traveling with a nigger and a whore. The only good thing to his credit is at least she was a white whore."

"The Henrys! They're not the best source for the truth mother. I would certainly..."

Jessica cuts her off. "I think if you have a look at Paxton Henry you'll see the truth."

Helen becomes irritated with her mother and says, "For the last time. Tell me the whole story. Please!"

"Very well. You'll just love this. Ike sent Paxton and his brother Pate to look at some bucks for sale over in the Shenandoah. On their way, they happened upon Mister Tanahill and his whore camped near Sapling Grove. Paxton told your father that Mister Tanahill almost drew down on 'em when they stopped to talk. Anyway, later that day, the Henrys were in Sapling Grove at a tavern, drinking, when Mister Tanahill and his nigger walked in with their guns drawn. Mister Tanahill accused the Henrys of beating his nigger and stealing his horse. So he pistol whipped Paxton, crippled him, and stole his horse and saddle with the whore's help."

Jessica pauses for a moment, enjoying the effect she can see the story is having on Helen.

Helen stares at her mother for a moment, measuring her words before she speaks. "Well Mother, that's an interesting piece of gossip you tell with such conviction. But I need to hear the other version before I hold it as the truth."

As Helen stands up to leave, Jessica smiles and says, "I am not finished with the guest list, if you have some names you would like to add."

Helen stops and looks down on her mother. "It's a shame you can't put your favorite on that list."

"And what does that remark mean?" Jessica asks.

Helen ignores her mother and calls out, "Petal, where are you girl?"

Petal runs out of the kitchen wiping her hands. "Right chere, ma'am."

Helen starts to walk out the door, leaving her mother silenced. "Come help me get dressed. I am going riding."

Petal follows Helen up the stairs. "Yes ma'am."

Helen quickly ties her hair up and gets dressed in her men's pants and shirt. She pulls the old leather boots on and tucks the shirttail in, reaching for her belt. Petal hands her the floppy hat and Helen dashes off down the stairs. When she hurries by the veranda windows, she catches her mother's attention. Jessica slowly stands up and glares at Helen. Helen abruptly stops walking, smiles a sweet, mocking smile, and does a low bow with the hat in her hand. When Helen finishes, she puts the hat on her head, pulls it down tight, and walks out.

Jessica sits down and goes back to her invitations. "Keep it up," she says to herself, "and you'll be the whore in the wagon."

When Helen walks through the gardens, she sees Rabbit leading the gray stud around in a circle down in front of the stables. Cordell stands in the middle, directing Rabbit to walk and trot the stud so he can watch the horse move. Helen cherishes the rare occasions when she has her father all to herself. If it weren't for their long rides together over Shannon Hill, she feels they would have never gotten to know each other. She stops at the stable doorway and quietly watches her father admire the stud.

"That's enough. Bring him here and let me check his legs one more time."

Rabbit leads the stud over to Cordell, looking nervous, and begins bumping the lead rope on the side of his leg. When the stud sees the rope hit Rabbit's leg, he goes ring-eyed, jerking Rabbit to the ground and dragging him. Rabbit holds on to the lead rope and struggles to get to his feet.

Cordell speaks to the stud and Rabbit in an even, soft voice. "Rabbit, be still. Don't fight him."

The stud quits running backwards, snorts loudly, and stands there trembling, watching Cordell, who eases toward him, talking softly. "Easy Blue Rock. Easy. Rabbit, don't get up. Just hand me the lead rope. Real easy."

Cordell reaches down and takes hold of the rope, then eases toward the stud. "Now. That wasn't so bad was it?" He walks closer to the stud, rubbing the side of his neck softly. "Easy now."

Cordell turns and leads the stud toward the stable, talking softly. Rabbit gets up off the ground, his eyes far bigger than the horse's were when he was spooked. Rabbit looks like he's about to take off running when Helen speaks to him.

"Rabbit." She can't get his attention so she speaks a little more firmly.

"Rabbit look at me. It's okay."

Rabbit is almost sick with fright. "I know better ma'am. Lord Jesus, I know better. If that hoss even thinks you're gonna hit 'im, he's leaving the country."

"Listen to me, Rabbit, and settle down. Go help my father, and get my horse."

Rabbit walks off with his head down talking to himself. "Lord Jesus, hep me survive this day."

Helen stands in front of the stable hallway, waiting on her father and Rabbit. The hallway is shadowy, making it hard to see much past the door. Cordell comes walking out, leading his horse, but Rabbit hangs back in the shadows holding what looks like the gray stud.

Cordell walks on to Helen, smiling, and stops. "I bought you something I think you'll like. Rabbit, lead her out."

Rabbit walks out of the dark hallway leading a gray mare that is a bookend match to the stud. She has a keen head, with a soft eye and a sleek bodyline that gives testament to her breeding.

Helen walks around the mare with her hand to her mouth, completely amazed and unable to speak. Her father has given her the best of everything growing up; clothes from Europe, jewelry from the Far East, but never a horse. Cordell watches her walk around the mare with a special pride and love for his daughter. She is the son he never had: bold, tough, and headstrong.

Helen walks around to her father and hugs him. "I love you with all my heart. Thank you is just not enough."

Cordell smiles, takes the reins from Rabbit, and hands them to Helen. "Here. They call her Analia. I hope you like her. She's like you."

"Like me?"

Cordell steps up onto his horse. "Yeah. One of a kind. Now get aboard and let's go."

Helen rubs the mare's nose, looks her in the eye, and speaks her name softly. "Analia."

"You've got all day to get acquainted. Let's go."

Helen walks to the side of the mare and raises her left leg. "Rabbit."

Rabbit cups his hands and lifts her by the ankle into the saddle.

They ride off, leaving Rabbit standing in front of the stable. He takes off his hat, wipes his worried brow with a ragged shirtsleeve, and walks back into the stable mumbling, "Lord Jesus, what a mornin'. I think sometimes the Lord himself is tryin' to frighten me dead."

As Helen and Cordell are riding off, Helen notices a bedroll tied behind Cordell's saddle.

Helen gestures toward it and asks, "Are we going to be gone longer than today?"

Cordell smiles. "No. I had Bell pack some bread and cold cuts, plus a bottle of wine. Thought we'd have lunch up on the Slick Fork."

"That's nice. Is there a reason behind all this?"

"Not at all. The cotton's in bloom, and it's time I made my rounds. Just thought it would give us some time together."

Cordell breaks his horse into an easy lope down the red dirt road headed toward the cotton fields, followed by Helen on the mare. When they reach the first fields, Cordell stops and gets down. He hands Helen the reins to his horse and walks out through the cotton, inspecting the plants and blooms with a gentle touch. The rest of the morning, he repeats the process at a dozen different fields, always returning with a smile on his face. He walks out of the last field, takes the reins from Helen, and steps up on his horse.

Cordell sits looking across the field. "If this crop makes, maybe we'll finally get over Jackson and Van Buren both. The damn fools need to leave us to our business. That whole bunch in Washington gets to where they meddle more and more every year."

They turn their horses and start down the road toward the Slick Fork. Cordell asks, "Enough of politics. How's the mare?"

"Great. She has a will to get along and does what I ask."

Cordell laughs. "Then I take back what I said. Y'all are nothing alike."

Cordell doesn't give Helen a chance to respond. He lopes off, headed for the tree line on Slick Fork. He reaches the creek first, rides his horse into the shallow water, and steps down, followed by Helen. When the horses finish drinking, they walk them back under the ancient oaks and tie them to a massive low hanging limb. Cordell rolls out the bedroll blanket by one of the oaks, and Helen goes about unwrapping the bread and ham. He opens the wine, then walks over to his horse and retrieves two tin cups out of his saddle pouch. He pours the wine and sits down on the blanket, looking off to the distant fields. Helen offers him a piece of bread and some ham.

"No thanks. Not right now."

Helen tastes the wine and begins to eat. She watches her father, because she knows there is something weighing heavy on his mind.

He takes a drink of the wine, swallows hard, and makes a face. "God, Sorrel. What is this?"

Cordell slings the cup empty, gets up, and goes back over to the saddle pouch. He digs out a flask of sour mash and walks back to Helen, pouring his cup level full. He sits back down on the blanket, facing away from Helen and staring back out into the cotton field.

"Something out there worrying you?"

Cordell takes another deep drink of sour mash and pauses. "Yeah. You."

"Me?" Then she thinks of her mother. "Is this about Sam Tanahill?"

"It is. Partly."

"And which part would that be?"

“Do you know how long the Meyers have raised their children on this land?”

Helen feels a little confused. “I don’t know. But what does that have to do with Sam Tanahill?”

“Nothing. It’s men like him.”

Helen feels like there is a lecture of some sort coming her way. “I don’t know what you’re talking about. But I wish you would just tell me, and get it out in the open.”

The mood is broken when Cordell suddenly laughs. Helen is now utterly confused and doesn’t know what to say. Cordell pours another drink of sour mash.

“That’s what I am talking about right there, Little Sister. That snap, that grit, that look in your eye.”

He shakes his head and takes a drink.

“Father, if I’ve disappointed you...”

“On the contrary. You’re my greatest accomplishment. I love your sisters, but they’re not you, and they never will be.” Cordell points to the fields and pauses to collect himself. “You’re my only hope that my family will continue to walk these fields.”

Helen sits there struck dumb beyond thought. “Everyone knows your feelings about Shannon Hill, but how do men like Sam Tanahill fit?”

“That’s just it. They don’t. They‘re dreamers. They‘re broke. They’re always looking to the horizon for their future, especially now. This whole country is broke and on the move west. And I don’t want you to be part of that. You don’t have to be.”

"So. You think Sam is a man like that?"

Cordell takes a drink. "No 'think' to it. You can see it in his eyes, in that arrogant walk. He's hungry for sure, and I'd bet there's no compromise in him."

Helen, not wanting to hurt her father, but also not wanting to live a lie, says, "I've always known you've wanted me here, but I want to be happy. If that means living on a dirt floor with a man like Sam Tanahill that loves me, then that's where I'll live."

Cordell sits staring off into the field. Helen goes to touch his shoulder, but stops and takes her hand back.

"Father, I know you won't like this, but I am going to say it anyway." Helen takes a deep breath and continues, "I don't want a man to ever touch me that I can't feel the love in his hands. That's what I am looking for, and when it happens, there'll be nothing that can stop me from being with him. No matter where he goes."

Cordell comes back to life. "I can't say if Sam Tanahill has that in his hands, but I know he has iron in his fist. Paxton Henry's face stands testimony to it."

Helen hears her father's wish to change the subject and inquires, "You believe their story?"

"Truthfully? No. Paxton wasn't pistol-whipped, but he was whipped, like no man I've ever seen. I don't know what went on and don't care, but that horse was mine. Now, if Mr. Tanahill stole him, then he has to answer for that. And so does everyone else involved."

"You're not going on Paxton's word about the horse are you?"

"Hardly. I sent a letter last night directing Lanham Hawks at the magistrate's court in Camden to make an inquiry into the incident at Sapling Grove. He'll be back in a couple of weeks or so. Then we'll know the truth."

"I personally don't believe he stole the horse."

"Based on what?" Cordell asks.

"I just know."

"Well. No matter whether he did or didn't, he had a woman traveling with him, and he's still not going to call on you."

Helen smiles and says, "Then, Father dear, you just may get half of your wish. I'll die an old maid right here on Shannon Hill."

Cordell stands up and laughs. "I doubt that, Little Sister. Collect up and let's go."

Helen stands up and hugs her father. "You're a good man."

Cordell laughs once again and says, "Now that is in doubt. Let's go."

Cordell ties the blanket back behind the saddle. Then he and Helen mount up and ride off toward home.

Later that same night, Cordell is in his office at the cotton gin, going over the cost of planting this year's cotton crop, when there's a knock on the door.

"Just a moment."

He closes the books, gets up, and locks them in the company safe. He walks back around his desk and sits down.

"Come in."

Ike Murphy opens the door and walks in. "You wanted to see me, sir?"

Cordell doesn't get up or offer a handshake. He points to a chair in front of his desk. "Have a seat, Mr. Murphy."

Ike walks up to the large mahogany desk and sits down across from Cordell.

"I'd like to discuss my wife with you, Mr. Murphy."

Ike becomes a little uncomfortable. "Your wife, sir? I don't quite understand what I..."

Cordell holds up a hand. "Mr. Murphy, I know you don't understand. That's the reason you're here. Do you remember that day you stopped Sam Tanahill on the road?"

"Yes sir. But I really didn't stop him. He stopped me."

"Okay. Do you recall how all that came about? How he stopped you and all?"

"I do, sir. But if I could, is this about my man Paxton, sir?"

"Why don't you share with me your encounter with Mr. Tanahill first? Then we'll get to Mr. Henry."

"Well, I was making my rounds, and I saw Mr. Tanahill leaving the house. I cut across the field so I could catch him on the road. Then..."

"Wait a minute. Why would you do that?"

Ike, hesitating: "Sir. It's common knowledge that Mr. Tanahill wasn't welcome on this place. I felt like it was my place to look out after your best interest, given the kind of man Mr. Tanahill is."

"What kind is that Mr. Murphy?"

"I think your assessment of his character has been proven correct. He's an outlaw who has niggers for friends and travels with whores."

Cordell sits and says almost to himself, "My assessment?" He pauses, then continues, "Did you tell Mr. Tanahill that I would ruin his father's business if he ever came back on the place?"

"Absolutely not, sir."

"Did my wife direct you to the road that day?"

"No sir. Like I said, I took that upon myself."

Cordell gets up from behind the desk and stands facing Ike. "Mr. Murphy, let me be clear about your position here at Shannon Hill. You are to concern yourself with only the directions I and I alone give you about the operations of this plantation. If my wife should impose upon you, you will direct her to me with that request. Am I clear?"

"Quite clear, sir."

"And for the situation with Mr. Tanahill. I will be the one to deal with Mr. Tanahill and not you, under any circumstances. Mr. Murphy, that means not you or anyone in your employ. Understood?"

Ike gets up. "Yes sir."

"Then goodnight, Mr. Murphy."

Ike goes to walk out, then turns back to Cordell. "Sir. Don't you want to know what was said on the road that day?"

Cordell answers, "I know all I need to know Mr. Murphy."

Ike turns to walk out. "Good night, sir."

"Oh, Mr. Murphy, the bucks that you sent Paxton to look at in the valley, I take it that you took that upon yourself also?"

Ike turns around, "Yes sir, I did. I hope that wasn't a problem?"

"Not at all."

"Is that all, sir?"

"It is. Goodnight."

Ike walks out.

Cordell walks back to his desk, sits down on the corner, and takes a cigar from a small wooden box. He sits there for a moment in reflective thought with a sly smile on his face.

"My assessment of his character. Interesting phrase."

He gets up, grabs a match, and walks out on the front porch of the mill. He lights the cigar, takes a deep drag, and blows the smoke to the heavens. The door quietly opens behind Cordell, but he continues to stare off into the night in thought.

Jolene walks up behind him, puts her arms around his chest, and lays her head on his back. "You okay?"

"I am. I am blessed beyond all of my requests, both past and present."

"He lied like you knew he would, didn't he?"

Cordell nods and answers. "He did. But it's just his breeding. Good never comes from evil."

"You need me to fetch you anything?"

Cordell reaches down and softly rubs her hands. "Naw. Go on to bed; I am coming. I need to sort out a few things."

Jolene turns Cordell loose and walks back into the mill.

Cordell looks to the heavens and says, "Father, forgive me of my sins." He pitches the cigar into the road, walks back into the mill, and locks the door behind him.

CHAPTER TEN

TWO WEEKS LATER, THE FULL AUGUST MOON HANGS HIGH IN the eastern sky, and a cool fall breeze is gently blowing through the entire Tanahill household. Sensing the first cool spell over the Carolinas, Mary Beth had raised every window in the house that evening before bedtime. She lies in bed next to Owen, reading her Bible by lamplight and listening to the night birds, when she hears a faint but familiar whistle. Mary Beth closes the Bible and nudges Owen who is sound asleep.

Mary Beth nudges him again and whispers, “Owen, wake up.”

Owen immediately raises up. “What is it?”

“Sam is driving in.”

Owen rubs his eyes “What time is it?”

“A little after eleven.”

Owen sits up on the edge of the bed listening. "At this hour. Are you sure?"

"Just listen."

Far off, on the cool night air, rides a faint, high-pitch whistle. Owen gets a sick feeling in the pit of his stomach. He hurriedly gets dressed and walks out on the back porch carrying a lantern, followed by Mary Beth. They stand on the porch listening to the distant rattling of a wagon approaching from town. After several tense minutes, the white cover of the wagon finally appears on the moonlit road coming up the hill.

Owen walks down off of the porch toward the barn while Mary Beth lights another lantern, hangs it on a post by her rocker, and sits down. She hums an old hymn and rocks easy.

Sam swings the team up by the barn and reins them up. "Whoa, now."

With their heads down and their big ears flopped over from pure exhaustion, the mules stop dead still in one motion and don't so much as twitch a tail. Owen walks up to the wagon holding the lantern up so Sam and Little Jim can see to get down. When Sam steps down and faces Owen, neither man speaks for a moment. Then Owen moves the light where he can look at Little Jim's face.

Owen speaks first. "Are y'all alright?"

Sam and Little Jim answer at the same time. "Yes sir."

Owen nods his head in approval. "Good. First thing I want you to do, Sam, is walk over to the house and speak to your mother. Go on now and get back, we got work to do."

"Yes sir."

He walks off toward the house and puts a smile on his face.

Owen addresses Little Jim next. "Little Jim, unhook the lead team. I'll get the next pair."

"Yes sir."

Sam walks up to the porch where his mother sits and rocks in the lantern light. "Maw."

"You okay, son?"

"Yes ma'am."

Mary Beth points to his face. "You get that doing what's right?"

Sam nods his head. "Yes ma'am, I did."

"Well, go help your paw. I'll get y'all some coffee and something to eat."

Sam smiles and answers, "Be nice to sit down at your table, Maw. We haven't eaten much in a week."

"I am glad you're home. Go on now. It'll be on the table by the time y'all finish and get washed up."

Sam walks back to the barn and Mary Beth thanks the Lord he's safe. She takes the lantern, goes to the kitchen, and starts cooking.

Sam walks back to the wagon, unhooks the last pair of mules, and leads them into the barn. He ties them up and starts taking their harnesses off. Little Jim is feeding and watering the other mules out back in the pens when Owen walks back in.

"Little Jim says you whipped Paxton Henry in a straight up fight."

Sam continues working. "Wasn't no way around it. He and his brother caught Little Jim off by himself and whipped him for no reason. And then they ran off your horse."

"I would guess all this trouble comes from your run-in with Ike Murphy down at Shannon Hill awhile back. Wouldn't you?"

"It looks that way, Paw, that's for sure. The Henrys knew what they were doing when they jumped Little Jim."

"You should have told me what Ike said that day at the forge."

Sam stops work and looks at his father. "I am sorry I didn't, but I thought I had it behind me. Besides, I didn't want to worry you with it."

"When a man threatens your family, it's something that's never behind you. We should have talked."

Sam goes back to pulling the harnesses off of the mules. "I know, but like I said, Paw, I thought it was finished. Who told you about Ike anyway?"

"Ira Paul did. He was by here with some letters for you. Came by two days after you left with the first one from Helen Meyers. Then he was back a few days ago with a letter from Bess Rayburn. Spence died a few weeks back. I'd guess her letter is about the horse."

Sam pauses for a moment, thinking of Spence. "What about the race? Did he get to match the gray before he died?"

"He did, and lost. Ira Paul said the gray out ran the bay by ten lengths. He said the loss left Spence broke in more ways than one. After the race, he took to his bed and never got up."

Sam is taking the last of the harnesses off the mules when Little Jim walks back up.

Sam says to his father, "You mind if I go on in and read the letters? Little Jim can finish up."

"Yeah, go on. We'll be in directly."

Sam turns and walks toward the house.

Owen and Little Jim finish feeding and tie the wagon cover down just in case it rains. When they walk up onto the back porch, Sam is sitting in a rocker reading the letter from Helen. Owen and Little Jim wash up and start into the house.

Owen says to Sam, "You coming in?"

"Yes sir. I'm coming."

Owen and Little Jim continue on into the house.

Sam rereads Helen's letter and sits in thought.

Mary Beth finally walks out on the porch. "Sam. It's getting cold, come on. We're ready to say the blessing, son."

"Go ahead and let Little Jim eat. I'll be in shortly, Maw."

After Little Jim finishes eating, he and Owen walk back out on the porch.

"I'm turning in, boss. See you in the morning."

Sam is still sitting in the rocker. "Good night, Little Jim."

Little Jim walks on to the bunkhouse over by the barn, and Owen sits down by Sam.

"Your mother has a plate fixed for you. Go on in and eat so she can clean up."

Sam gets up, walks down the porch, stops, and walks back to his father with the letter in his hand. Owen lights his pipe and rocks.

"I know you think all this trouble is about Helen Meyers, but it's not. It's about..."

Sam pauses, not knowing how to explain his feelings toward Helen. He can't even bring himself to tell his father why he has been so viciously angry.

Owen interrupts before Sam can continue. "It's about control, son. Plain and simple. They have it, and they work to keep it."

Sam turns to walk off, then stops. "I agree, but Ike sent Paxton Henry after me when there was no need. I don't know their reason, but they need to let it go. Because if they press the issue again, so will I."

Owen rocks for a moment. "I'd say what you do about that letter will pretty much decide that issue."

Sam works to hold his frustration in check. "There's no issue. I am going to get my horse and as soon as I have the money, I am going west. I don't care how many letters she writes me. I am leaving."

"Well until then, son, I have a lot of hauling for Cordell. But you're sure not going down there. I don't want this to go any further."

Sam becomes moody at his father's proclamation. "No disrespect. But I am going back down there, and everywhere else we have loads to haul, until I leave. Without exception!"

"Son..."

Sam cuts him off. "Paw. If that bunch wants to fight every day, then so be it. I will not be bullied by them or anyone else."

Owen admires his son's courage. "I understand. Just don't let that hot temper run your business."

"I won't. I give you my word, Paw."

"Good. Now go on and eat."

Sam remembers the other letter that came from Mrs. Rayburn. "Oh. Mrs. Rayburn wants me to come on and get the horse. So when my team is rested, I'll go pick him up, then swing by Shannon Hill for a load. If that's okay."

Owen reluctantly agrees. "Just watch your back."

"I will. I am taking Little Jim with me."

Owen looks off into the dark and nods. "Go eat."

Sam turns and walks into the house.

A week later, long about dusk, Cordell walks out of the mill with Lanham Hawks, a short, stout man of forty with piercing blue eyes and a straight forward way of doing everything in life.

Cordell extends his hand. "Lanham, I appreciate your help in this matter. Please tell the Magistrate I said thank you."

Lanham shakes Cordell's hand. "Any time we can help, Mr. Meyers, just call on us."

Lanham steps into the stirrup and swings up onto his horse. He points to the dun tied to the hitching rail and says, "Keep that one tied up tight. If he gets loose, he's hell to catch."

"I will," Cordell says, "Thanks again."

Lanham turns and rides off just as Ike is riding up. Lanham and Ike know each other, but they only nod in their passing.

Cordell turns his attention to Ike. "Evening, Mr. Murphy. Come in."

"Yes sir."

Cordell turns and walks into the mill.

Ike glances over at the dun when he dismounts and ties his horse up.

He walks into Cordell's office with his hat in his hand. Cordell stands with his back to Ike, looking out of his office window.

"Shut the door, Mr. Murphy."

"Yes sir."

"Mr. Murphy, do you know how long my family has been doing business in South Carolina?"

Cordell pauses and waits. Ike knows the conversation is going to Tanahill and the horse, so he needs to measure all of his answers carefully.

"Not sure sir. But I hear tell y'all been here awhile."

Cordell turns around, red-faced, and Ike is taken aback by the anger in his eyes.

Cordell keeps his tone level and even as he speaks. "A while indeed. For over two hundred years, sir, we've done business in this state. You know how, Mr. Murphy?"

"Like everyone else, sir. I would say hard work."

"That's the easy part, Mr. Murphy. The hard part is integrity, sir. The Meyers' name has always carried it, and I will not let it stop with me. This problem you and my wife have caused me with Mr. Tanahill is an embarrassment. And I..."

"Mr. Meyers, men like him..."

"Mr. Murphy! My family came from men like him. Do you understand me?"

Ike becomes angry but remains respectful. "Sir, with all due respect. Your family is nothing like him. He's an outlaw of the worst character."

Cordell regains his composure and asks, "You saw the man leaving?"

"Yes sir."

"I know you know who he is, but let me tell you why he's here with Sam Tanahill's horse. I had the authorities send an inquiry to Sapling Grove about the theft of my horse and the fight between Paxton and Sam Tanahill. And do you know what I found out?"

Ike knows he's in a tight spot. "No sir, I don't."

"I found out the goddamn truth, Mr. Murphy. The truth!"

Cordell paces and tries to keep his self-control. "The truth, Mr. Murphy, is that Mr. Tanahill has done nothing wrong. The young lady is a friend of his, not a whore. And as for the fight, he took your man Paxton Henry in the street and whipped him with nothing but his bare hands, fair and square. There was no pistol whipping involved, and as for the horse, well, Paxton bet my horse and saddle on the fight. And in the end, the man collected, which was his right. The right, Mr. Murphy, which he's been in all along. Even the right to call on my daughter. But it was my right to say no, for my reasons and mine alone."

Ike knows how hard times are right now, and he can't afford to lose his position at Shannon Hill for any reason.

"Mr. Meyers, I apologize for any dishonor I've caused you. How should I proceed?"

Cordell disapproves of many of Ike's qualities, but under his management for the past two and a half years, Shannon Hill has not only survived the Panic of '37, but has shown a profit. Ike's family plantation down in Atlanta had been one of the first places to go broke at the onset of the crash. Shortly after the Murphys' loss, Cordell's son-in-law, Miles, sent Ike to him with a sterling recommendation for a job. But Ike has struggled in his relationship with Cordell because Ike has always been in charge, and old habits die hard. Cordell likes Ike's management skills, but cares nothing for the man himself.

Cordell bluntly and to the point says, "I'll tell you how I want you to proceed. Just as I told you before. You will leave Mr. Tanahill alone. If he is sent here to haul freight, you will load his wagons and only involve yourself in those matters. And if he calls at my house, that is my business alone and no one else's, not even my wife's. So I strongly suggest you think twice before you act as her agent in any kind of future intrigues. Are we in agreement, sir?"

Ike extends his hand and says, "We are. I will personally see to it that your wishes are carried out. On that, you have my word, sir."

Cordell shakes his hand but believes Ike lives and acts in the moment. "Thank you, Mr. Murphy. I have one last thing. On your way home, stop and tell Bell I'll be home for supper in an hour or so. Oh, and put that dun horse somewhere until I can send him to Mr. Tanahill. Now if you'll excuse me."

"Of course sir. I'll see to it. Good night."

"And Mr. Murphy."

"Yes sir?"

Cordell stares silently at Ike until the tension between the two is palpable. "Mr. Henry owes me for a horse and saddle."

Ike's face turns crimson red. "Yes sir. I'll see to that also."

Ike stalks out of the office and shuts the door behind him. Cordell stands there for a moment, still consumed in a gripping mixture of anxiety and rage. Finally, he walks over to his liquor cabinet and pours himself a large drink of sour mash. In reflective thought, he takes the drink in hand, walks around his desk, and sits down. Cordell settles in the chair and begins to sip on the whiskey, thinking about the fight between Sam and Paxton. He leans back in the big chair and lets the whiskey settle over him. There is a soft knock on his office door, which makes Cordell close his eyes in thought.

Jolene eases the door open and steps in. When she sees Cordell's red face and his closed eyes, she stands silently still and waits.

Cordell doesn't open his eyes. "Jolene, honey. Go on and see to your mama. I won't be very good company tonight. Believe me."

"Yes sir." She remains standing by the door.

Cordell sits up, opens his eyes, and looks at her with an easy smile. "I'm okay; go on."

Jolene smiles an unsure smile and nods her head. She quietly eases out the door and shuts it behind her.

Cordell leans back in the chair and closes his eyes. His mind returns to the fight, and Lanham's detailed description of Sam marching Paxton into the street and whipping him with the whole town looking on.

Bell's house girls are busy cleaning up and getting ready for the next day when there's a knock at the kitchen's back door. Bell sits at the kitchen table having a cup of coffee and scribbling some marks on a piece of paper. The knock sounds again, and the girls all look at Bell.

Bell returns their look and says, "I got ears. Tend yo' business."

She gets up, walks to the door, and opens it. When she sees it's Ike, she straightens her spine and stares unwaveringly. She stands in the doorway, and doesn't invite Ike into her kitchen.

"Evenin', Mr. Ike. How can I help you?"

There are several pet niggers on Shannon Hill that Ike would like to whip, but none more than Bell.

Ike returns Bell's look of dislike. "Mr. Meyers wanted me to tell you he'll be here for supper in an hour or so."

Bell responds with a mammy-like tone of voice. "I appreciate you coming by and sharing that with us, Mista Ike."

Ike clinches his jaw at Bell's mocking tone and struggles not to slap her down. He stands looking at Bell, then turns and walks away. The demeaning disciplining from Cordell was hard enough to swallow, but a smart-mouthed, pet nigger is more than Ike can stand for one day. He walks down the back driveway of the mansion in a rage to where his horse is tied.

"From your walk, I'd say your day has been trying."

Ike recognizes the voice and stops walking. "Between your husband and your..."

He pauses and changes his tone. "Just an ordinary day, ma'am. Nothing special till now."

Jessica walks out of the dark into the shadowy light of the driveway. She walks up to Ike, then around behind him, dragging her index finger across the back of his broad shoulders.

She stops behind him and whispers in a seductive, catty tone, "Nothing special till now. Would that be an indication of interest, Mr. Murphy?"

"Ma'am, we've had that discussion. But I've had no indication of your interest."

Jessica reaches around Ike with her hand and rubs his crotch. "That is my interest, Mr. Murphy."

Ike turns around and reaches for her, but she steps just out of his reach, smiling.

"Mr. Murphy, I am not a comfort girl to be groped in the dark. I'll let you know when and where."

Ike stands there looking at her for a moment and responds, "Then be careful not to act like one."

Jessica takes a step backwards to walk away. "Good night, sir. And Mr. Murphy, for future reference, always remove your hat in my presence."

She turns and walks away, leaving Ike standing in the dark. He stands there until Jessica walks back out of sight, then unties his horse, steps up into the saddle, and rides away. When Ike and Jessica are both out of sight and hearing, Bell walks out into the driveway. She stands there for a moment, thinking, then she turns and walks back to the house.

The final ten o'clock chime is striking when Cordell walks into the kitchen to find Bell sitting in her rocker waiting on him. She starts to get up when Cordell holds up his hand.

"I'm going to bed, Bell. You do the same."

"You sure, sir? I got stuff set out for you, still warm."

Cordell walks out of the kitchen and says, "I'm sure."

Bell watches Cordell walk off and thinks about Ike talking with Miss Jessica in the dark. Bell knew Ike didn't have a good bone in his body the first day she laid eyes on him. He's fooled lots of folks with his smooth ways, but never Bell, and he knows it. Bell worries that someday she might come under his hand, which would only mean grief. She rocks and makes herself a promise not to let that come to pass.

Early the next morning, Cordell sits at Bell's kitchen table, drinking coffee and reading a week old Charleston paper. The warmth of the big kitchen stove cuts the morning chill from the cold drizzling rain that's falling across Shannon Hill. The early fall cool snap is welcome relief after a long, hot summer. Bell, Jolene, Petal, and the other two house girls are cooking breakfast, cleaning, and getting the house up and running for the day.

Ike knocks at the back door of the kitchen.

Cordell lays the paper down and says, "Come in."

Ike opens the door and steps just inside in a dripping wet slicker.

Bell and her girls don't look up from their work when Ike steps into the kitchen.

He takes off his hat. "Morning, sir."

"Morning, Mr. Murphy. Coffee?"

"No, thank you sir. I just wanted to let you know I put the field hands in the warehouses and barns today so they can be making repairs. If that's okay? No sense wasting a whole day."

"Mr. Murphy. Today is no different from any other day. Those decisions are yours. Now what really brings you here this morning?"

Ike hesitates when Jessica walks into the kitchen, cooler than the chilled rain that's blowing in the wind. She pours herself a cup of coffee and sits down at the table. Cordell doesn't give her a second look, and keeps his attention to the business at hand with Ike.

"Good morning gentlemen. Am I interrupting business this cold morning?"

"Not at all ma'am," says Ike.

Cordell is aggravated with Ike over his less than honest way of communicating in the past few months on several issues. The most damning indictment against Ike is his willingness to act as Jessica's behind-the-scenes agent. Cordell becomes more and more guarded regarding his interactions with Ike, because hidden agendas are becoming the order of the day at Shannon Hill.

"Mr. Murphy... the reason you're here?"

"Well sir, it's the matter of the horse. I want you to hold that money out of my pay. Paxton will pay me."

"The saddle also?"

"Yes sir."

Jessica looks up from her coffee and says with feigned kindness, "Mr. Murphy, that's nice that you take such an interest in your friends."

"Mr. Meyers wants it taken care of, I am just making sure that it gets done."

Cordell speaks directly to Ike, ignoring that Jessica has inserted herself in the conversation. "I am good with that. Go on about your day."

"Thank you, sir. Ma'am."

Ike walks out the door and Cordell goes back to his paper.

"Want to tell me why Paxton is paying you for the horse that Sam Tanahill stole?"

Cordell puts the paper down and looks at Jessica. "I tell you what I am going to do. Petal, come here."

Petal hurries over to Cordell. "Yes sir."

"Petal, go get Helen and tell her to hurry up and get down here."

Petal says, "Yes sir," as she dashes out of the kitchen.

"Why do you need Helen?" Jessica asks.

Cordell snaps. "Because I don't want this story used in the war of words around here. Okay? I am going to tell it one time, then I don't want to hear about it in this house again!"

Jessica raises an eyebrow. "Sure. Don't get touchy."

Cordell goes back to his paper, and several minutes later Helen walks into the kitchen, followed by Petal.

"You wanted to see me, Father?"

Cordell closes the paper. "I did. Sit down."

Helen walks around the table and sits down. "What is this about?"

Jessica replies, "It's your favorite bedtime story. The ongoing Sam Tanahill saga."

Cordell snaps at Jessica. "Enough." Looking from Jessica to Helen he says, "I want to tell both of you this story, and then I don't want to hear a word about it after today. NOT A WORD!"

Cordell pauses a moment, then he begins. "I had the magistrate in Camden send Lanham Hawks to Sapling Grove to make an inquiry on my behalf about the fight, and my horse. The short story, ladies, is this; Sam Tanahill is guilty of nothing. Paxton bet my horse and saddle on the fight, which he lost fair and square, with the whole town looking on. The fight itself was instigated by Paxton, who whipped Mr. Tanahill's nigger and ran off his horse. And there was no whore. The young lady in his company was a friend of his who owns a boarding house in Sapling Grove with her mother.

So, as I have told Mr. Murphy, I will tell you. The business with Mr. Tanahill is closed. Forever! Now I am going to have breakfast and read my paper, if there are no objections."

Helen immediately gets up and kisses her father on his forehead. "If I may be excused. I am going back to bed."

Cordell smiles. "Go on."

Jessica raises a finger and begins to say, "I think..."

Cordell cuts her off sharply. "Jessica, I am in no mood! So please."

Jessica sees the look in Cordell's eyes and quietly gets up and leaves the room. Cordell watches her with scorn until she walks out of the kitchen. Then he opens the paper and starts to read.

Bell walks over to Cordell with a plate of eggs, toast, and bacon. She can't help but grin. "Eggs just like you like 'em, sir."

Cordell puts the paper down, looks over to Jolene, then up to Bell, smiling easy, and says, "Thanks."

He opens the paper and begins reading and eating breakfast.

CHAPTER ELEVEN

SEVERAL DAYS LATER, THE EVENING SUN IS SLIPPING BEHIND the hazy Blue Ridge Mountains, turning the western sky into a fiery red panorama that stretches from north to south as far as the eye can see. Sam leans on the rail fence with his eyes fixed on the far off horizon, wondering what untouched wilderness lies under that blazing red sky.

Owen walks out of the barn toward the house when he glances up and sees Sam standing by the fence of the north pasture. He pauses for a moment in thought, turns, and walks down the fence to Sam.

When Owen approaches, Sam looks at his father, then turns back to the sunset and speaks. "Spence told me about the agony that the setting sun caused his son Ryland. How he felt left behind every day that the sun went west without him. I'll tell you the truth, Paw, I've come to know that agony."

"Son. Every man has to find his place in this world. I've seen too many men side-step the challenges that it takes to do that. And you know what? One of two things happens: they finally go looking for it, or they die a miserable human. There's no in-between, son."

Owen reaches out, puts his hand on Sam's shoulder, then turns and walks back to the house. Sam continues to watch the red sky until darkness settles over the mountains.

The next morning at four o'clock, Sam and Little Jim are walking out of the back pens, leading two mules each into the barn to be harnessed. Little Jim is leading his pair as he hums and dances a light shuffle.

"What's going on this morning with you, Little Jim?"

"We're going to Charleston boss. Dat's women. Lots and lots of pretty women."

"Well. We've got to go by the Rayburn's and Shannon Hill first, so put yourself into that harnessing. We need to get."

"Don't be moody boss. I am moving."

"I am not moody. Just quit talking and work. It'll be light soon."

"I'ma jumpin' boss. I'ma jumpin'."

Sam leads his pair out of the barn and hooks them up to the wagon. Little Jim walks out with his pair just as Sam is hooking the last trace chain to the single tree.

Sam turns to Little Jim. "Harness and hook the lead pair. I'll be right back. I need to see Paw, and then we're leaving."

Sam walks across the road to the house, and up onto the back porch. When he walks into the kitchen, Owen and Mary Beth are sitting at the table drinking coffee and talking. He can see the concern and worry on his parents' faces.

Sam sits down by his mother and puts his arm around her. "I know this isn't easy for y'all, but I have to do this. There's no way around it, and I am not looking for one."

Owen is fearful for his son, but he admires his character. "Son, the truth is, we know that. Just make sure you're in the right, no matter what happens."

Sam stands up, reaches across the table, and shakes his father's hand. Owen looks Sam in the eye and nods his head in approval.

"Yes sir. Y'all don't worry though. I'll be home in three weeks."

Mary Beth gets up and fetches Sam a knapsack of food. "Here's something for your midday stop." She pulls him down to her and hugs his neck. "You mind yourself and trust the Lord. He's the way, and there's no other."

"Yes ma'am."

Sam turns and walks out the door while Mary Beth sits back down at the table and opens her Bible.

When he gets back to the wagon, all of the mules are hooked up and Little Jim is sitting on the wagon seat holding the reins, smiling.

"That quick enough for you, boss?"

Sam steps up on the wagon wheel, trying to hide a smile. "Slide over, knot head, and give me those lines."

Sam takes the lines and whistles for the team to step up. The big mules all lean into their collars, the trace chains come tight, and Sam swings the team toward the road.

Later that same day, sometime around noon, Ike rides down a little-used road, following a fresh set of carriage tracks. The road winds off through the heavy timber for several miles, going deeper and deeper into the Santee River bottom until it ends at a hunter's cabin overlooking the river. The fresh smell of an oak fire is drifting off through the river bottom when Ike rides up to the cabin. A tall, thin, black man of forty plus years, dressed in a flat-brim black hat and a black coat, walks out from under a shed off to the side of the cabin. Benjie has been Jessica's personal carriage driver for ten years. His quiet, solemn ways make him Jessica's trusted and indispensible servant.

Benjie takes his hat off, keeps his eyes down, and nods his head in respect. "Mister Ike."

Ike is surprised and annoyed that Jessica would bring her carriage driver to their meeting. Now every nigger on the place will know about today. He steps down, pitches Benjie the horse's reins, and walks up on the front porch. Taking off his hat, he opens the door and walks in to find Jessica standing by the fireplace in a full-length red nightgown. Ike swings the door shut behind him and never takes his eyes off of her. Pitching his hat on a nearby table, Ike starts across the room. Jessica holds up her hand, but Ike keeps coming. When he gets close, she puts her hand on his chest and keeps him at arm's length.

"Mr. Murphy! You are here, sir, because you are a gentleman. So conduct yourself as one!"

Ike, still pressing into her hand, says, "I really don't think that's what you're looking for. Not today, anyway."

Jessica steps away from Ike and points to him with fire in her eyes. "Mr. Murphy, this will stop before it starts if you persist with your rough approach."

Jessica turns and walks away from Ike in fuming silence.

Ike, sensing he's made a huge misstep, says, "My apologies. That was very coarse of me."

Jessica turns around and faces Ike. "Mr. Murphy. I am a lady. Even under these circumstances, I will not act nor be treated like a whore. Are we clear?"

"We are. I promise you, I'll conduct myself accordingly."

Jessica walks to a rocker by the fireplace and sits down. Ike eases over to a bench close by and sits facing her.

"Before this goes any further, there are some things I want understood."

Ike knows better than to disagree at this point. "By all means."

Jessica turns to him. "The first thing I want is your word as a gentleman that our relationship does not become common gossip."

"I think you should have considered that before you had Benjie drive you here. Every nigger on the place will know before dark, including your husband's bed warmer."

"Mr. Murphy, its common knowledge that you spend a lot of time in the quarters. Have my activities ever been the subject of gossip?"

Ike concedes the point. "Not to my knowledge, they haven't."

"Then your word, sir."

Ike smiles a reassuring smile. "You have my word. Anything else?"

"There is. The quarters are off limits, and especially that little skinny girl, Switch."

Ike looks down, then back to Jessica. "I don't have any other arrangements. So you're telling me you're going to see me that much?"

"Sir. I am in one relationship where I have to make compromises. But here, I have complete control of this bed, and there will be no wenches."

Ike nods his head in forced agreement. "I am not sure how this is going to work, but okay."

They sit in awkward silence, neither one knowing what to say next. Ike finally pulls his shirttail out and reaches down to pull his boots off. Jessica gets up and walks to the bed, pulls the covers back, and gets in.

She props herself up in bed with several pillows and points to a bathtub sitting in a far corner of the room. "I heated the water myself."

Ike pauses and looks over his shoulder at the tub. "A bath?"

Jessica has a long ringlet of her blonde hair in her hand that she is rolling around her fingers. "It's your decision, Mr. Murphy."

He starts taking his clothes off again, with Jessica absorbed in his every move. Her eyes miss nothing, from the scars on his body to his oversized arms, and everything in between. When he is finally naked, he turns to face her, grinning slightly.

Ike holds his hands out from his side. "You sure you want to wait?"

She looks him over for a moment, then points to the tub again. "The bath."

Ike walks over to the tub and tests the water with his hand. The water is long past warm, but he doesn't say a word. He steps into the tub, looks over to Jessica, and smiles.

"From head to toe, Mr. Murphy."

Ike takes the soap and starts to bathe. "Tell me something, Jessica. When will we get to just plain Ike?"

Jessica, teasingly: "If you get invited back. Then we'll see."

"Want to hear a true story?" Ike asks.

"That's the best kind, Mr. Murphy."

Ike rinses off and stands up in the tub, facing Jessica. "I always get invited back."

Jessica points and says, "The towel is behind you, Mr. Murphy."

Ike reaches over, picks the towel up, and steps out of the tub. He starts drying off, walking toward the bed. Jessica sits up in bed and goes to take the nightgown off.

"No ma'am."

Jessica hears the authority in Ike's voice and stops. She looks him in the eyes for a moment, then smiles and lies back down.

"That's for me to do, and I'll get to it in my own time."

Ike pulls the covers back and slides in next to Jessica. He rolls over on his side, facing her, and begins to lightly trace the line of her lips with his finger.

"You have the most beautiful set of lips I've ever seen on a woman. Do you know how many times I've been in your presence and wanted to kiss those lips?"

His unexpected tenderness takes Jessica's breath away, a faint moan escaping her lips as she exhales softly. She closes her eyes and settles into the pillows. Ike runs his finger down her jaw line, leans over, and gently kisses her. Jessica can't remember the last time one kiss stirred such a feeling of anticipation. Her hips move on the bed as Ike kisses her again, trailing his hand down her neck to the side of her breast.

She arches her back as his hand softly moves down to her trembling stomach. When Ike's hand reaches the edge of her nightgown, Jessica raises her hips, allowing him to push it up around her waist. Her trembling turns almost to a spasm when his hand slides between her legs. He holds his hand there for a moment, then moves it back up to the nightgown.

"Take this off. I want to see you naked."

She arches her back and lifts the gown over her head with his help. When the nightgown is off, she pulls him to her and gives him a hot, passionate kiss. He eases between her legs, and the bed makes a slow rhythmic creak. They spend several hours trying to make up for something neither has had in a long time.

Later that afternoon, Jessica is asleep in Ike's arms when he gently touches her lips. "Hey. I have to go. My men will be looking for me."

Jessica opens her eyes and moans a soft sigh of contentment. "You surprised me today. But in a really nice way."

"How so?"

"I was looking for something I didn't think you had."

"Then why did you agree to see me?"

Jessica sits up in bed and says, "I wanted to be touched by someone who wanted me. I've seen that want in your eyes for a long time. You just always scared me."

Ike smiles. "So let's back up here. First, you didn't think I had what you were looking for, and second, I scare you?"

Jessica looks away and says, "You do. When you came in here, you were less than a gentleman."

"My apologizes again. I just wanted to kiss you. More than you can believe."

Jessica's mood changes to something a little more like everyday Jessica. "Given I've seen your other side, Mr. Murphy, I think my apprehension was well-founded."

Ike reaches up, takes her in his arms, and lays her back down. "I'll be Mr. Murphy when your feet touch that floor, but in this bed, I expect equal respect. I am Ike. Say it."

Jessica whispers his name and kisses him passionately.

The noonday September sun bears down, still holding South Carolina in its heated grip. The cool spell the week before was a sweet relief from a miserable summer that everyone thought was over, but today's heat is a cruel reminder that summer has a little more misery yet to offer.

With every step of the mules' twenty-four iron shoes, Sam's team and wagon are covered in dust. In the distance, down the lane leading to the Rayburn place, Sam can hear the ringing of the noonday bell. When they reach the house, Sistell is standing on the end of the porch. She has one hand up, shading her eyes, and the other on her slightly large belly, looking off to the distant fields. When she notices Sam and Little Jim, she waves, and then turns her attention back to the fields. The men return the wave and push the team on by the house until they reach the circle drive in front of the Rayburns' barn.

Little Jim smiles upon seeing Sistell. "Looks like there's a colt due 'fore too long."

Sam ignores the comment and reins the team up, looking around. "Wonder where everyone's at?"

Sam and Little Jim climb down off of the wagon.

"Unhook 'em and get 'em watered. I'll see where Teddy's at."

Little Jim goes to work. "Yes sir."

Sam walks into the barn and says, "Hey Teddy."

"Hey boss," Little Jim yells. "Come have a look."

Sam walks out to see Little Jim pointing toward a wagon coming up a field road beside the barn. Ira Paul is driving with Mrs. Rayburn sitting next to him, and Old Jeb and one of their house girls are riding in the back of the wagon. When they get a little closer, Sam notices they aren't dressed for a social event. He walks over to the edge of the road just as Ira Paul reins up the two rail-thin mules. He has a bright smile from ear to ear on his dirty face, which stands in stark contrast to the haggard smile of Mrs. Rayburn's. All four are sweat-stained and dirty from head to toe.

Ira Paul extends his blistered hand. "Good to see ya, Sam." Ira Paul looks around Sam and says, "Little Jim."

Little Jim waves and continues unhooking the team.

"You too, Ira Paul." Sam takes his hat off and nods to Mrs. Rayburn.

"Ma'am. I was sorry to hear about Mr. Rayburn."

Mrs. Rayburn gets down from the wagon. "Thank you kindly, Sam. He sure thought the world of you."

"The feeling was mutual. He was a good man."

Mrs. Rayburn, speaking more to the world than to Sam, replies, "He was a good everything, except gambler."

Sam can see the hurt and loss in her eyes.

Mrs. Rayburn looks to Sam. "I am glad you've come for the horse. Maybe with him off the place, my misery will let up a mite. I doubt it, but I hope."

Mrs. Rayburn takes off her sun hat, turns, and walks toward the house with exhausted steps. "Sistell has the table set. Y'all come on up and eat."

"Thank you ma'am."

"Bring your man there too."

"Yes ma'am."

Ira Paul looks to Old Jeb. "Y'all go on and get washed up."

Old Jeb and the girl get down and plod along after Mrs. Rayburn.

"I take it y'all are working the fields?"

Ira Paul answers, "There's nobody left, except the five of us." He ducks his head and looks off into the distance for a moment, then back to Sam. "Well, six, come late winter."

Sam smiles. "I saw her standing on the porch when we drove up. Congratulations."

Ira Paul shakes his head in disbelief. "Wasn't long ago I was coon huntin' without one thought past a hound, every day my eyes opened. Now here I am running a place, looking after folks, and waitin' to be a father. Life can sure sneak up on a fellar in some odd ways."

Sam looks around and asks, "All this over the horse race?"

Ira Paul gets down from the wagon. "Yes sir. He bet every dollar they had on the match, and it wasn't even close. Three quarters of the way, both jockeys went to the bat and the race just fell apart."

"How do you mean fell apart?"

Ira Paul explains. "Well, Blue Rock took off like a scalded dog, and Journey just slam quit tryin'. That's what Mr. Spence did after the race: he just plain quit tryin'. He came home, went to bed, and never got up again."

Ira Paul leads his team over to the water trough, where Little Jim is watering Sam's team two at a time. Sam walks over with him.

Sam instructs Little Jim, "Tie 'em in the shade while we eat, but leave the harnesses on. We're pushing on in a couple hours."

"Yes sir."

Then Sam asks, "What happened to Newella?"

Ira Paul smiles. "You'll like this story. The goofy bitch moved in with Paxton Henry three days after we buried Spence."

Sam's mind momentarily flashes back to the fight. "Paxton Henry? That don't figure."

"Yeah it does. She's the only person I know that hates niggers worse than Paxton and Ike put together."

"She's that crazy?"

Ira Paul looks at Sam. "She is and then some. But I'll tell ya what's really crazy: all the stories about you whipping Paxton. He says you pistol whipped him and crippled him."

Sam almost laughs. "That's his story?"

"Yes sir. Him and his brother both swear it for the truth."

Sam laughs outright. "He got whipped all right, but it was fair and straight up. Hell, the whole town of Sapling Grove was standing there watching."

"According to Newella, they're laying for you. So I'd watch where I go if I was you."

"Well, that's good to know. I'll ask 'em about all that tomorrow."

Ira Paul turns a little pale. "You headed down there, are you?"

"I am. But don't worry; I won't mention your name."

"I 'preciate that. But you best be careful. Ike's hired a bad bunch over the last year and half there at Shannon Hill. I mean some real cut throats."

"On the subject of bad people. You figure Jessica sent Paxton after me?"

"Naw. That was Ike's doing."

"How do you know that?"

"Because Ike and Paxton were drunk one night, and that's when Newella overheard them talking about you."

"Why would she warn me? When she's sleeping with Paxton?"

Ira Paul answers, "She didn't. She came to see her mama and got drunk on the porch one night talkin' to Sistell. She allowed how things weren't finished between you and Ike."

"I knew that when I whipped Paxton. But for the life of me, I don't know what's driving Ike so hard."

"Look, I don't know either," says Ira Paul, "but I can tell you for sure it's not Jessica. Because Helen and her parents did some horse tradin' on you."

Sam smiles. "What kind of horse trading?"

"Well. Jessica worked Helen and Cordell into a fight about you, and in the end Helen agreed not to ever see you again. But her mother and father had to agree to one condition."

Sam, anxious to hear that condition, asks, "Which was?"

"That no other man would ever be allowed to court her without her permission."

Sam looks off and smiles. "Checkmate."

"It's driving Jessica raving-ass crazy, but Helen won't give in. No sir. Says she's gonna die an old maid right there on Shannon Hill."

Sam laughs and says to himself, “An old maid. I doubt that.”

“I don’t want to pry, but what are you gonna do about all this? I mean this trouble with Ike and Paxton... and then there’s Helen.”

Sam answers matter-of-factly, “I am here to get my horse, and before the year’s out, I am headed west. That’s what I am doing about all this. Nothing. Nothing at all, unless Ike forces the issue.”

Little Jim is tying up the last pair of mules in the shade.

Sam says to him, “Go on up, Little Jim. We’ll be along.”

“Yes sir.”

“So what about Helen? You’re just gonna ride off and not even talk to her?”

Sam answers Ira Paul a little too quickly. “That’s right.”

Ira Paul shoots back a quicker answer. “Bullshit! That look in your eye gives you away, my friend. You may go west, but I can guarantee you won’t be going by yourself.”

“Oh! You reading voodoo fortunes down in the quarters now, are you?”

Ira Paul walks over and ties up his team by Sam’s mules. “Don’t need none to read you. All a body needs to do is say her name.”

Sam snaps, “Spare me the fortune telling, Ira Paul. Let’s go eat.”

“I see you’re getting moody now, so let’s go.”

Sam and Ira Paul walk off toward the house.

“Folks get that all wrong about me. I swear they do.”

Ira Paul laughs. "A hog's ass, they do."

Sam gives Ira Paul a hard look and Ira Paul bursts out laughing. They walk on toward the house.

Two hours later, Sam walks out of the Rayburns' barn leading the stud, followed closely by Ira Paul. Little Jim has just finished hooking up the team and is walking around, giving the rig a final check before they leave.

He walks over to Sam and reaches for the stud's lead rope. "Let me have 'em boss. I'll tie 'em to the wagon."

"Thanks," Sam says as he watches Little Jim lead the stud away.

Sam just can't believe that horse can't run. From the stud's muscled shoulders to his massive hips, it all says 'racehorse' loud and clear to anyone with an eye for horseflesh. When Little Jim finishes tying the stud up, he walks around and climbs up on the wagon. He releases the brake and takes the lines in his hands. Sam walks around the side of the wagon, followed by Ira Paul.

Ira Paul asks, "What are you going to do with that horse, Sam?"

"I was going to use him for breeding, but now, I just don't know."

"Well he's a mystery for sure," says Ira Paul. "We matched him three times before the big race, and every time he won. I mean it was something to see. Not one horse got even close to 'im."

Sam asks, "Y'all matched him before the race?"

"We did. And it made Spence bet a lot of money that he didn't have. Fact is Cordell is holding an IOU on this place."

"For how much?"

"He was two thousand short. No worry though, I got it covered. Between the money for Teddy and the others, plus this year's crop, we're gonna be okay."

Sam extends his hand to Ira Paul. "You know Ira Paul, I believe you. You take care."

Ira Paul shakes Sam's hand. "I will. You too, Sam." Ira Paul looks up to Little Jim. "Watch his back down there."

"Yes sir, boss. I shore will do that."

Sam steps up on the wagon and takes the lines from Little Jim.

He says, "Tell Mrs. Rayburn thanks again for the meal."

Ira Paul answers, "I will."

Sam whistles, and the team easily puts the empty wagon in motion.

Later that night, Bell is standing by her kitchen door, holding a lighted candle and quietly listening. The main house is shrouded in pitch darkness, unusually quiet for this time of the evening. Bell has a lot on her mind and is thankful for the day to be at an early end. Turning around, she walks back through the kitchen and on to her bedroom. When she walks into her room, she shuts the door behind her and places the candle on a nightstand next to a well-worn Bible. She picks up the Bible and reverently lays it down on the edge of her bed. She kneels down, places both her hands on the book, bows her head, and silently goes to the Lord in prayer. When she finishes praying, she says amen and stands up.

Benjie is laying in the dark on the far side of the bed, waiting on Bell. "Woman, you can't read that Bible. So why do you pray with your hands on it?"

Bell begins taking her clothes off. "Cause the Lord lives in it, dat's why. With my hands on it, he knows my heart and soul. Besides, readin' the book ain't everything. Prayin' is."

Benjie chuckles and says, "Well what you think the Lord feels about me visitin' with you?"

"Well if you be worried, get up, and we'll jump the broom right quick."

Benjie answers, "You know I ain't doin' dat. I ax you what you think."

Bell gets into bed naked and snuggles up next to Benjie.

"From what I heard," she says, "the Book says that the Lord made woman to keep a man company and help him. I figure I am doin' both right now."

"Look here, woman. You done invited me over here every night nare on a week. Cookin' for me and keepin' me company and all. You just livin' the Book, or you got a reason?"

Bell replies, "Let me ax you a question, sir. You like the cookin' and the comfort you been gettin'?"

"Land a mighty woman. I don't know what's better, bein' in yo' kitchen or bein' between yo' legs. Both places is pure heaven."

"Well since it's been pure heaven, I got a reason."

Benjie suspects he's been had. "Now woman, 'fore you get to pryin', there's somethings you know I can't talk about."

Bell sits up in bed. "And dat's exactly what I want to know about."

"Careful now, girl. You could get us both a bad whippin'."

Bell crawls over on top of him. "If you don't tell me what I want to know, you gonna be a gone nigger. Kicked straight out 'a heaven. No more cookin' and no more comfort. You hear me?"

Benjie pauses, not wanting to lose either one. "Alright, but you jest 'member, Mr. Ike is a bad man. You get caught foolin' around in white folks' business, you'll get us both hung dead."

Bell rolls off of Benjie and onto her back. "Well, come on over here to heaven and have your comfort. We got lots to talk about tonight."

CHAPTER TWELVE

THE EARLY MORNING SUN PUSHES A BLINDING GLARE ACROSS the shimmering white cotton fields when Sam makes the last turn on the main road leading to Slick Fork. The rolling red hills on both sides of the road will soon echo the mournful songs that accompany the grinding work of picking cotton. From can to can't, every able bodied man, woman, and child at Shannon Hill will soon be dragging a cotton sack, singing in unison like a church choir.

When Sam reins the team up at the warehouse dock, Pate Henry is standing there glaring, with his usual bullwhip in hand. Without taking his eyes off of Sam, Pate calls one of Sorrel's crew over and gives him an order that Sam can't hear. The young man runs down the warehouse steps and sprints off down the red-dirt road toward the distant Cotton Gin.

Sam keeps his eyes straight ahead and says to Little Jim, "Easy enough to know what that was all about."

Little Jim nods his head in agreement. "I think this is gonna be a little hairy, boss. Like a grown bear."

"No matter what they say, Little Jim, just keep working. You let me deal with 'em."

"You got it, boss."

"Now get down and untie the stud so I can back the wagon up."

Little Jim hops down off the wagon. "Yes sir."

He unties the stud and starts walking down to a hitching rail at the end of the warehouse. Pate arrogantly walks down the dock and stands above Little Jim, looking down on him. Little Jim doesn't look up, but he can feel the hate and anger coming off of Pate. He finishes and heads back to the wagon, followed by Pate up on the dock.

Pate can't hold his hatred any longer. "Hey, jumpy nigger. There's a day of reckonin' comin' for your black ass. That's a solemn promise, nigger."

Sam has backed the wagon up and jumped up on the dock with Pate, Sorrel, and his crew.

Sam walks toward Pate and addresses him directly. "Pate, we didn't come for trouble. We came to get a load of freight. Now what's done is done. Let's just let it go."

Pate shakes the rolled up whip at Sam. "Fuck let it go. You crippled Paxton."

Talking through clenched teeth, Sam works to hold his temper. "Pate. I am going to load my wagon and leave. Now somebody show me which grain sacks are mine."

Pate is instantly intimidated by Sam's sudden anger. He has his orders from Ike to load the Tanahill wagons and not to cause trouble with any of the drivers. It's just hard for him to believe that Sam Tanahill and his nigger would show up on the place after what they did to Paxton. Pate turns and walks away in silence, slapping the bullwhip on the side of his leg. He keeps looking off toward the cotton gin, not knowing what to do next. Sorrel, ever so easy, tries to break the tension.

"Mr. Henry, sir. The Tanahill sacks all be laid out. If'n you've a mind to, we can get busy."

With anxiety gripping him, Pate turns on Sorrel. "Goddammit, nigger, I'll do the thinkin'..."

Before Pate can finish, a young black boy dashes up the warehouse steps, out of breath. "Boss, boss. Cricket be peein' in the water buckets again, boss."

Pate flies into an uncontrollable rage and storms off the dock. "Son of a bitch. I am gonna kill that goddamn kid."

After Pate is gone, Sam looks at Sorrel and says, "Let's get it loaded, Sorrel. I need to go."

Sorrel smiles and says, "Yes sir, boss." Sorrel lowers his voice and says, "We all proud of you for what 'cha done."

Sam is still angry, but he smiles at Sorrel and his crew. "Thanks."

Sorrel turns to his crew. "Get a move on it. Man says he needs to go."

Sam, Little Jim, Sorrel, and his crew all go to loading the sacks of grain. When the job is about half finished, a small black kid of ten or so, with a deformed left arm and a sidling gait, dashes up the dock steps, giggling, with Pate close behind, grabbing at his ragged shirt. Pate lunges for the kid at the top step and falls headlong, gasping for air on the dock in front of everyone. Between no air and sheer embarrassment, his fat red face looks like it's about to explode. The kid dodges behind Sam while Pate staggers to his feet, swearing to beat the kid to death. The kid peeps around Sam, makes a funny face, and dashes into the back of Sam's wagon. Pate makes a fumbling but effective move around Sam and blocks the kid's escape. He stands at the end of the wagon, glaring at the kid, still struggling to catch his breath.

Pate shakes out his whip. "Time you learned what bein' a nigger is about, kid."

Sorrel steps up behind Sam and whispers, "Cricket ain't right boss. He be plumb dumb in the head."

When Pate draws the whip back to strike Cricket, Sam steps on the tail. He reaches down, takes hold of it, and jerks it from Pate's hand in one easy move. Sam rolls the whip up and throws it back in the warehouse.

"I don't have time for this, Pate."

Pate stands facing Sam in utter disbelief. Then just as he starts to speak, Cricket dashes by him, still laughing, and grabs him on the ass. Pate is startled and embarrassed to the point of insanity. Cricket stops at the far end of the dock, making funny faces at Pate and cackling.

Pate points at Cricket and yells, "Goddammit, Sorrel, y'all catch that fuckin' nigger."

Sam reaches out and catches Sorrel's arm. "Hold it Sorrel. Pate! I want this wagon loaded first."

Pate walks back toward Sam. "Fuck you, Tanahill!" Pate turns to Sorrel screaming, "NOW! I SAID NOW!"

With the anger rising in his voice, Sam looks holes through Pate. "You want him, you go catch him. We're loading this wagon!"

Pate starts to smile, looking past Sam. "We'll see about that, Mr. Tanahill. Yes sir, we shall see."

Sam looks over his shoulder to see Ike riding up the warehouse road on horseback, leading Slick, with Pate's messenger running alongside.

Sam turns back to Pate. "I don't care who rides up, Pate. I want this wagon loaded." Sam turns to Sorrel and says, "Sorrel."

Pate looks at Sorrel and says, "You better not move, nigger. Cause when he leaves, I'll peel your ass."

Sorrel and his crew all stand with their heads down.

Sam turns and walks into the warehouse. "Okay. Little Jim, come on."

When Ike reaches the warehouse, he steps down off his horse and hands the messenger the reins to his horse, as well as Slick's lead rope. He walks up on the dock and he notices right off that Pate doesn't have his bullwhip in hand. From Pate's agitated face, to Sorrel and his crew all looking like whipped dogs, Ike senses there's a problem.

Ike walks up to Pate first and says, "What's going on here, Pate?"

Pate points to the inside of the warehouse. "That goddamn Tanahill is interferin' with my niggers."

About that time, Sam walks right by Ike, carrying a sack of grain on his broad shoulders. "That's not the truth."

Pate starts to say, "The son of a bitch..."

Ike watches Sam walk to the wagon with an evil look in his eyes. "Shut up, Pate."

When Sam places the sack, he aggressively turns around and walks straight back toward Ike with a cold, blank look in his eyes. For an instant, Sam sees a flash of intimidation cross Ike's face. Ike regains himself and takes a commanding step toward Sam, but the damage is done. Sam now knows that the brutal whipping he gave Paxton has put a thread of doubt in Ike's mind. Sam walks right up to Ike and squares off with him, standing face-to-face.

Sam says, "Ike."

"I got my orders about you, Tanahill. There's your horse, and we're going to load your wagon." Without taking his eyes off of Sam, he says, "Pate, get them niggers busy."

"But Ike..."

"You heard me goddammit, Pate. Now get to it!"

"Yes sir."

Sam looks over at Old Slick. "You forgot my saddle."

Ike clenches his jaw. "Don't push me, Tanahill. You were lucky to get by Paxton, but you won't be that lucky with me."

"I'll tell you like I told Paxton after I whipped him. If you ever send anybody after me again, I'll do more than push on you."

The two men stand there staring at each other for a moment. Then Ike gets a sarcastic smile on his face, turns, and walks away.

Ike stops on his way to the steps and looks straight at Pate. "I said kick them niggers in the ass, Pate. I want this trash off the place."

Pate looks at Sam and smiles. "Yes sir." He then turns on Sorrel like a snake and says, "Don't jest stand there. Go get my goddamn whip. Hurry up, nigger!!"

Sorrel ducks his head and trots into the warehouse. "Yes sir, boss."

Pate starts violently shoving different members of Sorrel's crew. "The rest of you niggers go to work! NOW!!"

Ike continues on toward the end of the dock when Sam reminds him of the saddle. "What about my saddle?"

Ike stops but doesn't turn around. "I'll send it to you."

When Sorrel trots back out with the whip, Pate snatches it from his hand. "Now get them burr heads busy before this whip finds your ass."

"Yes sir, boss."

Sorrel and his crew go to loading the last half of the grain sacks on Sam's wagon.

Ike walks down the dock steps and gets on his horse. He rides back down the side of the dock to where Sam's standing.

Ike stops the horse and looks up at Sam. "Tanahill, don't think those orders will hold forever. Cause they won't."

Sam responds with a direct hardness. "Before you come lookin', Ike, you best think long and hard on Paxton."

Ike momentarily stares at Sam, a silent rage building in him at not being able to respond to yet another galling insult. Today's challenge has now escalated into a debt of honor with Ike, a fact that Sam can clearly see in his eyes. He knows without a doubt that Ike will not rest until he is personally able to settle the score. Ike jerks the horse around and lopes away toward the cotton gin, carrying an insult that no southern gentleman could ever tolerate nor forgive. Sam watches Ike ride off and wonders what orders were given to Ike and why. He's sure they came from Cordell, but he can't for the life of him figure out the reason for them.

Sam looks past Ike, to the main house on the distant horizon, and thinks of Helen and that last dance at the spring cotillion. The images of her he carries in his mind are still as fresh and new as a morning sunrise. Those hypnotic blue eyes as dazzling as the stars in the heavens. There is not a day in his life that those images of her don't linger in his mind and call to his soul. He struggles to find a place to leave her memory, but his heart will not relinquish that authority.

Little Jim walks over to Sam with a look of relief on his face. "We about finished boss. You ready?"

Sam is lost in thought and continues to look to the horizon.

Little Jim stands there for a moment, unsure of what has Sam's attention. "Boss?"

Pate hollers at Sam. "You're loaded, Tanahill! Now get gone."

Sam turns to Little Jim and smiles easy. "Go get the horses and let's go."

Little Jim turns, walks to the edge of the dock, and hops down by the horses. He unties them and leads them to the wagon.

Sam walks up the dock straight for Pate, and makes him step out of his way. He hops down off of the dock and turns around. "Thanks, Sorrel."

"Yes sir, boss."

Pate turns a crimson red over Sam making him step aside and then speaking to Sorrel.

Pate stalks to the edge of the dock and points at Sam with the whip in his hand. Sam turns his back on him and walks to the wagon before he can begin speaking.

"You and that nigger both gonna get yours, Tanahill. Sooner than you think. Mark my word! It's comin' real soon!"

Sam climbs up on the wagon and pulls it up so Little Jim can tie the horses to the back of it. When Little Jim finishes, he is in the seat next to Sam in a couple of quick steps. Sam whistles to the team, rattles the lines, and the wagon is in motion.

Sam glances over behind the seat of the wagon and says, "Get that rifle up here by us."

Little Jim breaks out his harmonica and smiles. "Ah, boss. I think you put the fear in 'em. Like a grow'd bear."

Sam, this time with an urgency in his voice, says, "The rifle, Little Jim."

Sam's tone makes Little Jim scramble. "Yes sir."

Sam keeps his focus on the road ahead and occasionally looks back. "May be nothing but Pate shooting his mouth off, but we're going to be right careful for a spell. So keep your eyes open."

Little Jim loses the smile. "Ike said he had orders. You thinkin' different?"

Sam whistles at the team. "I don't know what those orders are. But we'll be off of the place at the tree line."

Sam's hyper vigilance puts Little Jim on edge. "You think they a comin', boss?"

"Maybe. Just keep your eyes open."

Several miles past the tree line, off in the far distance, a rider on a gray horse appears at the edge of the road and stops. Little Jim points down the road.

"I see him," Sam says.

The rider sits there for a moment, then slowly turns the horse and heads straight toward Sam and Little Jim. Sam hands Little Jim the reins, reaches for the rifle, and stands it next to him.

Sam watches the rider approach. "May not be anything but a rider."

Little Jim says, "Feels like he was waitin' on us, don't it."

Sam pulls his pistol out and places it by him, under a jacket. "It seems that way. If he's on your side and goes for a gun, stay out of my way."

"Yes sir."

The rider slowly continues toward Sam and Little Jim, keeping to the far right side of the road.

Little Jim begins to get a little nervous. "I swear that man is looking straight at us, boss. I mean straight."

"He is looking, that's for sure. When I tell you, stop the wagon."

Little Jim turns and looks behind them. "He's by hisself, boss."

When the rider is several hundred yards away, he crosses over to the left side of the road and keeps coming.

"Pull 'em up, Little Jim, and let's just wait on him."

Little Jim stops the team, sets the brake, and lays the rifle across his lap.

The rider comes within a hundred yards and stops the gray horse. The horse's long, flowing white mane and tail are in stark contrast to his powerfully built, dappled gray body. Sam and Little Jim are momentarily distracted until the rider starts forward again.

"I don't know who he is. But it sure seems he came looking for us. Keep a watch behind us, Little Jim."

"Yes sir."

The rider keeps coming, and finally stops well out in front of Sam's lead pair of mules.

The rider tips his hat and speaks, "Mr. Tanahill,"

Sam reaches under the jacket and cocks the pistol. "Don't think I know you."

Little Jim grabs Sam's arm and whispers, "It's a woman!"

Sam starts to turn to Little Jim, when out of the corner of his eye he sees the rider take off his hat, and the long blonde hair falls around her shoulders. In an instant, Sam recognizes her. It's Helen.

"It's a dang woman, boss! Rigged out like a man."

When Helen rides the horse up to the wagon, both Sam and Little Jim sit silently, looking at the girl in the men's clothes and the magnificent dappled stud.

"I see you still have that terrible habit of staring, Mr. Tanahill."

Sam is almost at a loss for words, until Little Jim bumps his arm.

Sam smiles and points to her clothes. "That's just not what I thought you would be wearing when next we met."

"So you're planning on calling on me again?"

Sam looks off in the distance. "At one point," his voice trails…

He starts again, this time with his voice carrying a resolve he did not feel. "At one point I did."

Helen pushes the subject. "And now?"

"You know the answer to that, Miss Meyers."

Helen rides the gray a little closer to Sam. "Why don't you tell me? I've sent you letters. You know I wanted to see you again!"

"Miss Meyers! Your father throws me off the place, your mother threatens to ruin my father's business, and now I have Ike Murphy to deal with. What do you expect from me?"

Helen, in an abrasive tone, responds, "I expect..."

Sam cuts her off sharply. "I know what you EXPECT! YOU expect to have your way. Just because you write a couple of letters, you really think I'll show up with my hat in my hand? I don't think so."

Helen doesn't back down. "You know what I really think, Mr. Tanahill?"

Sam reaches over and takes the reins from Little Jim. "Save it!"

"I think you are an arrogant ass!"

Helen angrily kicks the gray stud with both boot heels and hits him across the rear with the reins all at the same time. The stud's response is instant, and takes Helen by complete surprise. In the flash of an eye, he takes the bit in his teeth, jerking both reins out of Helen's hands, and stretches out, running at a terrifying speed. She screams and grabs hold of the gray's mane with both hands, hanging on for dear life.

Sam franticly jumps down and runs around to the horses at the back of the wagon. He unties his bay stud, jumps on him bareback, wheels him around, and takes off after Helen in a dead run. When Sam gives the bay a loose rein, the horse responds with a powerful burst of speed. After a short distance, Sam begins to realize he's not gaining on the hard charging gray. In desperation and without thinking, Sam takes the end of the lead rope and hits the bay hard across his rear end on both sides. Before Sam strikes the second blow, the bay immediately starts to slow down.

In a panic, Sam leans forward, rubs the bay's neck, and talks to him easy. "Come on Journey, don't quit on me. Run, please run."

Journey responds in a way that surprises Sam. The more he rubs the stud's neck and talks to him, the faster and harder he runs. Sam can feel Journey's heart and effort as every muscle in the stud's body strains to overtake the gray. In less than half a mile, Journey is within a length of catching up. Helen looks back at Sam, terrified.

Sam hollers at her over the thundering hooves and the loud, rhythmic breathing of the two powerful studs. "Take my hand when I get close! And don't hesitate!"

"Okay!"

Journey closes on the other horse and is running with his nose at the gray's flank. Helen reaches back to Sam.

He hollers at her, "Not now."

The gray senses he's about to lose a race, and opens the lead on Journey by two full lengths with unbelievable ease. Like a seasoned racehorse, Journey matches the gray's grit and determination stride-for-stride and starts to pull even. Helen looks back at Sam as he gets closer, and her fears suddenly melt away when she looks into his eyes. For some odd reason, she has never felt safer.

Sam leans down close to Journey's neck and urges the stud on. "One more step Journey. Just one more."

Sam feels Journey respond and surge forward with a driving force. He reins him over next to the gray until the studs are almost rubbing shoulders, running stride-for-stride.

Riding bareback, Sam locks his legs tight around the horse and leans over, reaching for Helen. "Now!"

She looks into his eyes for a split second and then lunges for his outstretched arm. Sam catches her around the waist and pulls her to his side with all his strength. With his leg lock slipping, Sam fights to slow the stud enough so he can safely put Helen down. Just before the bay comes to a stop, Sam loses his leg lock, sending him and Helen both crashing to the ground at Journey's front feet. They lay there motionless, side-by-side, out of breath, looking up at the clear blue sky, and feeling more alive than any other day of their lives. They finally look over at each other, and after a brief moment of silence, they burst out in uproarious laughter.

They are still laughing when Sam stands up and offers his hand to Helen. When she reaches up and their hands touch, it is a meeting of two souls. She slowly rises, and stands looking into Sam's eyes. The gales of laughter are swept away by a moment that bonds them forever.

Helen smiles softly and pulls Sam to her. "From the instant you said my name, I was hopelessly in love."

Sam takes her in his arms, amazed that God has answered his prayers. When he kisses her, he feels a stirring of life deep within his soul.

As the kiss ends, he pushes her back slightly and looks into her eyes. "And I have loved you from that first day. I don't know how or when, but I will come for you. That is my solemn pledge."

Sam kisses her again, ardently, knowing he must take her home. The gray is probably back to Shannon Hill by now, and there will be riders looking for her.

When he finishes kissing her, he takes her by the hand, and they walk over to Journey. Sam grabs a mane hold and swings up onto the stud. He reaches down to Helen, takes her by the arm, and pulls her up behind him. She scoots up close against him, wraps her arms around him, and lays her head on his back. Sam puts his hand on hers, turns the stud, and heads for Shannon Hill.

"Just so you know," says Helen, "I pledge to be there waiting."

They both ride in silence, wondering what the other is thinking about the unexpected events of the day, from the adrenalin rush of near catastrophe to their shared pledge of a life together.

Helen, unsure of how Sam will receive her next request, feels a sudden surge of anxiety. "I'd rather not tell my father everything about today."

Sam smiles and asks, "And which detail would you like me to leave out?"

Helen can hear the teasing tone in Sam's voice without seeing his face. "Well, about Blue Rock running away with me."

Sam, still teasing her: "So the part about where you love me, and I am coming to take you away—we can tell all that?"

Helen pinches his stomach and laughs. "You know what I mean."

Sam whispers like they're telling a secret. "No, I don't. So what should I tell?"

"He won't believe the truth, that's for sure."

"Why would he not believe you?"

Helen answers Sam with a question. "This is the Rayburn stud, Journey, right?"

"It is."

"Well Blue Rock just beat him in a match by ten lengths. Now, do you honestly think my father will believe the truth?"

Sam finds himself between a rock and hard spot. "I guess not. So what's your story?"

"It's simple. The stud came by you on a dead run, without a rider, headed toward Shannon Hill. A while later, you came upon me walking, and were kind enough to escort me home safely. The end."

Sam presses her. "And how did you come about being on foot?"

"I got down to rest and he spooked."

Sam reluctantly agrees. "I don't like it, but you're right. The truth is even hard for me to believe."

Helen, in a mocking tone, answers, "And which truth would that be, Mr. Tanahill? That the nag you bought turns out to be a super horse, or that you were going to ride off without seeing me. Which one?"

Surprised, Sam tries to turn and see her face. "How do you know all that?"

"Your friend and mine."

Sam laughs. "I should have known. Ira Paul."

"Were you really going to leave without seeing me?"

"I was."

"Even though you knew you were in love with me?"

"Woman. You're making this hard."

"No I am not. Just tell me how you feel."

Sam struggles to find the words. "There's no doubt that I love you. But one day I am going west, and I want you to be with me."

"If your mind's that set on it, we can leave today."

Sam smiles. "Is it that easy for you?"

"No, it's not. It would break my father's heart if I ran off. But I won't let you leave without me."

"I have to have his permission, Helen. It can't be any other way."

As a matter of principal, Sam knows he must have Cordell's permission to call on her if he is ever to ask for her hand in marriage. He also realizes the hardships it would cause Owen if he took her with him without Cordell's blessing.

"I understand. We'll wait." She pauses for a moment. "I do have one pressing question I need an answer for."

"Sure. What is it?"

"Well." Helen pauses again, "Is there any reason you need to go back to the valley?"

Sam stops the horse. "None."

Helen squeezes Sam in her arms. "Good."

Sam pushes Journey onward. "Who told you about Dancy?"

"My father."

"You know that story Paxton told is a lie, near word-for-word. I sure hope your father doesn't hold any of that yarn as gospel."

"He didn't. That's the reason he requested Lanham Hawks be sent to Sapling Grove to do an inquiry."

Sam is a little puzzled. "Why did he go to the Magistrate?"

"Because the horse and saddle you won from Paxton in the fight belonged to him."

Sam nods his head. "And Paxton told him I stole it. So what happened when he found out the truth?"

"Oh, according to Bell, he talked to Mr. Murphy like a field nigger. Gave him strict orders to leave you be. Then he..."

Sam abruptly stops the horse. "Riders."

There in the distance, where the Slick Fork road meets the cotton fields at the tree line, four horsemen have suddenly ridden into view. They rein their sweat-drenched horses to a stop in the middle of the crossroads and scatter out, each riding slow and looking at the ground.

Helen glances around Sam's shoulder at the horsemen and feels a loneliness that has never been in her heart before. She puts her head on Sam's back and holds him tight in her arms. His pledge to come for her has stiffened her resolve to wait a lifetime if necessary.

Helen holds on to Sam, hoping by chance that the horseman will ride the other way. "What are they doing?"

One rider turns and rides toward Sam and Helen, then stops in the road and dismounts. He walks down the road a short distance, squatting down every so often and touching the ground with his hand. When he's satisfied that the tracks he's following are the stud's, he turns around and calls to the other riders. When they all ride up, and the man points down the road, they all see Sam in the same instant. The tracker quickly swings up into the saddle and the four riders start toward him in an easy lope.

"They're coming," Sam says to Helen.

Helen leans out around Sam, trying to get a better look at the oncoming riders. "If my father is not with them, I want you to take me home."

Sam recognizes Paxton riding just back of Cordell. "He's with them. The lead rider, with no hat."

Seeing her father, she leans back in and puts her hands on the back of Sam's shoulders, pressing her forehead in the middle of his back. "Promise me you'll write."

Sam keeps a stoic gaze upon the approaching riders, but answers with a gentleness in his voice. "I promise."

Helen reaches up and runs her hand through the hair on the back of Sam's neck. "Give him a chance Sam. Y'all are a lot alike, and I love you both."

Sam almost smiles. "I don't think I see the similarities, to be honest. Not just yet, anyway."

Helen wraps her fingers around Sam's hair and gives it a light tug. "I hope our children have this cold black hair."

Speaking through clenched teeth, Sam fights back a nagging smile. "Woman, be still. What are you thinking? He's ridin' up!"

Helen leans up and quietly whispers something in Sam's ear, which makes her blush to speak it.

Stifling a curt laugh, she adds, "THAT is what I am thinking, Mr. Tanahill."

Cordell, Paxton, and two rough looking renegades rein up their worn out horses in front of Sam and Helen. Paxton and his two cronies have "fight" written all over their hard-case presence. Sam passes a cool smirk of disrespect across the three with a dismissive glance. Everyone sits in momentary silence, waiting on Cordell to say something. The rush of anger and relief at seeing Helen safe gives Cordell pause. His gaze rests upon Sam and Helen, sitting on the horse bareback together. From the dirt on their clothes, their missing hats, and the stud's being covered in dried sweat, Cordell can see there's a story here that he doesn't really care to know.

"Mr. Tanahill."

Sam answers. "Mr. Meyers."

Cordell looks to Helen. "You okay?"

Helen slides off the horse and stands by Sam. "Yes sir. Thanks to Mr. Tanahill."

Cordell addresses Paxton, though his attention is still on Sam and Helen. "Paxton."

Paxton snaps to attention. "Yes sir."

"Have your men double up and give my daughter a horse."

"Yes sir." Paxton looks over at one of the men and says, "Slack. Give the lady your horse."

Slack dismounts and leads his horse over to Helen, handing her the reins. She takes the reins, but doesn't move from Sam's side.

Cordell's quiet, methodical way only increases Helen's guilt for the anguish she's caused him. She wishes with all her heart that she could tell him about her day, and about her feelings for Sam. His unspoken indictment of her planned deceit leaves her heart in shambles, but she grits her teeth, holds her ground, and does not avoid his piercing stare. The resolve in her eyes is a clear indication to Cordell, that one way or the other, where she stands at the moment is where she'll be for life: at Sam's side.

"Paxton, take my daughter and start home. I'll be along."

"Yes sir."

Helen looks up at Sam and smiles. "Thank you."

With a cat-like move, Sam slips off of the stud's back and stands in front of her. Her heart skips, and for a fleeting moment she can't breathe, unsure of what he's about to say.

He leans over and cups his hands. "May I?"

She smiles as she steps into his hands, and he lifts her to the back of her horse.

"Thank you again for everything, Mr. Tanahill."

Ever a gentleman, Sam nods. "Yes ma'am."

Cordell instructs Helen, "Go on. I am coming."

She rides off, followed by Paxton and his men. Sam grabs a mane hold and swings back up onto the stud. He and Cordell sit there facing each other for a moment.

When Cordell rides up a little closer, Sam can plainly see the seriousness of the impending conversation on Cordell's face.

"First, Mr. Tanahill, you have my deepest appreciation for coming to the assistance of my daughter. But I would hope, sir, that this encounter was not of your design. I very much remember a gentlemen's agreement that we shook hands on. Did we not?"

Sam, entirely formal and correct in his reply, answers. "We did. I am honor bound to abide by my word, sir, until you release me from it."

Cordell pauses in thought for a moment, completely taken back by Sam's pointed candor.

"Do you honestly anticipate my release?"

"I do, sir."

Cordell strikes a somewhat friendlier tone. "And why would you think that?"

"Because, sir, I am as fit of character as any man who would ever call on your daughter."

Cordell finds Sam's confidence and boldness intriguing. He begins to see why his daughter is so persistent about spending time in his company.

Cordell's voice hits a true note of honesty. "I have never doubted your character, son, or the merit of your family for that matter. It's just..."

Cordell's newly found respect for Sam makes him hesitate to damage his pride any more than he already has.

Sam presses Cordell. "It's just what, sir? And please be as forthright with me as I have been with you."

Cordell gathers himself up. "You're right, I should be. It's money, son. Money controls life. Without it, you just get ground up and spit out. I didn't raise my daughter to be butchered or raped somewhere out on the frontier, or..."

Cordell pauses, and now Sam hears a father almost pleading for his daughter. "Or used up before her time, living in the middle of God's nowhere. I couldn't bear that. I just couldn't."

Sam responds. "I would never allow those things to happen, sir. Whether I have money or not."

Cordell's mood stiffens. "Money is absolute, son. Out there, you'll always be struggling to have it. I know there's great opportunity for men like you in the West. But I won't allow my daughter to be sacrificed in that struggle."

Cordell rides up alongside of Sam and extends his hand. "For those reasons, sir, I expect you to honor your word on our original understanding."

Sam reaches over and firmly shakes Cordell's hand.

Still grasping Cordell's hand, Sam looks him square in the eye. "I will earn your release sir. On that you have my word."

Cordell acknowledges Sam with a gentlemanly nod, wheels his horse around, and lopes off toward Shannon Hill.

CHAPTER THIRTEEN

SAM SLOWLY TURNS THE STUD AROUND AND STARTS HIM BACK toward the wagon. The whirlwind turn of events that Sam has experienced in the last few hours has left him a changed man. When Helen leaned up and whispered in his ear, it ignited an inferno of determination in Sam that will not be quenched until he has Cordell's release. He rides, looking off down the picturesque red dirt road, and feels that at long last, his life has a true course.

He reflects on the events of the day and gives all the credit for his good fortune to Journey. The stud's speed and endurance were amazing to witness, especially from where Sam was sitting. When he thinks back to the moment when Journey actually ran Blue Rock down, it seems like he has witnessed something impossible. Suddenly, a fantastic thought clicks in Sam's mind. If Journey could overcome the huge lead that Blue Rock had on him today, then he could easily beat him in a heads up match.

Sam reaches down and rubs the side of Journey's neck with a newfound respect. "Thanks, old pal. I think you just unlocked the door."

Sam pushes the stud off into an easy lope, and Journey responds with a lively step. Their shared drive, determination, and toughness bond the man to the horse and the horse to the man.

Sam and Journey cover the last couple of miles to the campsite in short order. When Sam rides up to the wagon, he finds the mules all tied to a picket line on the edge of the woods, and Little Jim in the middle of cooking an early supper. The stew pot hangs over a roaring fire, and a fresh pot of coffee sits nearby.

Little Jim walks over to the wagon, wiping his hands on a cook rag. "Didn't 'spect you back yet, boss. I shore thought it would be near dark 'fore you was back. Everything work out?"

Sam slides off the stud and ties him to the back of the wagon. "It did, but you won't believe how."

Little Jim turns around and goes back to his cooking. "I'd say it's a story, from the looks of you and that hoss."

Sam goes to the water barrel and starts drawing up a bucket of water. "Let me look after Journey, and we'll talk."

Little Jim stirs the pot of stew. "No hurry. It'll be a mite yet 'fore its ready."

Sam goes about the care of Journey like a man on a mission. When he finishes up, he takes a step back, admiring the stud and formulating a bold vision for the future of their partnership.

Cordell pushes hard, and overtakes Helen and her escort on the field road that leads to the back of the main house and the stables. He rides around Paxton and his men, reining up his horse alongside of Helen. When they exchange a quick glance, Cordell is met with the same unyielding directness that he saw in her eyes when she was standing by Sam's side. He's not sure just what has changed, but he can sense a marked difference in his daughter. They ride on until they reach the turn-off to the cotton gin and the stables for the workhorses.

Cordell stops his horse at the crossroads. "Paxton. Y'all go on to work. I'll bring your horse back directly."

"Yes sir." Paxton and his men nod to Helen in respect. "Ma'am."

Helen nods and quietly watches the men ride away, waiting on her father's wrath. Cordell sits on his horse with both hands on top of the saddle horn, looking across the rolling hills of white cotton. He clears his throat and leans forward in the saddle like a man uncertain about who has the next move.

Cordell finds his thoughts. "We're going to have this talk out here. Just you and me."

Helen hears the tone of his voice and knows this won't be the scolding she was expecting. "I agree. We need to talk about what happened today. Because I want you to listen to what's in my heart."

"You set out with a plan today, didn't you Helen?"

"Yes sir, I did. I knew exactly what I was doing." Tears begin to roll down Helen's cheeks. She pauses to collect herself, determined that she will not speak falsely to this man with whom she has built a lifetime of trust. "You remember our conversation that day on the Slick Fork? Well, I've found that man."

Cordell looks across the wide expanse of Shannon Hill with the realization that his family's legacy may stop with him. He admires his daughter for having the drive and guts to go after what she wants in life. He just wishes her ambitions were directed toward Shannon Hill.

Cordell sighs. "I know. I've known that all along, just like you have. It's just hard when a man comes eye-to-eye with something he is unable to change. But you know what? When I finished talking to him, and we shook hands... well, I realized that what I wanted really didn't matter."

Helen fights back the tears. "I don't want you to be ashamed of me. But I want to spend my life with him."

Cordell takes a deep breath. "When I rode up today, and saw y'all together, there was no doubt in my mind what you wanted. I don't know that I agree with that... but I guess we'll see."

"We'll see what? He's lived on his word. We were together today because of me, not him. He's a good man, and you have to know that by now."

"I do. His integrity has never been a question with me."

"Then please tell me why you're so adamantly opposed to him! Why?"

"Because you have no idea about men like him. He's tough and driven. He's going to live a hard life. It's a life you know nothing about, because I wanted something better for you, a life that would be safer and more comfortable."

"I don't care where he goes or how hard it is there... that's where I want to be."

Cordell nods his head slowly and says, "I also remember the rest of our conversation. Especially the part where you said nothing could stop you from being with him."

Helen feels her father's hurt. "Father, I am not going to run off. I offered, but he said no. He'll never break his word, not even for me."

Cordell almost wishes Sam would come for her, so this agony tearing at his heart would come to an end. He knows that social formalities will not keep them apart forever. He knows the next step in this emotional deadlock belongs to him.

"He gave me his word that he would earn my release. I want to see that happen before I give my consent to anything."

Helen can hear the compromise in her father's voice, but she knows her mother will never yield to the thought of her marrying Sam. She would carry it as a glaring stain on her personal reputation. "What about mother?"

"You said you wanted to be happy. Did you mean it?"

"Yes sir, I did."

"Well, we both know how unhappy your sisters are... right? Then you just need to keep that in mind when you deal with her."

Helen flashes a heartwarming smile and says, "I love you."

"I know you do. But I don't want any more days like today. You hear me?"

Helen knows she's pushed her luck far enough for one day. "Yes sir, I hear you."

Cordell's attention is still riveted on the vast fields of white cotton and the dying dreams of his legacy. "That means none."

Helen sighs. "I know this is a special day. I hope I haven't ruined it."

"You surely haven't. Besides, today is special in more ways than you'll ever know."

Cordell pauses in thought and prays to God that his daughter has found a love that never goes cold.

He looks over at Helen and smiles. "Let's go home; your mother's waiting."

They both turn their horses in unison and ride toward home.

Just about the same time that afternoon, Benjie raises his hand to knock on the cabin door down in the Santee River bottom, but much to his surprise, the door suddenly flies open, and he stands face-to-face with a smiling Ike Murphy. Benjie quickly averts any eye contact, bows his head, and takes a couple of shuffling steps backward. The smile on Ike's face quickly fades when he looks around Benjie and sees the empty carriage.

Benjie twists his hat up with both hands, looking at the floor. "Mister Ike, sir..."

Ike pushes Benjie aside and walks to the edge of the porch. He stands there for a moment staring at the carriage. "You rotten bitch. You dirty, rotten bitch."

Ike wheels around, grabs Benjie by the front of his coat with one hand, and roughly jerks Jessica's driver to him. "Where is she?"

Before Benjie even hears the question, Ike viciously palm slaps him on the side of his head. "I am talking to you, nigger!"

The force of the slap buckles Benjie's knees and drives the pain deep into his ear. Ike pulls Benjie back up with his left hand and hits him again, this time with a brutal punch to his left eye. Benjie falls limp, like dropping a rag on the floor.

Ike stands over Benjie like a wild predator. "You tell that bitch I am not happy about this!"

He rears back and drop kicks Benjie in the stomach. "Can you remember that, nigger?"

Inflicting pain on another human gives Ike more pleasure than any woman could ever give him. "You better talk to me, boy!"

He draws his boot back for another kick when Benjie holds up his hand, struggling to catch his breath. "Please, boss... I can remember. Please!"

Ike's eyes glaze over, and he kicks Benjie with twice the force of the first kick, knocking him unconscious. "I bet you can, nigger. I just bet you can."

Ike walks back into the cabin and puts on his hat and coat. When he comes back out, he shuts the cabin door, steps over Benjie, and walks off the porch toward his horse. He steps up onto the horse, turns, and rides away easy.

Later that night, the fifty-candle chandelier casts a sparkling shimmer of light across the huge state dining room of the main house. Bell and the girls have worked all day preparing the lavish dinner for Jessica's birthday. She stands just behind Cordell, where she supervises the four house girls stationed around the room and tasked with serving the meal. The girls all wear crisply ironed black dresses and long sleeve white shirts, and each of them wears a white scarf wrapped around their head and tied on an angle above her left ear.

Cordell is seated at the head of the elegantly set table with Helen on his left and Jessica seated on his right. The house girls have just served the last course of dinner and returned to their stations. The tension hanging in the room all evening has felt like a stain on a wedding dress that no one dares to acknowledge, much less openly discuss. The emotional drain of the day's events was far easier for Cordell and Helen to endure than was Jessica's endless cross-examination before dinner. The temporary halt in hostilities between Helen and her mother is just that: temporary.

Adding to the evening's atmosphere of dysfunction, Switch is standing at Jolene's usual station, straight across from Cordell. He would like to question Jolene's absence, but given that it's Jessica's birthday, he continues with his dessert in silence and savors it almost as much as the brief lull in the seemingly endless conversational combat.

Jessica takes one bite of the dessert and lays her fork down. "Bell."

Bell looks over to Hattie, who is standing behind Jessica, and nods for her to respond. Hattie steps to Jessica's right and removes the dish and fork. Bell's cool composure has been of note to everyone at the table since long before they sat down tonight. She is unmoved by Jessica's stern look of reproach, and doesn't quickly yield eye contact with her either.

Jessica turns her attention to Helen. "Careful with that dessert fork, or you'll need some new dresses."

Helen gives her mother a coy smile.

Cordell points at Jessica with his fork. "Tonight is about you, Jessica. About celebrating your birthday and being together. So could we please be of good discourse for the remainder of the evening. Please?"

Helen queries her mother on the one subject that always touches a nerve. "And how old are we today?"

Jessica smiles like a bitch in control. "If I wanted that to be of general knowledge, the guest list would've been longer tonight."

Cordell looks from Jessica to Helen, throws his napkin in his dessert plate, and stands up. "Ladies, I said please. Now if you will try to be civil, I'll be back momentarily."

Helen and her mother look at each other for a moment and both nod in agreement to Cordell's request.

Cordell looks from Jessica to Helen. "Fine."

Both women watch Cordell leave the room and then immediately pick up their conversation where they left off.

Helen speaks first. "I just can't imagine the world at forty-five."

"Well dear, I assure you, if you persist with your current intrigues, you probably won't see twenty-five. Which just amazes me, because for the life of me I can't understand something."

"And what would that be, Mother? That I could trade all of this, JUST to be happy?"

Jessica slides up to the edge of the table. "Your arrogance is almost intolerable, young lady! Given the events of the day, I'd say you have increased the rumors substantially."

"Let me be clear about Mr. Tanahill, Mother. My feelings for him are not rumors."

Jessica's look of condemnation is pushed back by Helen's unyielding stare of arrogance. Sam's pledge turned a page in Helen's life today, and she has no intention of allowing her mother to turn it back.

Jessica takes a moment to control her emotion before she speaks. "Your feelings? Surely you wouldn't gamble your life away on a simple feeling. What could you possibly feel that makes you so self-destructive?"

"Don't pry, mother."

"What is it about this young man that's driving you? What? Do you think you're in love with him? Is that it?"

Helen slides up to the table. "I am in love with him, and do you know how I know? Because he makes me want to take my clothes off."

Helen's graphic boldness makes Jessica livid. "I would pray to God that you never deliver that shame upon this family. I raised you to..."

Bell suddenly puts her hand over her mouth and tries to stifle her cough, knowing it sounds like a reaction to Jessica's lecturing at Helen. She bends over, turns her back on everyone, and forces the choking cough to continue to hide her dangerous slip of emotion.

From the minute Helen drew her first breath, she was handed over to Bell for the duration of her childhood. The two became inseparable, which Jessica encouraged because of her busy social calendar with Helen's older sisters. Between Bell and the tutors Cordell hired, Helen had more than enough affection and attention to make up for Jessica's lack of interest in her youngest child. She blossomed into an educated young woman, a woman not afraid of living her life by her own accord. Bell's open and honest discussions with Helen about life instilled in her a true north compass that neither Jessica nor the world will ever bend.

Helen immediately gets up and goes over to Bell, who continues to cough and gasp for air. Jessica reaches for a glass of wine, totally indifferent to everything but the irritating thought of Sam Tanahill. She drains the wine glass in one throwback gulp and fumes over the glaring fact that a backwoods wagon driver of low breeding could make HER daughter want to take her clothes off.

Helen puts her hand on Bell's back. "Bell, are you okay?"

Bell stands up, takes a deep breath, and fights back the galling urge to speak her mind. "Yes ma'am. Just a touch of winter in my bones."

Cordell walks back in about the time Bell steps back to her station. He is carrying a small bright red package with a curly red bow on top. The package is evidently a birthday present, which catches everyone's attention but Jessica's, her mind still reeling with the idea of a wedding guest list that would include multiple North Carolina families.

Cordell walks around the table to Jessica. "I see everyone is still alive, and no blood on the floor."

Helen smiles and sits back down, looking first at the present, and then over to her mother "As you requested, we're of good discourse."

When Cordell places the present in front of Jessica, her transformation from heartless bitch to heartless southern belle is instant. She places her hands up to her face and muffles a squeal of childish delight while tapping her shoes on the marble floor under the table.

The red wrappings charm Jessica into a hypnotic stare. "For me?"

Cordell takes pleasure in her surprise. "It is. Open it."

When Jessica picks up the gift, a flash of lightning coupled with a rolling clap of thunder rattles every window and china cabinet in the house. The violently breaking rainstorm gives everyone in the dining room pause, that is, everyone except Jessica. She looks up to Cordell and feels a sexual rush that has long been dead.

"I've always loved the unexpected."

She holds the gift in her left hand and sensually caresses the red ribbon with the fingertips of her right, oblivious to the rising crescendo of the storm. Jessica relishes any occasion to hold a room in suspense with her southern theatrics, and tonight is no different. The urgency to be finished with opening the gift is pushing Bell to her limits.

Bell hesitates, then speaks. "Mr. Meyers, sir."

Cordell hears the concern in her voice and turns to her. "What is it, Bell?"

Bell, with her eyes on the floor, answers, "No disrespect sir. But most of the windows be open in the house."

Cordell looks around for a moment, and then realizes how viciously the wind and rain are pounding the house.

Cordell looks back to Bell. "By all means, see to the house."

Bell looks at the house girls and signals with a nod of her head for them to leave the room.

Before they all reach the kitchen door, Bell is barking orders. "Hattie, you and Pearly close all the windows on the bottom floor. Petal, you and Switch shut everything upstairs. Mop up all the water and bring me the wet curtains. GO! Hurry up with you!!

Bell walks back into the room and takes her station just as Cordell is placing a dazzling diamond and emerald necklace around Jessica's neck. He hooks the clasp and steps away, leaving Jessica spellbound.

In a soft, seductive tone, chosen to allure Cordell, Jessica asks, "Where did you get this?"

"In Paris. I ordered it last year when I was there on business."

Sensing there is a moment coming between her parents, Helen gets up, walks around to her father, and kisses him on the cheek. "It's magnificent, father."

"Thank you."

She then walks over to her mother and kisses her on the cheek. "The necklace is perfect... now that it has a beautiful woman to wear it. Happy birthday."

In a tender moment, with tears in her eyes, Jessica hugs Helen tightly and whispers in her ear. "I hope one day that you find a man like your father."

Helen steps away from her mother, politely but with meaning, and replies, "I have."

She turns her back on her mother and starts from the room. "Goodnight, mother." Helen reaches out to her father on her way out and they briefly touch hands. "Goodnight, father. I love you."

"And I love you."

When Cordell looks back to Jessica, it's easy to see that she burns with a desire that she wants him to fill. Her breathing is coming in waves of lust, making her full, round bosom rise and fall in a long, sensual rhythm.

Her hand trembles slightly when she offers it to Cordell. "Shall we?"

For a calculated moment, Cordell stands looking into her eyes. "I'll be along. I am going to have a brandy."

Jessica doesn't like being turned down, but she continues with the seduction. "Don't drink two. The best part of the evening is upstairs." With a sweet, beckoning smile, she turns and walks from the room, leaving Cordell standing there lost in thought.

Jessica's passionate sexual advances only add to Cordell's tendency to be guarded in his relationship to her. Her appetite in life has always been far greater for acquiring social skills than sexual skills. He can't remember a time in their married life that he's seen such a begging sexual need in her eyes.

Cordell stands there motionless, until he hears Bell speak. "You be takin' that brandy in the study, sir?"

The sudden arousal that Cordell feels is being swiftly smothered by the ache of a long ago broken heart. He walks from the room like a man looking for a place to unburden his soul.

Bell waits for him to respond then answers her own question, "Yes sir, I guess you do."

Bell walks over to the liquor cabinet and pours Cordell a glass of brandy. She then takes a sideways look at the glass and says to herself mischievously, "What the hell." She picks the bottle back up and begins pouring again, until it's an extra stout double, plus some. She smiles, sets the drink on a silver tray, and follows Cordell to the study.

When she walks in with the brandy, Bell takes quick notice of Cordell's dark mood. She has no illusions about its source. He sits in his favorite chair, rolling an unlit cigar between his fingers and staring into the fireplace. She places the brandy on a small table beside his chair and steps back.

"Will that be all, sir?"

Cordell doesn't respond, and Bell dreads having to stand silent and wait while her girls work unsupervised. The raging storm that's tearing at Shannon Hill is trivial compared to the raging storm that's tearing at Cordell's heart.

"Where is Jolene?"

Bell is straightforward with the truth. "Miss Jessica sent her to the fields."

Cordell smiles easy, and reaches for the brandy. "Quite a storm, isn't it Bell?"

"Yes sir, it is. But they always pass."

"Goodnight, Bell."

"Goodnight, sir."

She turns and hurries off to her girls, making a mental note to check on Benjie just as soon as her duties will allow.

When Bell walks into the kitchen and sees the piles of curtains on her kitchen floor, it only adds more difficulty to an already trying day. Her patience snaps when Petal hurriedly walks in carrying another armload of dripping wet curtains, drops them on the floor, and turns to leave.

Bell reacts swiftly. "Come back here. We don't wash clothes in the kitchen." She opens the back door and points to the washtubs out on the porch. "Girl, you know better. Pick up all that shit and put it where it belongs!"

The storm continues to rack Shannon Hill with sheets of chilled, driving rain. Multiple lighting strikes rip gaping holes through the pitch-black sky, bathing the house and gardens in flashes of blinding white light. The jarring thunder nips at the heels of the jagged lightning, slamming the holes shut with a crushing force.

Petal squeezes the material on each side of her dress and changes feet like she's about to wet her pants with fright. "Oh God! I can't go out there, Mama Bell. I done seen a ghost devil out there!"

"You gonna think a ghost devil done got you, if'n you don't mind me, girl."

Petal is just about in tears, pointing toward the back driveway. "Please, Mama Bell! He be sittin' on his black hoss right in the back there. Honest to God. I ain't lying! Go look."

Bell reluctantly steps out on the back porch just as the lightning flashes. She sucks in her breath sharply at the sight of a shadowy rider sitting in the back driveway. Panic grabs her by the throat until she realizes who she sees, then fire and brimstone come to her eyes. She walks to the edge of the porch and waits on the next flash of light. When it comes, Petal squeals loudly, right behind Bell, because the rider has disappeared.

"See, Mama Bell! It be a ghost devil! He done turned to darkness."

Bell turns on Petal, grabs her by the arm, and shakes her hard. "Hush up that ghost devil nonsense and get to work. That kinda talk'll have every nigger on the place killin' chickens and doin' them damn voodoo chants."

"But Mama Bell..."

Bell points her finger in Petal's face. "Hush up! It was a man! You hear me! Just a man! Now get on with you."

Petal walks back into the kitchen, nervous and looking over her shoulder out into the night.

"Go on now. Pick all them curtains up and put 'em where they go."

With fright all over her face, Petal obeys Bell's orders. "Yes ma'am."

Bell walks back to the edge of the porch and stands looking off into the dark, thinking how correct Petal was about what she saw. Indeed it was a devil, a devil by the name of Ike Murphy.

CHAPTER FOURTEEN

WITH THE MANSION BEHIND HIM, IKE RIDES THROUGH THE driving rain and fits of lightning with a single purpose that will not be denied. He aims his worn out horse far down the road toward a faint speck of light that blinks in the darkness.

Ike pushes hard through the relentless storm until he reins the horse up in front of an old moss-laden oak, its long arching limbs shrouding the front of a clapboard frame house. The mossy limbs sway in the driving wind and rain, making the one dimly lit window in the shack blink like an ocean lighthouse. Ike steps down from the horse and ties him up at the hitching post by the flapping picket gate. When he walks up on the front porch, he is startled by the sudden vicious growling and barking of a dog from inside of the house. He instinctively reaches for the pistol in his belt.

From in the house he hears, "I got a shotgun and Cur in here, so you best be about your business!"

Ike smiles and relaxes. "It's Ike, Newella, don't shoot."

There's a long pause of silence and then Newella answers. "Take off your hat and step over to the window."

Ike removes his hat, runs his hand through his wavy brown hair, and steps in front of the lighted window. "Satisfied?"

Newella opens the front door with one hand and holds the Cur by his collar with the other. "Paxton ain't here, if you be lookin' fur 'im."

"I know he's not here... and I am not looking for him."

An awkward moment of silence passes between them. Newella shoves the dog outside and looks up at Ike. "Come in."

Ike takes off his slicker and hangs it on a peg by the front door, along with his wet hat. He then steps inside and closes the door behind him without taking his eyes off of Newella. His stalking focus leaves little doubt in Newella's mind about the reason for his unexpected visit. She moves off toward the kitchen table with Ike following her step-for-step.

She cautiously looks back over her shoulder. "Like a drink to cut the cold?

"I think you know what I need to cut the cold."

Newella turns and faces Ike. "Is that the reason you're here?"

The light of the fireplace behind her outlines a much slimmer Newella than Ike remembered. His eyes follow her clean cut body line from bottom to top, until his gaze comes to rest on her hard nipples pushing against the thin cotton gown. He slowly reaches to touch her and Newella takes an easy step back, smiling.

"I guess that's a hand signal for yes."

Ike snaps out of his fantasy. "I hope that smile is a yes. Cause it'll be a lot easier for both of us."

"I can't say I hadn't thought about you a lot. Fact is, most every time I see you... But I don't think this is doing right by Paxton."

Ike takes an aggressive step toward Newella, and she nimbly backs around the table until she has it between them.

"Let me clean your conscience up for you. You don't have a choice."

Newella measures his bravado with her own. "I know I don't... But you do."

Ike has to choke back a laugh. "I have a choice? Listen to me, I am going to do you, and there's nothing you can do about it. Nothing!"

"That's true. That's one way to go about things for sure, but not the best."

Ike begins to lose his patience. "Then make your point. What's the best?"

"Well. You can chase me down in here, break me over, and hit it a lick, which is no fun for anyone. Or … you can shuck them wet clothes and get in that bed over yonder, where we'll all have some fun."

Ike puts his hands on the table and leans in toward Newella. "Bitch! Are you horse trading with me?"

"I am. It's either fun or no fun. Your call."

"If it's fun, what do you want?"

"I want a paying job somewhere on this place. I don't care what it is, as long as I get paid. You do that, and we'll have some real fun."

Ike stands there looking at Newella, amused, but not knowing what to think. He finally nods his head yes.

Newella extends her right hand. "I guess I didn't hear you. Did you say deal?"

Ike reaches across the table and shakes her hand. "Deal."

Newella drops her nightgown on the floor and walks around the table naked. Ike stands there watching her cross the room in stunned silence.

Newella pulls the covers back and gets into bed. "For a man in full rut, you sure seem stalled out."

Ike hastily strips and crawls in beside Newella.

Later that night, the ten striking chimes of the foyer clock arouse Jessica from her hypnotic trance. She sits in the study across from a snoring Cordell who's lapsed into a deep, brandy-induced coma. Her fixation is not on Cordell, but a four-inch silver cross lying on the arm of his chair with a red ribbon tied around it. The gift is a blatant reminder of the neglect she has inflicted on her marriage, both in the bedroom and out. The love and passion that ignited her relationship with Cordell is a long ago buried battlefield casualty of her youthful quest for social rank. Jessica quietly rises, reflects on the day's events, and walks from the room like a monarch absolved of all sins.

The next morning, just at the break of light, Ike sits on his black horse in front of the barns and pens for the mules and plow horses, issuing orders to eight of his hard case overseers. The barns and pens are the morning departure area for all of the Shannon Hill work crews. This particular morning is busier than usual because of the preparations being made to start picking in the next few days. Ike is momentarily distracted from talking to his men when he sees Jolene helping harness a team of mules.

He finally turns his attention back to his men. “Everyone clear about the day?”

The men answer in unison. “Yes sir.”

“Alright then. Let’s get them niggers moving.”

Ike turns, rides over to the mill office, and dismounts. While tying his horse up, something off in the distance toward the main house catches his attention. The house girls are hanging out a lot of white linen on the backyard clotheslines. The linen triggers his mind to replay Newella’s white nightgown falling from her shoulders, and her walk across the room, naked, to the bed. For a day that started terrible, it ended better than any fantasy he ever had riding to meet Jessica.

Ike is brought back to life by the sound of Cordell’s voice coming from behind him.

“Come in, Mr. Murphy.”

Ike turns and follows Cordell back into the mill. “Yes sir.”

When he walks in, Cordell has his back to Ike and is looking out of his office window. “I want Jolene assigned to the kitchen here at the mill.”

Ike is not sure as to why Jolene’s at the barn harnessing a team, but he doesn’t ask. “Yes sir.”

Cordell reaches into the pocket of his coat and takes the cross in his hand. The combination of sleeping in his chair and drinking too much brandy has left Cordell in an ill mood.

"I want that to be this morning, Mr. Murphy."

"I'll make that happen, sir... Speaking of the kitchen, sir. I wanted to discuss that very issue with you."

"The kitchen is an issue?"

"Well, in a way, sir. It comes down to cost, sir. We need an overseer to manage the kitchen. Make sure we feed our overseers and not every buck on the place."

"You're going to put a man in the kitchen?"

"No sir, a woman. In fact, I've got a girl right here on the place."

"Who?"

"Newella Rayburn."

"Now wait a minute, Mr. Murphy..."

Ike respectfully interrupts, "Sir, just hear me out. She can run the kitchen here until the cotton is picked and shipped. Then I'll send her to the logging camps up on the Moore sections in the spring. It's..."

Cordell's patience is short. He holds up his hand and says, "I got it. How much do you want to pay her?"

"Overseer wages?"

Cordell abruptly shakes his head no. "She's a woman. Pay her half."

Ike has gotten what he wanted, and knows to back off and leave Cordell alone. "Thank you, sir." He turns to leave.

Cordell snaps in a harsh tone. "Mr. Murphy."

Ike turns back around. "Yes sir?"

Cordell has turned around and stands looking out of his office window once more. "Make sure Miss Rayburn knows who Jolene is."

"Yes sir."

Cordell's tone turns even colder and more calculating. "One last thing, Mr. Murphy. I care about one thing and one thing only, sir. I want every ounce of cotton picked and shipped. From first light to lantern light, everyone picks cotton. Am I clear?"

"Yes sir."

Cordell dismisses Ike with a wave of his hand. "Good. Go about your day."

"Yes sir."

When Ike walks out of the mill, the distant white linen at the main house catches his eye again. He stands there enjoying the sinister contentment he feels in knowing that he now owns Newella.

Several days later, the entire slave population of Shannon Hill is marshaled into their assigned positions like an invading army. They stand in the chilled morning darkness, shivering in tattered clothes and waiting for that first break of light from the eastern sky. The early October days are mornings that chill the bones and afternoons that scorch the flesh, both of which the slave soldiers will endure in silence, or Ike Murphy will make sure they pay the price for their insolence.

As Cordell stands and looks over his readied army, he can't help but think that if prayers were light, the cotton fields of Shannon Hill would be awash in the brightness of a thousand heaven-bound comets.

Like Shannon Hill, the cotton harvest is in full swing all across the Deep South. The New England and British textile merchants will soon have their contracted Clipper ships anchored in every port on the East Coast and the Gulf of Mexico, all waiting on the first bales of white gold. The port of Charleston, with its deep water and abundant supply of cotton, make it the preferred choice of many New England and British buyers.

Because of the port's heavy traffic, the local taverns are filled with colorful sea captains from around the world. Their embellished tales of exotic lands and bold adventures keep the liquor flowing until the wee hours of the morning in many pubs. It's a celebratory time in these parts, and one that few men can ignore, including Sam Tanahill.

He sits and listens, along with a group of other men, as Conall O'Shea, an Irish sea captain, entertains the crowd with his tales of the high seas. What the brash, hard drinking Irishman lacks in size, he has tenfold in pure guts. His scars, tattoos, bangle earrings, and mane of wiry red hair look more like the marks of a Caribbean pirate than those of a gentlemanly sea captain. His tall yarns of the unsettled world only fuel Sam's desire to get on with his life. When Sam's imagination finally takes a rest, he realizes how late the hour is, and remembers that his planned departure for home is in just two hours. Sam stands up, catches hold of the table, and waits for the world to get level.

He increases his grip on the table with one hand and extends his other to Conall. "Captain, it's been a pleasure sir."

The feisty Irishman jumps to his feet and grasps Sam's hand. "The pleasure is mine, laddie. If ever you tire of the grass under your boots, and you want to see the world, I've always room for another bold lad."

"Thank you, sir. But I have a dream and a woman, and I can't let go of either one."

The Captain smiles and says, "Well then be true to both, or they'll quit you for sure, laddie."

Sam turns the Captain's hand loose, reaches for his hat, and jams it on his head. "Thank you, sir."

Sam takes a deep breath and starts for the tavern door. When he reaches the door and opens it, he loses his balance and stumbles outside in a free fall toward the edge of the porch. Sam feels someone catch him from out of the shadows with a bear hug tackle. When he finally pulls his hat from over his eyes, he comes face to face with Little Jim. Sam catches hold of a nearby porch post and pulls himself upright.

"What the hell?... Little Jim?"

Little Jim straightens his crushed hat. "Well boss, it got near time to go. So I got up, hitched the team, and drove on down here."

Little Jim points over his shoulder to the wagon and team parked down the street.

Sam squints his eyes, trying to focus on the wagon. "Well damn, Little Jim."

Little Jim puts his head under Sam's shoulder. "Come on boss, I got a bed made right there in the back so's you can puke real easy."

The pair stagger off of the porch and over to the back of the wagon. After several tries, Little Jim finally gets Sam over the back of the wagon and into bed. He then walks around to the front wheel, steps on the wheel hub, and vaults up onto the wagon seat.

Little Jim picks the reins up and rattles them at the team real easy. "Let's go. Little Bill, Henry, step up."

The trace chains come tight and the empty wagon easily rolls forward. Before they clear town, Sam is hanging over the back of the wagon and, true to Little Jim's prediction, puking.

Little Jim smiles. "Tastes a mite different coming up than it does going down, don't it boss."

Sam goes to say something when the heaves make him quickly hang his head back out of the wagon again. Little Jim points the team north, up the King's Highway, toward North Carolina and home.

After a few hours of sleep, Sam awakens to an icy chill that has settled over the night air. He climbs up into the wagon seat and spells Little Jim so he, too, can get some rest.

Sam's high-pitched whistle can barely be heard over the groan of the icy north wind. With their harnesses draped in glistening icicles and billowing white clouds of hot breath, the mules lay into their collars and assault the last hill before home. When they reach the crest and the barns come into view, the bone weary cold of ten days on the road fades quickly. The team steps up their pace, and needs little guidance to the front of the barn. When Sam reins them up, Little Jim is down on the ground unhooking the lead pair before Sam can set the brake. The closing darkness is only adding to the cruel force of a temperature in free fall. Sam climbs down and hurries around the wagon to get Journey and Slick out of the cutting wind.

He walks back around the wagon leading the horses just as Little Jim unhooks the first pair. "Get 'em all in the barn, Little Jim, then we'll pull the harnesses."

"Yes sir."

Little Jim takes hold of the barn door handle and fights with the wind for control of the door. When he finally has it open, he leads the first pair in, followed by Sam and the horses.

Sam and Little Jim quickly return for the other two pair who are standing with their heads down, trembling. No sooner than they have the team in the barn and the doors finally shut, there comes a hard banging on the doors. Sam hustles over and puts his shoulder to the door, cracking it just enough for Owen to slide in.

Owen stomps his feet and tries to shake the cold. "Gosh almighty, I ain't seen cold this early in a spell. You boys okay?"

Sam shakes hands with his father. "Yes sir. Just near froze stiff."

Owen is relieved they're home. "I been a mite worried. How'd it go at the Meyers' place?"

Sam goes back to pulling the harnesses off of the mules. "Aside from all the loud talk, we got loaded and left. Not much else."

Owen walks over to Little Jim, who's standing on his tiptoes trying to pull a collar over the head of one of the mules. "Here, let me give you a hand," Owen says.

He responds to Sam. "That's good to know, son. I hope Cordell keeps a hand on that bunch."

The thought of Ike doesn't trouble Sam near as much as it once had, not since he'd seen the intimidation and fear in his eyes at the dock.

"Yes sir, seems he has. But it ain't finished in Ike's mind. Personally, I don't think he'll ever heal."

Little Jim takes a stiff step out of Owen's way with his shoulders slumped against the cold.

Owen takes notice of his unusually slow step. "Little Jim, you alright?"

Little Jim nods his head. "Yes sir. Jest got the cold miseries, Mr. Owen."

Sam walks around to Little Jim. "You got the chills?"

Little Jim quickly goes back to work. "No sir, boss. Jest a mite cold."

Sam and his father trade a look.

Owen gives Little Jim an order that he can't ignore. "Go on to the house and warm up. The stew's on the stove. No need to wait on us. We'll finish here."

Little Jim stops work and looks at Sam, who nods for him to go on. He reluctantly pulls his hat down, walks over to the barn door, and with Sam's help, cracks it enough to get out.

Owen goes to hurriedly unbuckling the harnesses. "Let's get this done and get in the house."

Sam looks at Owen and asks, "You cook the stew?"

Owen smiles. "I did, and it's pretty fair."

"Where's Maw? She get tired of you?"

Owen laughs. "Naw. She's gone over to the Deason place to deliver another young'un. That poor little old Maple has one every year about this time."

"How many is that now? Eight, or nine?"

"Not quite sure, but there's a passel of 'em. Anyway, Jewett asked her to help out for a few days, and I am glad he did. Give this ice storm a chance to blow out."

"Don't take this wrong Paw, but I am glad she's not here."

It's the second time tonight Owen's heard that matter-of-fact tone in Sam's voice. Owen felt like Sam was holding something back when he'd asked him earlier about his stop at Shannon Hill.

Owen stops work and walks around to Sam. "Son, you got a look in your eye. You want to tell me about it?"

"Nothing bad, Paw. Just a business deal I need your help with. It can wait."

"Fair enough." He nods his head toward the back pens. "Put your team under the west shed, and Old Slick in with the saddle horses. What about the stud there?"

"He stays in the barn, if that's alright?"

Owen smiles. "From the looks of him, I'd say he's been getting some special treatment."

"He has that. He's a pretty special horse."

"I am not sure I understand how. Knowing what he cost Spence."

Sam continues working. "Wasn't Journey's fault. Spence didn't know what he was doing."

"That's strange. He raced horses for thirty years, and he didn't know what he was doing?"

Sam stops work and takes a deep breath of anticipated aggravation. "I am not saying he didn't know horseracing. I am saying he didn't know how to make this horse run."

"Sam. I hope your business deal doesn't concern racing this horse."

Sam looks his father in the eye. "It does. But just hear me out. That's all I ask."

Owen pauses, and then nods his head. "Alright." He can plainly see the resolve in his son's eyes. "Let's get finished. We can talk about this in the house."

Two hours later, Owen sits across from his son at their kitchen table in stunned silence. With his eyes and hands on his coffee cup, Owen tries to remember the days of his own reckless youth, when an insane risk seemed normal in every detail. Sam's adventurous spirit makes Owen envious of a time in his life before caution had a voice.

Owen finally looks up at Sam. "Son, let me get this straight. You want to send Cordell Meyers a match invitation for five thousand dollars?"

"Yes sir."

"Then you plan on marrying his daughter, and y'all going west. Did I, uh, leave anything out?"

"No sir. That's pretty much it."

"Well, I can't help you with Miss Meyers. So I guess the five thousand dollars is what you want to discuss with me."

"Not all of it, just some of it."

"How much is some of it, Sam?"

"I am not going to lose this race. Believe me."

"I am trying to, son. But why are we having this discussion if you're not going to lose?

Sam raises his hand in the air in desperation. "If by... whatever, Journey were to lose? Which he won't! I need to be able to pay Cordell, or he'll never let me marry Helen."

Owen's laugh takes Sam by surprise. "Son. That gray's unbeaten. If you win, he may never let you on the place again, much less marry his daughter."

Sam leans in toward his father. "Journey can beat the gray, no question. And as for Helen, she'll marry me with or without his blessing, and he knows it."

"You know your maw won't take to all this."

"I know she won't. But Paw, she's lived her life with a strict set of beliefs. Most of them are mine, but some of them are just not."

"I understand that son, but back to the money. How much?"

"I am short four thousand."

"That's a lot of money, Sam."

"It is. But if I lose, I'll not go west until it's paid back in full. That's my word."

Owen looks off for a long moment, then back to Sam. "Then let's get that invitation on the road."

Sam smiles and extends his hand to his father. "Thank you."

The two men shake hands, each with a prayer that rides on the back of Journey.

Owen points toward his study. "There's pen and paper on my desk. Help yourself."

Sam gets up and walks out of the kitchen.

Early the next morning, as Sam steps off the back porch headed to the barn, he is unaware of the polar ice blanket that covers every structure on the Tanahill place. He checks his inside coat pocket for the invitation one last time before pulling the wide leather belt tight around his bearskin coat. The dark shadow of his hat brim falls across a bearded jaw that's set in unyielding determination. Sam pulls on his gloves and turns up the hairy collar of his coat while walking on toward the barn.

Little Jim is pounding the ice-bound latch on the barn door with a hammer when he notices Sam out of the corner of his eye. What mission he's on, Little Jim isn't sure, but from the look of Sam's walk, Little Jim knows that there is a mission. Just about the time Sam walks up, Little Jim finishes beating the ice and weakly struggles to raise the latch from its frozen notch.

With his head down, and his weight leaning into the barn door, Little Jim pauses, trying to catch his breath. "Mornin, boss."

"Morning," Sam says. He reaches and puts a hand on Little Jim's shoulder. "Here, step out of the way and let me give you a hand."

Little Jim nods his head and shuffles to one side.

Sam jerks the latch free, and after several tries, he pries the barn door open.

Sam pauses for a moment to breathe. "Little Jim, I want you to help me a bit. Then I want you out of this weather."

Little Jim follows Sam into the barn "Boss, I can..."

Turning on Little Jim, Sam's tone is quick but friendly. "I want you out of this weather. Hear me?" Sam looks off, then back to Little Jim "You need to be well so you can ride Journey for me."

Little Jim smiles when he finally realizes what's driving Sam. "We got a hoss race boss?"

"Maybe. You never know what a man like Cordell will do."

Little Jim comes to life. "Well whatever the bet, boss, I got five dollars saved, and I want to bet it all!"

Sam walks over to the saddle room and opens the door. "How about fifty for riding Journey in the race?"

Little Jim is momentarily speechless. "Boss, does you mean fifty whole dollars?"

Sam smiles and says, "I do."

Little Jim stares off with visions of wealth. "Gosh almighty... Fifty whole dollars."

Sam takes two halters off of a peg on the saddle room wall and hands them to Little Jim. "Here. Go catch Old Slick and that sorrel gelding with the frostbit ears for me."

"Then I guess you be headed to Shannon Hill to see the man?"

Sam walks over to the back doors of the barn, flips the inside latch, and shoves the frozen door open. "I am. Soon as I can get saddled. So go on and catch 'em up."

Little Jim walks out of the barn door and down to the horse pens, grinning and shaking his head. "Fifty whole dollars."

Sam lingers at the barn door, thinking of his last encounter with Helen. The look in her eyes when he reached across and pulled her from the back of the hard running Blue Rock... he saw the unwavering trust in her eyes and knew then and there that he'd always be there to save her.

Journey's gruff squeal brings Sam back to life and makes him smile. "Yeah, I know you're hungry. Me too."

Sam walks to the feed box and starts measuring up grain in several buckets.

In a lively step, Little Jim walks back into the barn with both horses. "Why two hosses, boss, if you be going alone?"

Sam carries one of the buckets over to Journey. "I am going to ride straight through." Sam points to the horses. "Brush Old Slick off and saddle him. Then give 'em both a measure of grain. I'll be right back with my gear."

"Yes sir."

Sam strides by Little Jim, headed to the door. "Step it up Little Jim; it's near full light."

Sam walks out of the barn and on toward the house.

"I'ma steppin' boss. I'ma steppin.'"

An hour later, Sam rides out of the barn on Old Slick with the sorrel in tow. The frozen dirt road makes both horses highly cautious with every cat-like step. The fiery orange glow rising out of the frigid Atlantic is breaking the eastern horizon with streaking beams of light that dance across the icy landscape. Sam pulls the tall furry collar of his coat up around his neck and settles in for near three days of hard riding.

Little Jim stands at the front of the barn watching Sam ride off. When he suddenly remembers his bet of five dollars, he yells, "Don't forget my five dollars, boss!"

Sam raises his hand in acknowledgement and keeps riding.

Little Jim watches until Sam rides into the hazy morning light. He turns and walks back into the barn, talking to himself.

"Fifty whole dollars," Little Jim says. "Lord Jesus, what a blessin' for a nigger. Yes sir, a pure blessin.'"

CHAPTER FIFTEEN

THREE DAYS LATER, A HIGH NOON NOVEMBER SUN SENDS A welcomed relief of warmth streaming through the rustic colored canopy of the dense hardwood forest. Jessica leans back in the carriage, closes her eyes, and basks in the random patches of sunlight that dot the narrow road winding off through the Santee bottom country. The sleek team of black horses long-trot with a timed cadence that only heightens her sexual fantasies. With her hands in her lap, she gently rubs the front of her dress until the tingling waves of pleasure make her tremble with a low moan of anticipation. When she opens her eyes, the thought of being naked for the entire afternoon only adds to the ache beneath her pristine white gloves. The absence of a man's controlling touch has fueled a pent-up neglect that draws her near to madness. The sound of Benjie's voice saves her from the agonizing torture of her relentless imagination.

"We here, ma'am."

Jessica slides over in the carriage seat and tries to look around the team.

She anxiously strains to see the cabin. "Is he there, Benjie? Do you see his horse?"

"No ma'am. I don't sees him anywhere."

When Benjie reins the team up, Jessica is out of the carriage before the wheels quit rolling. She picks up each side of her long dress and dashes up the cabin steps like a smitten schoolgirl. With her heart in confusion and her mind in turmoil, Jessica bursts through the cabin door to find the room cold and empty. Even though there isn't a witness to her foolish infatuation, it spirals her downward into a dark hole of embarrassment. He assured her that the afternoon was hers, and he vowed to be there waiting. Jessica turns around, walks back out on the porch, and sits down on a small bench by the door. She stares down the wooded road, angry that she has put herself in such a vulnerable position, allowing yet another man to control her emotional and sexual needs.

After tying up the team, Benjie approaches her on the porch with nervous caution. "Ma'am, you wants me to start the fire and heat some water?"

Jessica's mood is turning darker by the second. "No, I don't! Go get my carriage; we're going home."

Benjie hesitates. "Ma'am, dem hosses are plum worn. They needs some rest."

Jessica jumps to her feet, pointing furiously at Benjie in a rare loss of control. "I don't give a goddamn. DO AS I TOLD YOU BEFORE I WHIP YOUR NIGGER ASS!"

Benjie turns and hustles off to get the carriage. "Yes ma'am."

Jessica paces back and forth on the porch, talking to herself. "I'll not be kept waiting like a common whore." She continues to pace. "Every time he keeps me waiting and waiting. Well no more. By God, never again!"

When Benjie pulls up in the carriage, Jessica storms off of the porch and climbs in before he can get down to help her.

Jessica snaps, "Go!"

In less than a mile, Benjie turns to Jessica. "Ma'am, he be coming up the road."

Jessica catches hold of the front of the carriage and stands up, looking around Benjie. There in the shadowy distance, coming up the road, is a black horse and a rider that can be no other.

Jessica sits down. "Don't stop!"

"Yes ma'am."

When the carriage gets close, Ike stops his horse on the side of the road and sits, waiting on her. When Jessica unceremoniously passes him by, Ike wheels his horse around and loops up alongside of the carriage.

"Hey Lady. Where you going?"

Jessica continues to ignore him. "Keep driving, Benjie!"

Jessica opens her parasol and tilts it over toward Ike where he can't see her face. His patience fails him, and he spurs his horse up alongside of the team, taking hold of the reins.

Ike pulls them to a stop. "Whoa, now."

He puts on his best gentlemanly smile, turns around, and rides up to the carriage door. He sits there waiting for Jessica to come out from under the white lace parasol.

"Benjie, let's go," she says.

Ike shakes his head. "Not until we talk. Now come out from under there."

"Benjie..."

"Jessica, what are you so mad about?"

Jessica comes out from under the parasol like a cornered lioness. "What am I so mad about? How many times have I told you not to keep me waiting? How many?"

"Listen..."

"No, you listen! A gentleman doesn't keep a lady waiting. Especially when she's agreed to share her bed with that gentleman!"

"Look. Let's go back to the cabin and talk."

"You want to talk? Go talk to your kitchen whore."

"Oh, so that's what this is all about. Newella."

"Not hardly, Mr. Murphy. This is about the one thing in this world I can and will control—who gets into my bed!"

"Come on now, enough of this! We're going back to the cabin."

"Don't you think for a minute, Mr. Murphy, that you can bully me into opening my legs. Because my weaknesses have limits, and you've reached that limit, sir."

"So I am a weakness?" Ike asks with a boyish grin.

"Unfortunately."

"Well, will I get to see you again?"

"Only if you learn to tell time, sir."

Ike pauses for a moment and looks off. "Fair enough. Take her home, Benjie."

Ike looks back at Jessica to find the storm has passed in her eyes. They share a moment, then Jessica slowly raises her parasol and blocks him from her view.

"Benjie."

Jessica never turns around to look back, but Ike watches her drive out of sight.

That same day in the early afternoon, Bell is dealing with her own set of aggravations in life. The unseasonably cold weather has put her wash day a full week behind. On top of everything else, Cordell has taken all of the house girls except old Aunt Hattie to the cotton fields. Bell has her sleeves rolled up and is walking through the clotheslines, taking down dry clothes, and hanging up wet ones in their place. She hums an old Negro spiritual and takes comfort in the Lord even though her life of drudgery never knows a day of rest.

Aunt Hattie is scrubbing laundry on the back porch when she sees a rider coming up the back driveway.

She calls out to Bell, "Bee."

Bell stands on her tiptoes and looks over the clothesline at Aunt Hattie. Aunt Hattie nods toward the rider.

Bell walks out of the clotheslines with a large wicker basket propped up on her hip. When the rider gets closer, she instantly smiles. If there's one trait Bell has, it's an intuitive judgment of human character that never misses the mark. Bell has a deep abiding respect for Sam Tanahill that's founded in his respect for all humans.

"My, my, Mr. Tanahill. What brings you to us?"

Sam rides on up to Bell. "Hello, Bell. I knocked on the front door, but nobody answered. Mr. Meyers home?"

"No sir, he's not." Bell turns and walks toward the house. "Hold on jest a minute, sir."

Sam yells after her. "Bell. I just need to speak with Mr. Meyers."

Bell walks up on the back porch, sets the basket of clothes down, and turns to Sam. "I know you do, jest hold on."

Bell turns around and walks into the kitchen, and almost immediately Helen dashes out of the kitchen door onto the porch. She stands there for a mesmerizing moment, smiling and wiping her flour-covered hands on the front of her apron. If he offered his hand, she would swing up behind him this very minute and ride off with never a look back. It's been only a month since she had her arms around him, riding double on Journey, but on the calendar in her heart, it's been an eternity. She walks up to him as close as she can get and looks up at him with a longing that knows no rest. They are both lost in a silent moment that the spoken word would only ruin. Sam reaches down and lightly brushes a spot of flour from her cheek. His gentle touch speaks volumes to her heart.

Bell loudly clears her throat. "Alright, enough of that. Get down and come in, Mr. Sam."

Sam would like to do just that, and to take Helen in his arms as well, but business nags at his mind.

Sam looks over to Bell. "I can't, ma'am. I just need to see Mr. Meyers and get on."

Helen takes hold of his hand. "Come in. I am baking some pies."

Sam laughs. "You're baking?"

"I take it you don't believe me?"

Sam kills his smile quickly. "Oh no, ma'am, I believe you." Sam points to her flour-covered apron and says, "You're sure doing something in there."

"Let me tell you something, Mr. Sam Tanahill. I am not some sweet little innocent southern belle. I can cook, ride, hunt, and fish with the best of 'em. You included."

Sam mockingly holds up his hands. "I believe you, ma'am."

"Well then get off that horse and come in."

"Like I told Bell. I need to see your father on business, then I have to push on."

Helen is reluctant to tell him where her father is, because she knows he'll ride off. "You can find him at the mill, if you're just bound and determined."

Sam pauses for a moment, then tips his hat to Bell and Aunt Hattie. "Ladies." Sam looks back to Helen for just a moment. "I have to go."

"Don't ride off... please. Just stay for a little while."

"I gave my word I wouldn't come calling without an invitation. I have to live on that."

Helen nods her head. "I know." She turns and walks toward the back porch. "Hang on before you go."

Helen walks into the kitchen and comes back carrying something wrapped in a piece of paper.

She hands it up to Sam. "It's still a little warm, so be careful. I hope you like apple."

Sam smiles and says, "It's my favorite."

Helen walks back up onto the porch and stands next to Bell. "Now go on, Sam Tanahill, before I do something totally unladylike."

Sam turns Slick around easy and rides off, leaving the two women standing side-by-side on the back porch. When Sam is almost to the mill, Bell puts her arm around Helen's shoulders and lovingly pulls her close.

Helen looks at Bell. "Mama Bell, you raised me to be a lady. But that man gives me some powerful urges."

"Don't you worry none on them urges, Missy. 'Cause the Lord couldn't have blessed you with a better man."

Helen looks back at Sam who's nearly out of sight, then she takes a slow, deep breath. "If that's true, Mama Bell, then why do my mother and father hate him so?"

"I think hate is a little too strong a word. He's just not like them, and that always makes folks uncomfortable."

"I don't care how uncomfortable they are. I won't let him go, Mama Bell. I won't."

"I know. Now quit that frettin', child." Bell turns to Helen and looks her in the eyes. "I taught you to trust in the Lord, didn't I?"

Helen nods her head. "Yes ma'am."

"Well then, get your head up and show the Lord that trust. The Lord helps them..."

Helen laughs and interrupts Bell. "I know. The Lord helps them that helps themselves."

Bell smiles, reaches up, and tenderly pushes a blonde curl behind Helen's ear. She takes Helen in her arms and gives her a hug that comes straight from the depths of a mother's heart.

Bell whispers in her ear, "He'll be back for you."

The moment is broken when Benjie swings the team of black horses on to the back driveway with a rattling clatter. The team's high stepping gait and lather covered harness are sure indications to everyone present that Jessica is in an ill mood. When Benjie reins the team up, Jessica steps out of the carriage and avoids Bell and Helen by walking through the gardens to the back veranda. Helen watches her mother until she hears the slamming of the veranda door.

Helen looks over at Bell. "I hope you're right, Mama Bell. I hope you're right." Helen turns and walks back into the kitchen.

When Jessica marches off, Benjie gets down to shut the carriage door. He notices one of the team slightly holding up a front leg. He kneels down and rubs the horse's leg, cussing and swearing under his breath.

Bell walks up behind him carrying a basket of wet clothes. "Watch yo'self, nigger. All dat will come to no good."

Benjie stands up and faces Bell in the hard grip of a rage that is near to overruling his fear of the whip.

"Dat woman needs a Juju curse put on her."

Bell steps up in Benjie's face and hisses a whisper. "Watch yo' mouth nigger with that ignorant talk. That voodoo shit scares white folks to death. Now go on and put them hosses up and get back here. Go on, nigger. I'm talkin' to you. GET!"

Benjie climbs back up into the carriage seat, looks at Bell, and moves the team off easy.

As Benjie drives off, Bell starts toward the clotheslines when she suddenly hears Jessica holler her name from inside the house. Bell stops for a moment and looks off to the cotton fields, wondering what it would be like to take one step in life that she totally owned. She sets the basket down on the back porch and walks into the house.

Jolene and Newella are on the porch of the mill, giggling, clowning around, and being girls, when Sam rides up. The camaraderie of the two laughing and holding on to each other surprises Sam. He never thought he would see the day that Newella could look past color and just see another human. Sam rides up to the hitching rail, steps down, and ties up Old Slick. Both girls are trying to catch their breath when Sam walks up on the porch.

Jolene puts her hand to her mouth and tries to say Sam's name, but instead she and Newella both burst out laughing again.

Sam finally holds up his hand. "Ladies, please. Is Mr. Meyers here?"

Jolene points to the office door and nods her head yes. She and Newella turn and walk off down the porch, trying to contain themselves for whatever reason.

Sam knocks on the office door with a nagging burn in his gut that he may be making a terrible overreach. A thousand dollars won't ruin his life, but it would sure make him limp for a while. Sam grits his teeth, shoves the sudden twinge of doubt to the back of his mind, and knocks on the door a second time, his jaw locked in determination. The seconds tick away to eternity until finally the door opens, but to Sam's surprise it's Lanham Hawks who opens it.

A crooked crack of a smile crosses Lanham's stoic features when he extends his hand to Sam. "Mr. Tanahill."

Lanham's reputation of unbending integrity and disciplined enforcement of the law makes even an honest man careful in his presence.

Sam shakes his hand. "Mr. Hawks. I was looking for Mr. Meyers."

Lanham nods toward the back office. "He's back there. Come in."

Sam steps by Lanham, takes his hat off, and walks down the dark hallway to the back office. When he walks in, Cordell is sitting at his desk with a tall glass of honey-colored sour mash in one hand and a cigar in the other. Lanham follows Sam into the office, shuts the door, and remains standing by the back wall.

Cordell gets up and comes around the desk to shake Sam's hand. "Mr. Tanahill, what a coincidence. I was just telling Mr. Hawks here I could sure use some help hauling bales to Charleston. Would you be available in the morning?"

Sam hesitates, and Cordell intuitively senses that something else is driving him. Cordell's day has been trying, to say the least, and he has no desire to wrangle old issues with Sam.

Sam answers Cordell with a gentlemanly but candid reply. "I would be glad to help, sir, but I am horseback at present."

Cordell walks back around his desk, settles down in his big leather chair, and reaches for the glass of sour mash. "I would hope, sir, that we're not going to tread worn ground."

"If you mean your daughter, sir, I will admit that she is never absent from my thoughts, but that is not my business for today."

Cordell takes a stout pull off of the drink and sets it back on the desk with a gentle bump. "Then praise be. A new problem would be a welcome relief around here." Cordell raises his hand and says, "Proceed, sir."

Sam opens his coat, pulls out the invitation, and hands it to Cordell. "This will explain my business here, sir."

When Cordell opens the letter and begins to read, humorous disbelief softens his hardass posture. After he reads the letter twice, he looks up at Sam and starts to speak, but Sam's cool disposition indicates there is no intent of humor in his challenge. In fact, his whole confident demeanor leaves Cordell puzzled and suspicious. He pauses in judicious thought on how to proceed. He knows a response is required, but the ramifications of that answer may set up an event that he cannot control.

The possibility of Blue Rock losing, Cordell could manage, but the loss of the race would very likely mean the loss of his daughter. If Sam has a thousand dollars, which Cordell is certain he has, or he wouldn't be standing in this office, then a win would give him two thousand dollars, making Sam's dream of going west an instant reality.

"A thousand dollars is a lot of money, Mr. Tanahill. I didn't know you were in the race business."

"I assure you, sir, I have the money to cover the bet."

"There's not a doubt in my mind, son, that you do. But tell me something. What horse do you plan on running?

"The bay stud, Journey."

"That's the horse you bought from Spence's widow."

"Yes sir."

"Mr. Tanahill, I don't want you to take offense, but I have to decline your offer. Because..."

"But sir..."

"Mr. Tanahill, hold up. I've agreed to a few rematches, but the stakes far exceed a thousand dollars. If someone wants another crack at Blue Rock, I make 'em pay for it, and pay dearly."

"But sir, you and I have never made a wager."

"It's the horse, Mr. Tanahill, not you. Blue Rock won that race by ten lengths. So where's the doubt? I could understand all this if it were a half a length, or even two lengths... but ten lengths? What are you thinking, son?"

Cordell's tone stiffens Sam's resolve. He presses Cordell. "Then what's the required wager for a rematch, sir?"

Cordell would desperately like to end the conversation. His aggravation shows when he puts his cigar out in an ashtray with four or five hard rubs instead of just one.

"Mr. Tanahill, let this go. That horse has caused enough destruction. You'll just be next."

Sam pushes back a bit. "I'll be the judge of that, sir. Now as I have requested before, please be as forthright with me as I am with you. What have you required of others?" Sam waits for the answer he already knows is coming. He came to this table with two things; money and information on just how much Cordell Meyers would require for a rematch.

Cordell gets up and walks to the window behind his desk. He stands there with his back to Sam, thinking.

Cordell turns around and says. "Five thousand! And that's firm."

Cordell looks into Sam's eyes with the arrogance of an over-confident card shark. The two men are locked into a battle of ego-driven personalities, a deep line drawn in the sand, with both men waiting to see who will blink first.

Cordell thinks he has Sam bluffed, and pushes on him aggressively. "It's five thousand dollars, Mr. Tanahill. And that's cash!"

Sam knows he's arrived at a long awaited fork in life's road, the fork that will take him to Helen. "I'll accept the bet on two conditions."

Cordell snaps. "Mr. Tanahill! There're no conditions, sir. It's either call or fold."

"I think you should hear the conditions before you answer in absolutes, sir."

Cordell is taken back by Sam's bold courage and raw tenacity. "By all means, let's not speak in absolutes. I am listening."

"When I win this race, I expect to be paid in cash, and I want your release from our agreement."

Cordell shakes his head in pure disbelief. "When you win? How about when you lose? What happens then?"

"Simple. I'll pay you in cash, and disappear into the West... without your daughter."

Cordell stands there in silence for a moment, realizing that he is being baited, but the gambler in him cannot resist. "You have a match, sir."

Sam's hard exterior doesn't change. "One last item. I would also like your word as a gentleman, sir, that you will never reveal the conditions of this wager to anyone, especially to your daughter."

Cordell walks around his desk and extends his hand to Sam. "You have my word. And I pray, sir, that you will live by yours."

Sam shakes Cordell's hand. "No need for prayer, Mr. Meyers. I'll see you in Camden on the tenth."

"I look forward to it, Mr. Tanahill."

Sam turns around and shakes Lanham's hand on his way out. "Mr. Hawks."

Lanham nods. "Mr. Tanahill."

When Sam walks out and shuts the door, Cordell walks back around his desk, sits down, and reaches for the glass of sour mash. Cordell motions to Lanham with the drink in his hand to have a seat.

"It's breeding, Mr. Hawks. It always has been and always will be."

Lanham walks over to the desk and sits down across from Cordell.

"Are you referring to men, or to horses, sir?"

The liquor is catching up to Cordell, unleashing memories of a deep-rooted streak of regretful errors from some of his youthful judgments.

Cordell leans into the desk and points at Lanham. "There is not a man on this Earth who does not pray from the depths of his heart for a son like Sam Tanahill. Not a man. And after my first two daughters were born, I was that man, praying for a son, seven days a week, never giving God or my wife a rest on the subject."

In all the years that Lanham has worked for and been friends with Cordell, he has never known the man to speak one word about his personal life, to anyone. But Lanham's keen sense of human nature tells him this man is about to unburden himself of his darkest, most deeply held sins and regrets.

"You said your first two daughters, sir. What of your third daughter?"

Cordell raises his class in a toast to himself. "To three daughters, sir–three lovely, brilliant gifts from God."

"That's surely a blessing, sir."

"Indeed, and no man felt more blessed than me in the beginning. In our first two years of marriage, my wife presented me with two beautiful daughters. Jessica and both the girls were all healthy, and I so looked forward to having more children, especially the sons I was praying so hard for. Then she just said, 'No more children.' No reason given other than just no."

Cordell pauses and blindly stares off at a blank spot on the wall. The pain in Cordell's eyes is plain enough to read, but Lanham feels out of place and struggles for something to say.

"Mr. Meyers?"

Cordell takes a deep breath. "Five years went by, and as a husband, I had more than lived up to my obligations. She and the girls had everything imaginable. Everything. I swear, I just felt denied, Mr. Hawks. Denied of the only thing I really wanted in life: a son. And to make things worse, she seemed to take pleasure in it. It got where I couldn't stand the sound of her voice, much less her company."

"Then one night, it happened. Five years of pent up anger, unleashed in a blind alcohol rage. God, what a sin. I not only raped her, I threatened to kill her if she didn't have another child. Anyway, when she had Helen the next year, it was the fork in the road for our marriage. She gave Helen to Bell to raise, and we went our separate ways, her to her social life, and me to my mistress, Shannon Hill."

Cordell reaches for a cigar and sits at his desk, resigned to the fact that his actions were never justified. When he looks over at Lanham, Lanham can see they are back to business.

Cordell smiles easy. "Let's get back to your report, Mr. Hawks. Where were we?"

Lanham comes to attention "Why don't I start at the beginning, sir?"

"By all means."

Cordell lights the cigar and reaches for the glass of sour mash.

Sam walks out of Cordell's office with an adrenaline rush that wipes away three bitter days of bone weary travel. He walks up to Slick, loosens the girth on the saddle, and walks the horse across the street to a watering trough. Slick has just finished drinking, and Sam is tightening the saddle back down when he hears someone call his name.

"Mr. Tanahill."

When Sam turns around, Newella is walking across the street toward him, smoking a small cigar and carrying a small covered pot by the handle. She is noticeably thinner, with a self-assured look in her eyes that speaks of an inner happiness. Her once common haircut is now replaced with a long growth of wavy brown hair, pulled up high on her head. The multitude of renegade ringlets that have fallen out and hang about her neck only add to her persona of a free spirit. Sam smiles and can't help but notice the marked changes in her.

"Miss Rayburn, it's..."

"Mr. Tanahill, it's just Newella. Things have changed quite a bit for me."

"I can definitely see that. I hope they're all for the good."

"Most of 'em. Where you headed?"

"I am going home."

"Mind if I walk with you to the cut off road?"

"Sure," Sam says. "It'll give us a chance to talk. I'd like to catch up on your family."

With Old Slick in tow, Sam and Newella start off down the road together.

"Ain't seen 'em in a while. Been too busy now that I manage the field kitchen. Feedin' twenty-five men breakfast and noonday leaves no time."

"The girl I saw you with earlier. She's your help?"

"She is, that's Jolene. She's a little more than my help. Her main job is Mr. Cordell's bed warmer."

"I was a little surprised by..."

Newella cuts Sam off, stops walking, and turns to face him. "By what, Mr. Tanahill? That she's black or that she's my friend?"

"Well, both, in fact. Best I can remember, your views of blacks were a little radical."

Newella takes a long drag off of the cigar, turns, and blows the smoke over her shoulder, away from Sam. She smiles, and they resume walking down the road together.

"Things change. Like I said, I've changed. Believe it or not, coming down here was the best thing that ever happened to me. You know why, Mr. Tanahill?"

"It's Sam, Newella. Just plain Sam. The truth is, I can't be anything but curious."

"Well, Sam... life opened my eyes long before Paw died. I realized that we didn't have money, and I sure didn't have the looks to ever be the lady of a plantation. So the way I saw it, I had only one of two options left. Hang around until some broke ass redneck knocked me up like Sistell, or light out. Three days after Paw died, I lit out."

"But why Paxton? Why here?"

"Paxton and I had spent a little time together when he'd pass through on occasion. He wasn't my first, but he'd been the best up until then, so that's where I headed. Besides, back then I had bought into all that nigger craziness that he's always peddling."

"And I take it from watching you and Jolene together that's not the case anymore?"

Newella takes another drag off of the cigar and stops in the middle of the road.

"That's right. I'd been around niggers all my life, and I'd always seen 'em as something less than human. Then I went to work with Jolene every day, working shoulder-to-shoulder and step-for-step. It sure opened my eyes. I came to understand that she was just a woman like me, with all the same hopes and dreams that God's given us all. The sad part is she can never live hers, and all just because of the color of her skin."

Sam and Newella stand in the middle of the road in awkward silence.

Newella finally smiles big and points to the cut off road. "This is where I leave you."

Sam smiles. "You take care of yourself, Newella."

Sam goes to turn away when Newella has an afterthought. "You goin' home by way of Beech's Crossing?"

Sam turns back to her. "I am. Why?"

"Your old friend, Paxton, and some of his bunch are waiting on you. That's why."

Sam's mood takes a dark turn. "Why are you telling me this?"

Newella answers in a matter-of-fact tone. "Just because I have to deal with some rotten people, don't make me one of 'em."

Newella can see the hard grit coming to Sam's eyes.

Newella lightens the mood. "There's another way out of here, if you're interested."

"Which way would that be?"

Newella smiles and points up the road. "See that big white oak right yonder? Just past it is an old tram that turns off into the woods. It cuts through by the Garrett place and comes out on the wagon road just below Beech's Crossing at Rita's."

"I know where that place is. It's a..."

Newella smiles. "It's a whorehouse, Mr. Tanahill. I know."

"You do?"

"And I know Rita too. When you get there, tell her I said to put you up for the night and take care of you."

"How is it you know her, Newella?"

Newella doesn't hesitate with her answer. "I work there on and off a night or two during the week. You see, Mr. Tanahill, just like you, I don't plan on being broke all my life either."

"And how does that work with Paxton?"

"He likes it. I never make him pay."

Sam smiles in amusement and steps up on Slick. “I won’t forget this. Thank you.”

Sam rides down to the oak, stops in the road, and looks back at Newella. He touches the brim of his hat in a gentlemanly southern fashion and rides into the woods.

CHAPTER SIXTEEN

THE BACK DOOR OF THE KITCHEN STANDS WIDE OPEN, ALLOWing a cool evening breeze to sweep the aromatic smell of sizzling beef steak into every corner of the elegant mansion. Bell cautiously steps up to the kitchen stove with another slab of flour-covered meat hanging on the end of a long fork. As she gently lowers it into the deep, black iron skillet, the scorching hot grease bubbles and pops, and then the massive steak settles to the bottom of the skillet. Bell takes a quick jig of a step back and feverishly wipes the specks of hot grease from her face and arms with her crimson-stained apron. The stinging burns are of little consequence compared to Bell's state of physical exhaustion, which is near complete.

She starts toward the back door for a breath of fresh air when the floor takes a sudden blurry spin. Bell catches herself on the corner of the kitchen table and pushes back on the visual darkness until she can lower herself into a chair. Just as Bell's head settles into her hands, Jessica crashes into the kitchen with the blunt force of an Atlantic storm. She looks beyond Bell's obvious physical distress and starts straight into her point of business.

"Bell, I want you to hold dinner until Mr. Meyers gets home tonight. My patience with this filthy house is at an end. I want my girls..."

Bell doesn't raise her head, and barely raises her voice. "He be home already."

"He's what?"

Bell points to the back porch and whispers. "He be out there, ma'am."

Jessica marches past Bell, headed for the back door. "What in God's name is he doing back there?"

Bell strains to be heard. "Drinkin' and talkin' to Cricket."

Jessica walks out of the back door. "That's not surprising."

Once on the porch, she turns to her right, starting toward the garden and the veranda, when she hears Cordell's voice from behind her.

"What's not surprising?"

Jessica wheels about and doesn't miss a step as she heads back down the porch toward Cordell. She walks back by the kitchen door and stops near the lighted kitchen window. She can barely see him sitting on the far end of the porch, down among the washtubs, in an old broke down rocker that wears a threadbare blanket for a coat. Cordell is stretched out in the old chair enjoying its worn-out, lopsided comfort, and sipping on a glass of sour mash.

Jessica snaps. "Are you coming in for dinner?"

Cordell answers her question flatly. "I am." He pauses, letting his silence remind her of who she's speaking to. "Is there something rubbing your ass raw?"

"I would rather the discussion not be out here in the dark. And I don't particularly like you speaking to me in that fashion, either, Mr. Meyers."

"And I don't particularly like you cracking that whip on my ass either, Mrs. Meyers."

Jessica steams with indignation. "Are you coming in, SIR?"

Cordell doesn't respond, and she can feel, through his renewed silence, a piercing stare that transcends the dimly lit back porch.

Cordell leaves no doubt that he will not be taken to task. "I sent Cricket down to the quarters to fetch me Rabbit. Now when he gets here, and I finish talking to him, I'll be in."

Jessica tries to call forth her sweet southern belle façade, but her annoyance with Cordell seeps into her tone. "Dinner will be served at your convenience, sir."

"I thought so."

Jessica detests Cordell when the liquor shades his southern etiquette with a common vulgarity. She takes a deep breath, turns, and walks back into the kitchen, resigned to the fact that he owns the moment, but resolving that he will not own the evening. Jessica stops in the middle of the kitchen and stands there in contemplative thought until Hattie places a bottle of red wine on the counter.

Jessica comes back to life. "Is that the wine I ordered for tonight?"

"Yes ma'am."

"Open it."

"Yes ma'am."

Hattie grabs a corkscrew, opens the bottle, and carefully sets it back on the counter. Her nerves are stressing every fiber in her body, and she doesn't dare make a mistake or look up. Jessica's caustic silence has draped her in a dark dress of caution.

"It's been a trying day, Hattie. But not to the point of drinking out of the bottle. Pour me a glass!"

"Yes ma'am."

Hattie steps down the counter, picks up a wine glass, and pours it half full.

Jessica reaches for the glass. "This isn't what I really want, but..."

When the wine washes a warm tantalizing tingle over her body, Jessica regrets not going back to the cabin when Ike asked her. With her social barrier dropping like a plate to the floor, she picks up the bottle of wine and turns to leave.

"Uh... ma'am."

Jessica turns around and Hattie nods toward Bell, who still has her head in her hands. Jessica looks Bell over for a moment, then turns back to Hattie with a slight glint of smugness.

"Hattie, I am going to freshen up. Hold dinner until Mr. Meyers comes in, and then come get me. Oh, and Hattie, I also want Helen to dine with us tonight."

"Yes ma'am. I'll fetch both of you when he be ready to eat."

With an eye on Jessica, Hattie goes back to getting dinner ready.

Jessica turns her attention back to Bell. "Bell, I want you and Hattie to serve tonight and do precisely as I tell you."

Bell weakly looks up. "Yes ma'am."

"I want both of you to stand at your station, and don't leave it until I release you. Understood?"

Bell nods her head without looking up. "Yes ma'am."

Jessica walks out of the kitchen with more concern for the bottle in her hand than for Bell's condition. When she is out of hearing, Hattie walks over to Bell and gently takes her by the arm.

"Come on Miss Bee. You needs to lay down a spell."

"I can't do dat. Ma'am won't like it."

"You go on back there to yo' room and lie down. I'll fetch you in time for the serving."

"Hattie, be sure you fetch me."

"I will. Go on now."

Bell shuffles off down the hall to her room, and Hattie goes back to working around the kitchen, getting dinner ready. She shakes her head when she catches a glimpse of Cricket darting by the back door. He is an underfoot menace. One minute you want to kill him and the next you think you'll die of laughter on account of his crazy ways. Cricket dashes up onto the back porch and plops down next to Cordell, laughing between breaths.

"Cricket! Enough of that now, be still! Now where's Rabbit?"

Cricket slaps his hands down by his side on Cordell's command, closes his eyes, and stiffens his body out like he's dead.

Cordell looks down at him. "Cricket!"

Cricket tries to choke back the giggles and says, "He be comin', Mr. Boss. Soon as he and little Switch finish fightin' the old devil. He be on."

"Fightin' the devil? He tell you that?"

Cricket springs up into a sitting position and becomes animated. "Don't have to, Mr. Boss. When I runs up on they poch, I hear little Switch wit my own two ears, callin' on Jesus to hep her."

Cordell can't help but laugh. "Was she now?"

"Yes sir. Like this." Cricket rocks back and mimics the passionate moans of a woman having sex. "Oh Jesus!! OOOOH JESUS!! GOD ALMIGHTY, HEP ME JESUS!!"

Cordell holds his hand up and tries to be gruff. "Cricket! Stop it now and listen to me! Go back down there and tell that nigger he better be stepping light, cause I am waiting. You hear me? Now get!"

Cricket jumps up and starts galloping in place with his one good arm flapping wildly by his side like he's riding a horse. He looks over at Cordell, laughs, and makes a noise like he farted.

"You means fast like old farting Blue Rock, boss?"

Cordell stomps his boot on the porch and makes a quick move to get up, which launches Cricket off of the porch in a rush of giggling fright. Cordell leans back in his chair, smiles, and watches Cricket gallop away into the darkness on his imaginary horse, making sordid farting sounds, and cackling hilariously.

The thought of Blue Rock jars Cordell's mind, leading him to ponder the match with Sam. His reflex turns back to his drinking, only to find his glass shallow in liquor. He spins the last teasing taste around in the glass and throws it back like a salute to a destiny that's known but not yet revealed. With his first breath of air past his last drink, Cordell calls to Bell.

"Bell girl. Where are you?"

Bell doesn't respond, nor does anyone else, which only adds to his present state of aggravation. Between Rabbit's drag ass ways and his own empty glass, it's not a good time for Bell to be slow of foot. He starts to holler louder when Hattie makes an appearance at the back door.

"Bell, where the hell..."

"Mr. Cordell, sir…"

"Hattie! Where in God's name is Bell?"

"She be down in bed, Mr. Cordell."

Cordell snaps, "Since when? She just brought me a drink a bit ago."

"I know, sir. But the wearies just hit her hard, and she had to lay down."

Cordell looks off in silent thought for a moment. "Is she sick?"

"No sir. She jest be needing some rest, that's all, boss."

Cordell motions to Hattie with the glass. "Here, fill this up. I'll be in soon as I finish with Rabbit."

Hattie walks down the porch and takes the glass from Cordell. "Yes sir." She turns around and starts back to the kitchen.

"Hattie."

Hattie stops. "Yes sir?"

"Petal, Switch, and two of the other girls will be back up here in the morning. So tell Bell I said to rest up. You can oversee the house for a day or two until she's up and around."

"I'll sure try, boss."

Cordell's tone is acquiring a sour mash level of anger that makes Hattie a little edgy.

"Ain't no try to it, Hattie. That's what better happen!"

"Yes sir."

Cordell waves Hattie to go on. "Now bring me that drink."

Hattie walks on into the kitchen and soon returns with the glass brimming full of sour mash. When she hands Cordell the drink, it is quite evident that his mood is in quick decline over having to wait on Rabbit. Hattie stands in guarded silence, with her eyes riveted off into the hazy darkness, waiting to be dismissed.

Cordell waves her off again. "Set the table, Hattie, and summon her majesty. I fear the court jester has delivered my message to a deaf ear in rut."

"It been set, sir. All I needs to do is fetch Miss Jessica and Miss Helen."

Cordell stands up and walks to the washbasin that Bell had set out for him. "Well then, by all means, fetch 'em."

"Yes sir. They jest be one other thang… it's 'bout the servin', sir."

Cordell sets the drink down, splashes his face with the cool water, and washes his hands. "Hattie, I heard Jessica talking to Bell. You never mind that, and go about your business."

Hattie hands Cordell a towel. "Yes sir."

Cordell dries his face and hands. "Now go on, I am coming."

Hattie turns and walks into the kitchen, relieved that she doesn't have to inform Jessica that Bell won't be serving. She is the strong right hand of Bell running the house, but she's not Bell when it comes to dealing with Jessica. Hattie was born in the Shannon Hill quarters and has spent her entire fifty plus years in constant service to some member of the Meyers' family. She was just a girl when Cordell's father assigned her to the main house staff. Hattie has known great sorrow, but nothing compares to the fear of being sold off, or sent to the fields, should she fall out of grace with Jessica.

Cordell pitches the towel down by the bowl, picks up his drink, and turns to go in the kitchen, when Rabbit dashes up to the edge of the porch, out of breath. He's bent over, trying to speak, and gasping for air.

"Boss, I'ze..."

Cordell turns around and points to the porch. "Rabbit! Sit down there and wait."

Rabbit takes a deep breath. "Yes sir, boss."

Cordell turns to walk into the kitchen.

Rabbit points over his shoulder toward Cordell's saddled horse, standing tied at the hitching post in the edge of the dim light. "Wants me to puts yo' hoss up, boss?"

Cordell continues into the kitchen. "Are you deaf? Sit down! I'll be back directly."

"Yes sir, boss."

When Cordell walks into the kitchen, Helen brushes by him, holding up each side of her dress as she heads to check on Bell in a double-quick hurry. A little unsteady in his balance from an afternoon of sour mash, Cordell almost spills his drink.

Helen doesn't pause and hurries on. "Sorry, Father."

"We're sitting down..."

Helen, over her shoulder, says, "I'll be right there!"

Hattie eases back into the kitchen and begins to get ready to serve the first course, with a cautious eye on Cordell.

Cordell shakes his head and walks on toward the dining room. "There'll be no serving tonight, Hattie. Just put it in bowls and get it on the table. I need to go."

"Yes sir!"

When Helen quietly steps into Bell's bedroom, she finds Bell fully dressed, lying on her back in bed with her arms by her side and her eyes closed. For an instant, Helen feels a chilling rush of fright that steals her breath away. With her hands pressed lightly to her trembling lips, Helen's eyes seek refuge on the crudely fashioned cross on the wall above Bell's bed.

Bell opens her eyes and looks up at Helen. "What's you doin' Missy?"

Helen quickly turns her back to Bell, wipes the tears from her eyes, and gathers herself.

Bell reaches out to her. "Come read to me child. I needs to hear the Word of the Lord."

Helen walks over and picks up the familiar old Bible with its broken binding and disheveled pages. She walks back to the slat board bed and sits down next to Bell. Since her early childhood, Helen has spent many nights reading the Word to Bell.

Helen holds the Bible in her lap and smiles at Bell. "What would you like to hear?"

Bell's eyes come to rest on the cross. "Anything in Mark where Jesus be talkin'. I jest needs to feel 'im in my heart."

Helen reverently opens the tattered book and straightens the pages as she turns to the book of Mark. She pauses when Hattie appears at the bedroom door.

"Mr. Cordell wants you at dinner, Missy."

Helen gently closes the Bible and hands it to Bell. "I'll be right back."

Bell puts the Bible on her chest, folds her arms across it, and closes her eyes.

When Helen walks into the dining room, the hostilities are mute for the moment, but the mutual rancor is palpable. Each of her parents are lingering over a drink—Jessica, a full glass of red wine, which is noticeably not her first or second, and Cordell, his usual glass of honey-colored sour mash. The verbal brawls between her parents are beginning to take on the unforgiving tones of enmity and bloodshed.

Helen turns to her father, ever so ladylike, and says, "If I may be excused, Father? I would like to look after Bell."

Jessica answers for him. "Your father requested your presence. Now be respectful and sit down."

Helen looks at her mother then back to her father, "I'd..."

Cordell points to the chair on his left. "Please. Sit down."

Jessica waves her hand in the air in a grand gesture. "By all means, sit down. We were just about to discuss The MAGNIFICENT Mr. Tanahill. But first, why don't you tell your father what you told me about him. Go on!"

Helen remains standing, smiles, and ignores her mother. "Father, I'm worried. Bell is..."

Jessica continues her rant. "No, No, No! Tell your father how he makes you want to take your clothes off. Tell him!"

Jessica leans in on the table, fumbles her silverware to the floor, clangs her empty plate, and points at Helen with her glass of wine.

Cordell begins to turn an even darker shade of red. "Jessica!"

"Go on, Helen. Tell him. Is that the reason he came by here today? For another quick sample!"

Cordell jumps up, pounds the table, and spills his drink all over his place setting. From out of the invisible realm of her station, Hattie is wiping the liquor up and resetting the table. Cordell throws his napkin down and steps out of her way. He paces the room, rubbing his hands through his hair while the drunk and the sober alike fall silent. Hattie finishes and quickly steps back to her station.

"Get me another drink, Hattie."

"Yes sir."

Cordell finally walks back around the table and stands behind his chair, facing the two women. He places his hands on the back of the chair and clears his throat, more to choke back the rage than to find his voice. When he begins to speak, his knuckles turn white from gripping the chair.

Cordell motions toward the chair in front of Helen. "Please! Sit down."

During her mother's accusations and her father's sudden violent response, Helen has held on to the sweet composure she entered the room with, just for her mother's entertainment.

"Yes sir."

Helen pulls her chair out and sits down with an elegance that would impress the most seasoned diplomat at any state dinner. Her genteel radiance casts an unwelcomed stream of light across the alcoholic darkness her mother is wallowing in.

Cordell turns his attention to Jessica. "I strongly suggest, madame, that you maintain civil decency while at my table. And I can't stress that strongly enough."

Hattie walks up behind Cordell with the drink and stands, waiting. When he finally sits down, she places the drink on the table, along with a clean napkin, and steps back to her station.

"Civil decency, sir?" Jessica laughs. "The grass has long grown over civil decency around here." She takes another drink and continues. "And I STRONGLY doubt sir that you could ever dig it up again."

Cordell waits for Jessica's tirade to end, then says, "Are you finished?"

Jessica raises her glass in a toast with a defiant silence to his authority. Cordell sits staring at her for the eternity of a few seconds. He reaches for his drink and returns the silent toast. When he places his glass back down, there is the distinct feeling that the well-worn dinner table truce is finally in effect.

Cordell takes a deep breath and tries to smile. "Well, ladies, it seems we're going to Camden after all. I have a match for Blue Rock."

Jessica is thrilled to the point of almost becoming sober in one breath. The festive Christmas season in Camden during the races is a must for anybody who's anybody of social standing. But when the shipping of the cotton dragged on and Cordell couldn't get a match for Blue Rock, he made the decision that they were staying home.

Helen is thrilled also, but for a wholly different reason.

Jessica looks down at her dress and gasps. "My God! I don't have one new dress to wear, and..." She looks up at Cordell, "We don't have a place to stay."

Cordell's mood is pushed closer to a smile with pleasant thoughts of old friends, cards games, and past victories at the Camden races.

"I've made arrangements with Lanham Hawks. He has an out building for our help, and we'll stay next door with his Aunt Mavis."

Jessica tries not to ruin the moment, but says, "Well... that's, uh..."

Cordell knows exactly what the "uh" means. "It's not The Camden House or Royal Hills, but it is in Camden. So what's your pleasure? Would you rather just stay home?"

Jessica, in a slurred sweetness, answers, "I think I am going to Charleston to buy some dresses. That's my pleasure."

"Well. If you're going, then it has to be in the morning. I am sending Mr. Murphy down there on business. He can be y'alls escort."

Helen perks up at that. "Y'all? I am not going."

Jessica responds to Helen's declaration. "Oh, I think that's a terrible mistake, honey. A lady never wants to get caught dead in an old dress."

Helen holds to her air of superiority and says firmly, "I am not going."

Jessica prods her with the intellect of a drunk. "You never know! The dancing wagon driver could..." She belches, "could possibly make another grand entrance!"

Cordell responds to Jessica. "If you're referring to Mr. Tanahill, he'll be there."

Jessica zones in on Cordell. "By whose invitation?" she demands.

Cordell takes a casual drink, savoring his next statement. "We're attending the races at Mr. Tanahill's invitation. That's why he came by here today."

Helen's voice breaks with excitement. "Your match is with Sam?"

"It is. We'll be one of the last matches of the week. So I would suggest you reconsider the shopping trip."

Jessica is the last to process Cordell's answer. She sits in stunned silence, then holds up her hand and speaks. "Hold the hell up right there. You really didn't agree to a match with Sam Tanahill, did you?"

Cordell loves to rag on Jessica's nerves about Sam, especially when she's drinking.

"I did. We..."

Jessica levels a scolding look at Cordell and asks, "He agreed to a thousand dollar match? Why, that broke ass wagon driver can't spell 'a thousand dollars,' much less cover it." She points at Cordell. "You should've pushed the bet, and you'd own them goddamn Tanahills."

Cordell measures his speech for impact. "I did push it, but not for that reason. We agreed to five thousand."

Jessica breaks up laughing. "Five thousand dollars! Oh my God!"

She turns to Helen. "When your wagon driver loses this race, you'll see what I've being telling you about him. The only thing that's bred into him is cut and run."

Helen looks straight ahead, speaking more to the world than her parents. "He won't do that. If he agreed to the bet, he will honor it!"

Jessica's alcohol-driven tirade presses on. "For that kind of money, you can bet your ass he'll honor it!"

Helen sits up in rigid defiance, with no intention of backing down. "Bet my what? I've just about had enough of your..."

Cordell points a paralyzed finger at Helen, commanding her to stop in mid-sentence. While the sour mash dulls Cordell to a physical lameness, it strangely sharpens his intuitive intellect to a razor's edge.

"The discussion around this match is closed, ladies. Final."

Jessica leans back in her chair, sipping on her wine with that same old sparkle of contentment. Helen grits her teeth and holds her silence, while a light red flush of color floods her face and neck. From the depths of her being, the anger rises and fights to escape her locked jaw, demanding to be voiced.

Helen looks to her father. "If I may?"

Cordell pauses, and then nods his head. "Be respectful."

Helen turns to her mother. "Do you believe a lost bet to be a binding debt of honor?"

Jessica leans in and locks into a stare with Helen. "Let me tell you something about honor. It's the only thing that separates us from the niggers and the rest of the trash in this world. It's who we are. It's how we live, and I would pray that you never forget that!"

When Jessica finishes her rant, Helen turns to her father. "If I may be excused, I'd like to see to Bell."

Helen's elitist snub of her mother sends Jessica to the brink of madness. "Haven't you anything to say?"

Helen never takes her eyes off of her father when she answers, "I don't."

"When you speak to me young lady, I expect you to look at me!"

Helen turns to face her mother. “Yes ma’am. I asked you a simple question, and you answered it. What else is there?”

Jessica is furious at Helen’s disrespect. “I’ll tell you what else there is...”

Cordell intervenes. “No, you won’t. That’s enough, Jessica. Now let’s...”

Jessica points at Helen and yells, “A bet is a debt of honor! Win or lose!”

Cordell is anxious to be finished and on his way. “I said ENOUGH, goddammit!”

A gripping stillness surrounds the dining room table and even Jessica, in her drunken stupor, knows it time to be silent. Helen finally breaks the tension and stands up.

She looks over to her father. “May I please be excused? Bell needs looking after.”

Cordell takes a deep breath and searches for his sanity. “Are you going with your mother to Charleston?”

“No sir.”

“Then you need to look after the house while she’s gone. That includes Bell.”

“Yes sir. Am I excused?”

Cordell nods and Helen walks away.

He turns his attention back to Jessica. “Sorrel will be your driver tomorrow. I need Benjie here at home.”

Jessica immediately sits up in her chair. “I would...”

Cordell cuts her off with a hard look that makes her pause. They sit locked in an eye-to-eye stare, both with the full knowledge and understanding of her knee jerk objection to Sorrel. Sending Sorrel instead of Benjie is a clear indication that Cordell knows about her current affair with Ike. Benjie has held silent for years about Jessica's recreational sex, which is something Sorrel will never do. Cordell doesn't particularly care for her bedroom escapades, but he does want her to be safe traveling to Charleston.

Cordell raises his glass in a toast. "You'll be safer traveling with Sorrel. And of course, Mr. Murphy will be an added bonus to your safety on the road."

Cordell slides his chair back and stands up.

"Are you not going to have dinner?" Jessica asks.

Cordell nods to Jessica, excusing himself from her presence. "I am not."

Jessica is aware of where he's going, and her question rings hollow with indifference. "Well, where are you going?"

Cordell picks up his drink, ignores her question, and starts from the room "Mr. Murphy and Sorrel will be here at five sharp in the morning. I suggest you don't be late. It takes a long, hard day to make Taylor's Roadhouse by dark."

Cordell walks out, leaving Jessica staring into space with a smirk of anticipation and a tingling that overrides all of her alcohol-numbed senses. She reaches for the bottle of wine on the table as her mind spins off into sexual fantasies of Ike stripping her of all her clothes and cultural inhibitions. With a soft grip on the neck of the wine bottle, Jessica continues to stare into space, giving Hattie pure misery in not knowing what to say or do next. Hattie finally summons her courage, clears her throat, and steps forward.

"Would you like me to fetch another bottle of wine, ma'am? That one be empty."

Jessica smiles, turns her attention to the neck of the wine bottle, and tenderly strokes it with the tips of her fingers. "No, Hattie. It's the only thing I've had enough of tonight."

Hattie stands silently waiting while Jessica's mind returns to her obsessive fantasies of sexual adventures.

Cordell walks on through the kitchen and steps out onto the back porch, where Rabbit is nervously pacing. When Rabbit turns around and sees Cordell, he drags his floppy hat off in a lighting reflex.

"Boss, I'ze shorely..."

In aggravation, Cordell holds up his hand for Rabbit to be silent. "Rabbit, it's late. All I want you to do is listen, and do what I tell you."

Rabbit nods his head, while rolling his hat in a twisted knot and busting at the seams to speak.

"I want you to wait right here for Benjie. He'll be in later tonight from up on the Moore place. Listen to me now! You tell him to look after the saddle horses for a few days while you're gone." Cordell reaches and takes Rabbit by the arm and looks him in the eye. "You got that Rabbit? I want him to tend the horses while you're gone with me."

Rabbit hesitates, and then asks, "Where we's goin', boss?"

Cordell turns and starts to walk off. "Never you mind that. Just hitch a wagon up in the morning and be at the mill before six, with Blue Rock."

"Yes sir. I gots it. At the mill befo' six with Blue Rock."

Cordell stops and turns back to Rabbit. "Oh, and bring your bedroll and a week's grain for Blue Rock."

Rabbit starts to walk off. "Yes sir. I..."

"Rabbit, where the hell you going? I said wait here for Benjie!"

Rabbit does a quick about-face and sits down on the porch. "Oh, yes sir, boss."

Cordell walks over to the hitching post and steps up onto his horse. When he rides back over to Rabbit, Helen walks out on the porch.

"Heard you tell Rabbit that y'all were leaving in the morning."

"We are. I am going over to Sherm Palmore's place and breeze Blue Rock against his mare. We'll just be a few days. You need anything, send Benjie after Paxton."

"We'll be okay."

"How's Bell?"

"Just worn out. Few days in bed, she'll be fine."

"The girls'll be here in the morning. Make sure she stays in bed, and they do the cleaning."

"Yes sir. You coming up for breakfast in the morning?"

Cordell turns to ride off. "Naw. We're leaving first light."

Helen stands on the porch watching her father ride into the shadowy darkness.

Cordell touches a spur to the big bay gelding, breaking him off into an easy lope down the moonlit field road. The cool November evening is settling in with a crisp edge that clears Cordell's head with every chilled breath. As his attention is drawn to the distant lights of the mill, his thoughts turn to Jolene. He feels a rush of passion that has only the blessings of his own heart, knowing it will never be sanctioned by God or by man. She has awakened his scarred soul, and he has no intention of returning to those feelings of hollow loneliness. He rides on with a hard-driven determination to live for today, with no questions for tomorrow.

CHAPTER SEVENTEEN

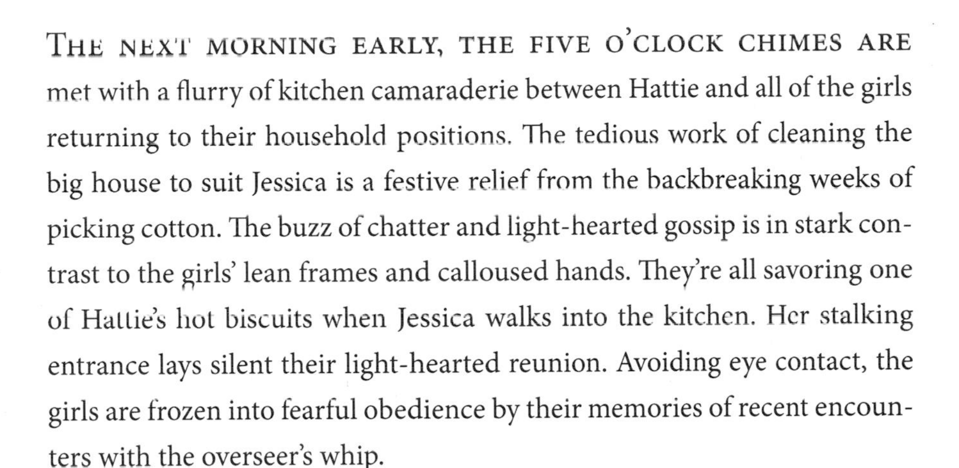

The next morning early, the five o'clock chimes are met with a flurry of kitchen camaraderie between Hattie and all of the girls returning to their household positions. The tedious work of cleaning the big house to suit Jessica is a festive relief from the backbreaking weeks of picking cotton. The buzz of chatter and light-hearted gossip is in stark contrast to the girls' lean frames and calloused hands. They're all savoring one of Hattie's hot biscuits when Jessica walks into the kitchen. Her stalking entrance lays silent their light-hearted reunion. Avoiding eye contact, the girls are frozen into fearful obedience by their memories of recent encounters with the overseer's whip.

Jessica asks, "What's going on here, Hattie? And where's Bell?"

Before Hattie can answer, Helen walks into the kitchen carrying a serving tray. She walks by her mother and places the tray on the counter behind the girls.

"Bell's in bed resting. I am managing the house until she's up."

"Well. If you're in charge, then you know these girls don't eat breakfast in this kitchen. EVER!"

Helen stands her ground, because her father made it clear that she would be in charge.

"They know that, but I told them they could. I mean, look at them. They're a bunch of scarecrows. Besides, this is not the cotton field."

Jessica points at Helen's dress with a mocking gesture. "Speaking of scare-crows, I think you should reconsider accompanying me to Charleston. You definitely could use some new dresses."

Helen smiles and avoids the bait. "I am fine, Mother."

Jessica prods. "But dear, I think you should look your best when you give Mr. Tanahill a send-off after the race."

"A send-off? And where would he be going?"

Jessica delights in the moment, knowing she has pushed Helen to take the bait. "Who cares?"

Helen knows exactly where her mother's conversation is going. "I guess I am missing your point here."

"Well, these are the cold hard facts of life, dear. Mr. Tanahill will lose the match, and that's absolute."

"I don't agree, but go ahead. Finish."

"When he can't honor the bet, I'll see to it that your father forgives the debt for a certain concession from Mr. Tanahill."

"Which is?"

"That he leaves the Carolinas. Without you! Never to be seen in these parts again."

"That's a great story, Mother, but it's not ever going to happen. Not ever."

"What's not going to happen? Him losing?"

"None of it. None of your fairy tale is going to come true."

"Don't be so cocky and sure of yourself."

"It's just a fact."

"Helen, that's pure damned delusional. Do you really believe that that nag of his will outrun Blue Rock?"

"I do. But the question is, how strongly do you believe Blue Rock will win? Strong enough to place a bet?"

Jessica laughs. "A bet? With you? I know you don't have any money. So what could you possibly wager?"

Helen smiles. "The one thing that you want most in life right now."

"Which is?"

Helen teases her mother. "Mr. Tanahill."

Jessica loses her smile. "Mr. Tanahill? Evidently you've thought this out, so let's hear it. I'm game."

Helen turns and looks her mother square in the eye. "If Mr. Tanahill wins the race, I alone select the men in my life, which will include Mr. Tanahill.

All of this will be with your blessings and without your interference, including whom I decide to marry."

"And if he loses?"

"Then you alone will select the men in my life."

"Plus who you marry?"

Helen extends her hand to shake in agreement. "Absolutely."

Jessica shakes Helen's hand and is overwhelmed with joy. In her excitement, she pulls Helen close and hugs her tightly. When she finally steps back and takes Helen by both hands, she can barely find her voice.

"Oh God, I've prayed for a miracle of some kind. I just pray, honey, that you don't get your heart broken over all this."

"You know, mother, that's the same exact prayer I have for you."

Jessica wipes the tears from her eyes. "Oh God, I have to go. They're probably waiting."

She starts from the kitchen, then abruptly turns and comes back to hug Helen again. "If I see something gorgeous, I'll buy it for you." She waves her arms in the air, hurrying out of the kitchen. "Hell, I'll buy you a dozen."

Helen smiles with thoughts of Sam and Journey running Blue Rock down and saving her. She turns to the girls who all stand in awe of what they've just heard.

"Hattie! Bacon and eggs for everyone—then let's get to work, girls. It's a good day."

Hattie goes to cooking and the gossipy chatter resumes.

Early that same morning, the barren cotton fields from tree line to tree line are covered in a ground hugging fog that shrouds the line of sight to barely one long step. The breaking sunrise is slowly burning the heavy gray veil down to a thin, cool mist that reveals a long line of wagons parked in front of the mill. Rabbit pulls up with Blue Rock in tow, just as the field crews finish tarping the wagons and hooking up the teams. He nods his head in recognition and speaks to Newella, who stands on the porch wrapped in her shawl and smoking a slender cigar.

"Mornin', ma'am."

Newella nods. "Mornin' Rabbit. Breakfast is long past, but I have a couple biscuits on the stove. You're welcome to 'em."

Rabbit sets the brake, hops down off of the wagon, and tips his hat as he walks by Newella. "Thank you, ma'am."

The sight of the stud takes her back to that disastrous race that destroyed her father and set her life on a course far removed from the social circles of her early childhood. She thumps the cigar into the road, draws the shawl tightly around her shoulders, and walks off of the porch, out to the stud. Newella stands there admiring the sleek gray stallion with not the slightest inkling of how much more he would impact her life. With an absence of malice in her heart, and content with the hand she's been dealt, Newella reaches out and gently strokes the horse's silvery mane. She's lost in memories of her father when she hears her name called.

"Newella! The boss wants to see 'ya."

Newella turns around just as Paxton walks by her and the stud. He heads on toward Slack, who is sitting on his horse over by the last wagon.

Newella hurries onto the porch. “My bags are on the wagon. I’ll be just a minute.”

Paxton comments casually over his shoulder, “No hurry. You ain’t goin.”

Newella stops and turns around. “What?”

Paxton ignores her and walks up to Slack. “When you get to the Moore Place, Benjie, put the repair lumber and tools in the old barn. Boss wants all the fields cleaned up and the repairs done to the house and barns first. I’ll be up in a day or so to check on you. Oh, and throw her bags off that last wagon.”

“Yes sir.” Slack turns, rides over to the wagon, and has the driver pitch Newella’s bags in the road.

Newella starts toward Paxton. “Damn it, Paxton! What the...?”

Paxton turns on her. “Them goddamn bags ain’t got legs. The boss is waitin’ on you. So you best get your ass in there! Now!”

Newella knows that something has changed her relationship with Paxton because he has treated her so roughly of late. It’s something deeper than his occasional jealousy, or the pain of a crippled step.

Paxton steps toward her. “You better get your sorry ass movin’, bitch. And I ain’t gonna tell ‘ya again.”

Newella turns and walks into the mill, totally consumed with worry. When she opens the door, Newella is startled to hear a loud, muffled voice echoing down the hall. Halfway to Cordell’s office, she realizes it’s Jolene, and then there is silence. Newella stops at the office door, hesitant to knock, when the door suddenly flies open to reveal a Jolene that Newella has never seen before.

Jolene pushes by her. "Careful. He's hatin' on women today." Jolene disappears down the hall.

A red-faced Cordell stands behind his desk with a haggard look—another thing that Newella has never seen before. He takes a deep breath, runs his hand through his hair, and sits down.

He motions to Newella. "Come in, Miss Rayburn, and shut the door."

Newella shuts the office door and walks forward, unsure of how she fits into all that has unfolded in the last few minutes. Cordell pauses and his continued silence pushes on Newella's nerves. If she's going to lose her job, she means to have it out and be on her way.

"If I am being dismissed sir, I would like to know why before I leave."

Cordell shakes his head in disbelief. "God almighty, this isn't my day. It's anything but that, Miss Rayburn. I want you to move up here and live at the mill, plus I am giving you a raise. You have a problem with any of that?"

Newella stands there relieved for many reasons. "No sir. No problem. Just one question, why?"

"Won't be much going on around here for the winter. I don't want Jolene here by herself. Plus, I know about your, er, other job, so maybe the raise will let you cut back on some of that."

"Thank you, sir," Newella answers, not the least bit embarrassed by Cordell's knowledge of her work with Miss Rita.

Cordell gets up from his desk, walks over and collects his hat and coat, and says, "I feel better knowing you'll be around here."

"I'll look after her, sir."

Cordell walks out the mill and over to the hitching post where his horse is tied. When he steps up onto the horse and turns around, he finds Jolene and Newella standing side-by-side on the porch. Jolene's smile speaks her forgiveness louder than words ever could.

Cordell finally smiles and nods in respect. "Ladies."

He turns and rides off, followed by Rabbit and the stud.

Watching Cordell ride off, Jolene reaches over and takes hold of Newella's hand. The tension in her grip increases as Cordell disappears from her sight.

Newella tries to reassure her. "He'll be okay."

With a tear rolling down her cheek, she looks down at the ground and shakes her head. "No he won't. Doctor down in Charleston done told 'im dat liquor's killin' 'im. He passed out in my bed last night. And when I said sumpin' this mornin' 'bout it, he said he done had one naggin' bitch in his life, and he didn't need two. Dats when you came in."

Out of the corner of her eye, Newella sees Paxton walking back up from the barn. She turns to Jolene with a definite concern in her voice.

"Go on in the mill. I've something to take care of."

Jolene looks over Newella's shoulder and sees Paxton carrying a whip, walking toward them.

"No, I am goin' to stay."

"Don't. It'll just make it worse."

Jolene turns and walks into the mill just as Paxton walks up behind Newella. She turns around to face him with blood in her eyes, determined to stand her ground, whatever his problem.

"You a little on the prod this morning, aren't you?"

"Pretty much. I..."

Newella cuts him off. "If it has anything to do with me, just cut to it."

Paxton steps up in her face. "One of my men was leaving Rita's this morning and seen Tanahill riding off. You sent 'im around us, down that cut to Rita's, didn't you?"

Newella stands looking eye-to-eye with Paxton. "Anything else hung in your neck?"

Paxton leans in with hate dripping from his eyes. "Word around Rita's is that you fucked a nigger. That TRUE?"

Newella doesn't give any ground. "None of that's any of your business. Especially who I fuck!"

"We both know I can't right now. But you know this, I owe you an ass whipping, and I will pay up. You can count on it."

"That won't come to pass, because I'll fucking kill you before I let that happen. That's what you can count on, Paxton."

The creator endowed Newella with a unique gift, one that her present occupation has sharpened to a keen edge. She has come to trust her uncanny ability to know what she doesn't know. Her intuitive judgment is validated again when Paxton's cowardly nature forces him to take a step back.

He shakes the rolled up whip at Newella. "You have your shit moved out before I get home tonight."

She stands unflinchingly still, with a stoic stare that forces Paxton to turn and walk away, cussing violently under his breath.

Late the next day, the evening sun slips behind a crystal horizon, leaving a rear guard of light to temporarily cover its westerly retreat. With less than a mile to go, Sam pushes his bone weary mount on through the encircling darkness. His urgency to get home has left both the horse and himself at the rock bottom of their endurance. When Sam rides up to the barn, the open doors are a dark silhouette against the failing light. He steps down and stomps his numb feet before starting into the barn to find a lantern. With the gelding fed and put up for the night, Sam walks out of the barn and heads for the bunkhouse, when he hears his mother speak to him.

"You not coming in?"

He turns and walks back toward the back porch where she's sitting.

"I didn't see anybody moving about. So I figured y'all had turned in early."

"Nobody here but me. Your paw and Little Jim are picking up a load of freight that goes across the Cumberland."

Sam walks up on the porch and sits down in a rocker by his mother. There's definitely a stiffness in his mother's tone. It's one he knows all too well, a tone she takes when she has something weighing on her mind. The subject is usually preceded by an uncomfortable rocking silence, which is currently underway. Sam sits and waits, because he knows his father told her about the match race with Cordell. She lives by the Book, and will never give her blessing to gambling in any fashion. Sam wishes there was another way around Cordell to Helen, but the match is the only way.

"The rider who delivered that order to your paw came by way of Sapling Grove."

Sam is totally caught off guard and confused about her mention of Sapling Grove. His fight with Paxton was long back in the spring, and it has never been discussed since by his mother or his father.

"Sapling Grove? I hope you're not still worrying on that fight. Because there's no need."

"That fight ain't my worry. Seems Dancy Higgins is close to having a young 'en, and she ain't got a husband."

It hits Sam like a bolt of lightning on a clear day. "A baby?"

The effect on Sam and the tone of his voice leaves him no defense of his mother's next question.

"Is it yours?"

Sam sits silent, with his mind lost in thoughts of those nights in his wagon. When she came to his bed, she asked for nothing past that moment in time they were together. His continued silence answers the question more than any spoken word.

Mary Beth stands up. "I am going in. I guess you need a spell to figure on this."

She walks over behind Sam and places her hand on his shoulder. "The Lord's the best place to start, son."

Sam reaches up and places his hand on hers. "Yes ma'am."

Mary Beth walks on into the house "Goodnight, son."

The next morning early, by the light of a lantern, Sam is saddling a horse in front of the tack room. He is just finishing tying his bedroll and slicker behind the saddle when his father walks up on the opposite side of the horse. Sam pauses for a moment, and then goes to tightening the cinch on the saddle.

"It's three in the morning, son. Where are you going?"

Sam, without looking up, answers. "You know where I am going, Paw."

"But what about the race?"

"I am committed to it. I'll be back in time to leave for Camden. Have Little Jim work Journey while I am gone. Work him hard a day, light a day, rest a day, and then start all over. He knows how."

"Son, you'll have to ride day and night to make it back for that race."

"No I won't. I am going over the mountains."

"That's tough traveling this time of the year. You know that."

"Got no choice, Paw. And I am not putting this off. Not for one day."

"I know you're struggling with all this. I just wish I could help you."

Sam turns to his father. "You already have, Paw. You taught me to always do what's right. That's what I am going to do all the way around. By Dancy and everyone else."

Sam steps up onto the horse. "Tell Maw to keep me in her prayers."

Owen extends his hand to Sam. "You know she does that, every day."

Sam shakes his father's hand and rides out of the barn into the cold darkness, headed for Sapling Grove and Dancy.

Later that same day, just after noon, Sorrel is doing a precarious balancing act, walking up a flight of stairs with an arm load of packages that he strains to see around. Jessica stands at the top of the landing with her parasol resting on her shoulder, nervously spinning it round and round. Sorrel's massive feet carefully search for one step at a time, dreading Jessica's wrath should even one package fall from his grip. When he finally reaches the top, beads of sweat from the stressful climb are glistening on his forehead. Aggravated with Sorrel's slow progress, Jessica turns around and walks down the balcony to the door of her room.

She aggressively digs through her purse for the room key. "I swear, Sorrel. You move slower than old Aunt Hattie!"

"Yes ma'am, dat be a fact."

Jessica finally opens the door and walks into the room followed by Sorrel. She walks straight to the wine decanter, ignoring Sorrel while she pours herself a large glass of wine. With no thought of savoring the taste, Jessica turns the glass up and drains it dry in one long drink. The ache in Sorrel's arms from hours of carrying packages is beyond measure. His arms begin to tremble and tie in knots, begging for relief.

Sorrel is near collapse. "Ma'am?"

Jessica pours another glass of wine and doesn't turn around. "Put them over there on the couch, and don't drop anything."

"Yes ma'am." Sorrel slowly kneels down on one knee, and gently places the packages on one end of the couch.

Jessica downs the second drink in the same fashion as the first, and follows it with a deep breath of satisfaction. She refills the glass and dismisses Sorrel without ever turning around.

"Go on down to the stable. I'll send for you if I need you. Oh, and have that house girl, Sweetie, come up here and help me with this dress."

"Yes ma'am."

Sorrel turns and walks out, glad to be loose from her clutches. The trip down to Charleston with Jessica has been a minute-by-minute torturous experience. Sorrel can't remember a time since Jessica's first day at Shannon Hill that she hasn't forced the world to revolve around her every whim. If one of her whims ever got derailed, the wrath of God was preferable to being the guilty party.

Jessica takes her glass of wine, then walks over and sits down on the couch next to her packages. She barely gets comfortable and starts to relax before there's a knock on the door.

"Come in."

The door doesn't open, and her earlier aggravation with Sorrel flares up again when the second knock sounds at the door. Jessica takes a sip of wine. She has no intention of getting up for a house girl too stupid to open a door. When the third knock rattles the door, it sends Jessica flying off the couch in a huff.

"I said come..."

Jessica pauses mid-sentence when she jerks open the door to reveal a dapperly dressed Ike Murphy, holding a bouquet of flowers and a bottle of wine.

Ike smiles and slightly raises his hands. "I'd remove my hat, my lady, but as you can see…"

Jessica stands there mesmerized by the sight and smell of Ike while her body and mind experience a sudden emotional shift. Her hot temper instantly falls prey to a hungry sexual need that takes no prisoners. Her breath comes short with anticipation, and she is plainly defenseless—completely vulnerable to his illicit intentions.

Jessica's continued silence leaves Ike feeling a little uneasy given some of their volatile past rendezvous. Under normal circumstances, he would press the issue after cornering a woman of his desire alone and in private. But in dealing with the tigress, there is no such thing as a normal set of circumstances. With a fading smile, and a serious feeling of social overreach, Ike looks as if he's about to excuse himself when she touches his arm.

With mischief twinkling in her eyes, Jessica asks, "Did you knock on the wrong door, Mr. Murphy, or is all that for me?"

Ike feels transparent as glass under her persistent gaze. He is passionately drawn to her, but her controlling temperament is always in force. Even when he is on top of her in bed, the sex becomes more of a contest to her than a source of pleasure. Ike pulls his mind back to his objective and bows, as southern etiquette requires when in the presence of the fairer sex.

"Make no mistake. My heart knew exactly what door to knock on."

Jessica loves a courtier, especially a handsome one. "Come in, Mr. Murphy. My life could use some gallantry today."

When Ike walks by Jessica, she reaches for the bottle of wine. "Here, give me that."

She glances at the vintage of the bottle while shutting the door. When Ike hears it lock, he immediately turns around and removes his hat. Jessica walks by him and places the bottle of wine next to the near-empty decanter. The sexual tension in the room is escalating like an epidemic fever with no cure.

Anxious to be free of the flowers, Ike looks around the room. "Where should I put these?"

"Here, give them to me."

Jessica takes the flowers and places them in a vase by the bed. She adjusts the flowers and steps back, admiring their color. She feels Ike's hyper-vigilance, which only heightens her sexual arousal. Her coy masking of her lustful needs is taking a toll on whatever confidence locking the door had given him.

Ike feels compelled to relinquish his afternoon quest and leave. "My apologizes for my unannounced visit. You were definitely expecting someone else."

"Matter of fact, I was. I was expecting a house girl to help me with my dress. But I seriously hope I don't need her now."

Jessica reaches behind her head and gathers up the blond ringlets that obscure the top buttons of her dress. She smiles seductively, bows her head slightly in submission, and turns her back to Ike.

"Mr. Murphy, would you be ever so kind?"

Her soft, honeyed whisper spins a fantasy of erotic pleasure through his mind that instantly brings him under her spell. When he steps up behind her and touches that first button on her dress, his hands fumble like those of an inexperienced youth. With a few, tender words, she encourages him,

"You've been here before, so take your time. For once, we don't have to hurry. It's okay, just relax."

When the last button nimbly slips from Ike's fingers, he leans in, kissing her lightly on the back of her neck. Jessica releases her hair, allowing him to gently pull her dress and petticoat straps down off of her shoulders. The dress and petticoats fall away to the floor, leaving her standing there in her lace-trimmed silk underwear. From behind her, Ike slides his hands across her round hips and up her sides until he gently cups her beautiful, full breasts, pulling her to him. With a gentle touch, his fingers teasingly stroke the ends of her upright nipples. She lays her head back onto his chest, arches her back, and loses herself in an erotic fantasy. The moans that escape her lips are short-lived, as Jessica reaches around behind her and rubs Ike's crotch. He senses something is wrong when Jessica falls silent, and her body becomes rigid.

"Is there something wrong?"

"I don't think you're ready."

Ike kisses her softly on the side of her neck. "Don't let that worry you."

When he tries to pull her silk underwear down, she steps away from him and turns around.

Jessica's mood takes a quick change. "Then you're not, are you?"

Ike begins taking his shirt off. "It's nothing a little help won't cure."

Jessica picks up her dress and petticoats and holds them in front of her. "Like what kind of help?"

With his shirt unbuttoned, Ike reaches for her and she takes a quickstep back. "Well. You have been down there before."

Ike's matter-of-fact cockiness is a little too much for Jessica. "I have. And I did enjoy it." Jessica drops the dress, steps into her petticoats and pulls the straps over her shoulders. "But I've never had a limber cock in my mouth. And I never will, Mr. Murphy!"

Ike's cockiness is replaced with a pleading tone that only increases Jessica's irritation. "Come on Jess, let's get in bed. It'll be okay. You'll see."

"I've told you before not to call me that!"

"Okay. What can I do here to make things better? Tell me."

Jessica finishes getting dressed and looks up at Ike. "I'll tell you what you can do. You can start by stripping them pants off and showing me you're ready. If you are, then I am getting in bed. If not, you're going out the door."

Ike works to control his anger. "What the hell is going on here? We've waited three whole days coming down here to be together, and now this. Why are you so mad?"

"That's a stupid question! Why am I so mad? Because you've had your hands all over me, and you're limp. Then to top all that off, you want me to suck that son of a bitch. I think you have me confused with that kitchen whore that's been warming your bed."

"Just listen a minute..."

"No, you listen. If you had any kind of feelings for me at all, we wouldn't be having this conversation."

"That's not the truth, and you know it."

"The only thing I know, Mr. Murphy, is that you still have those pants on."

Jessica walks to the door and opens it. "I think that in itself says everything. Good day, Mr. Murphy."

Ike picks up his hat and coat and silently walks out. When Jessica shuts the door behind him, the closing door leaves another painful scar deep within her heart. She walks over to the decanter, pours herself a glass of wine, and returns to the couch.

Later that night, long past the hour that decent folks have stopped moving about in Charleston, Sweetie has just finished entertaining Sorrel up in the hay loft at O'Malley's Livery Stable. Sweetie is just a girl, barely past her teens, but with the tall, lean build of a blacksmith in his prime. She pulls her dress over her head and starts buttoning it up the front when Sorrel reaches over and runs his hand down the inside of her thigh.

"What you doin', girl?"

Sweetie pushes Sorrel's hand away and continues to button her dress. "I's gots to go. It be long pass my time to be in."

"Come on, now. Just stay a bit longer."

"I can't. My Missy ain't gonna be happy wit me now."

"Just once more. Dat's all. Den you can go."

"I swear you some man, Mr. Sorrel. I bet your Missy wishes her beau was like you."

Sorrel sits up. "What beau you talkin' bout?"

"Why Mr. Ike. Dat be her beau."

"Girl, why you sayin' dat?"

"Cause I seen him all dressed up in his sportin' clothes, goin' into her room with flowers and a bottle of liquor."

"Dat don't make him a beau."

Sweetie smiles. "It do when she let him get her naked."

"Girl! Tell me what you know to be truth, and not any silly gossip."

"Well, right after you told me Miss Jessica wanted me, I see Mr. Ike goin' up the stairs with liquor and flowers. So I gives him a minute, then I sneaks up to her door and listened. They was goin' at it hot till Miss Jessica found out he was limp."

"He was limp?"

Sweetie stands up and straightens her dress. "Yes sir, limp. Dats when all hell happened."

"What kinda hell? Mr. Ike got mean with her?"

"No sir. All Mr. Ike wanted was her to suck his limp pecker. Dats when she got really mean."

"Mean how?"

"I ain't sure. Cause when she told 'im to leave, I took off."

Sorrel suddenly gets a little nervous. "After Mr. Ike left. Did 'ya ever go back like you was told?"

"I did. But she wouldn't open the door. I got down like before and listened on her door. She was cryin' sumpin' awful."

Sorrel lays back in the hay. He can find no way of ever imagining that Jessica could shed one tear over anyone or anything. If she ever has, Sorrel is sure there is not one witness to it on God's Earth.

Sweetie walks over to the loft ladder, and Sorrel realizes she's leaving.

He raises up on one elbow. "You comin' back tomorrow night?"

"If I ain't too sore."

"I done seen your Missy. She ain't the whippin' kind."

Sweetie starts climbing down the ladder, then stops. "I ain't talkin' bout my Missy soren' me up. I'm talkin' bout the rollin' in the hay you jest give me."

Sweetie disappears down the ladder. "Night, big man."

Sorrel smiles and lays back down in the hay. "Limp. Ain't that jest somethin'?"

CHAPTER EIGHTEEN

THE MOON'S LAST QUARTER HANGS HIGH IN THE MIDST OF A glittering gallery of stars. The lively banjo and fiddle tunes that carry off across the valley only add to a majestic evening. Sam stops his horse at the edge of Sapling Grove and sits for a moment, breathing in the music that speaks to his mountain heritage. Exhausted and numb from the endless hours of saddle-bound travel of the last three days, Sam pushes on, bound by a personal sense of responsibility and a sense that his family's honor is at stake.

When he rides up to the Higgins House, he pauses in the saddle, listening to the uproarious barn dance that's going on at the far end of town. Maw Higgins speaks to him from the swing on the darkened front porch.

"My Dancy loved to dance. She'd stay till the last song played, then dance all the way home, humming to herself."

Maw's words carry an unspoken message of a heart that's lost its last ray of warm sunshine.

Sam can hear the struggle in her voice as she holds back her tears. "You're two days late, Sam. I buried your son with his mother this past Sunday morning."

The words, "buried your son with his mother," send a storm that rages through his heart with a pain more terrible than any he has ever known. With tears rolling across a week of rough beard, Sam squeezes the saddle horn with both hands, trying to hold his balance until he can muster the strength to step down.

Sam clears his throat, looking for the right way to express his thoughts, "Why didn't she send me word?"

"She knew you'd come, but it wouldn't be because of her. She said she couldn't bear having you around, knowing your heart didn't belong to her."

"I would've been here sooner, Maw, if I had just known."

"She knew that too, but it's all done, Sam. There's no sense in letting it be a burden to you. Dancy made her own choices in life, not you or me. From the nights she told me she was going to spend with you, to having her baby and living by herself. She was happy with what life had given her, and she never grieved over what it denied her. She told me to tell you that, with the last breath of life in her body."

Sam steps down from the horse and holds on to the saddle horn until he can find the strength to walk up onto that porch and face Maw. When he finally approaches her, his hat in his hand, Maw pats the seat of the swing next to her.

"Come sit with me."

Sam sits down by her, at a loss for what to say or do next. Side-by-side, they are united in a common grief. Only the passing of years will heal the empty space Dancy's passing has left in their hearts. Maw gently reaches over and touches Sam's hand.

"She loved you so."

Sam's voice almost fails. "I know."

Maw stands up, wipes the tears from her eyes with her apron, and tries to smile. "Course, we've all loved you, Sam. I guess that's never been a doubt. Has it?"

Sam takes a deep breath, grits his teeth, and pushes back on the tears that well up in his eyes.

"No ma'am, it hasn't."

"Well, I am going in and have Mr. Bill get you a room ready. If you're hungry, I'll get you something."

"No need. I doubt I can rest or eat. I am just going to sit here a spell, if that's okay."

"I understand. I sat there the whole first night they were gone." Maw turns to walk into the house, then pauses and says, "Your room is the first door at the head of the stairs when you have a mind."

"Yes ma'am."

"Sam, I know you probably haven't thought about it. But they're both buried in the cemetery up on the north road."

Sam nods. "Thanks Maw."

Sam sits staring off into the night, paralyzed with rage and searching every corner of his mind for a reason why. Even though he knows all of this is God's will, it doesn't release him from the burden of guilt that weighs heavy on his heart.

Early the next morning, Sam's horse stands saddled and tied to the hitching rail in front of the North Road cemetery. Off down the way, under an ancient oak, Sam is kneeling down beside two graves with his hat in his hand, saying his goodbyes in a hushed tone. When Maw walks up behind him, she can see that the night has taken a brutal toll.

"Folks said I should have buried him in her arms. But I couldn't do it. She gave him a name long before he was born. So I thought it fit and proper that he had his own marker."

Sam looks up at her. "How did she know it was a boy?"

Maw smiles. "She didn't. It was Samuel if a boy and Samantha if a girl. Either way it was Sam."

Sam stands up and points to his son's marker. "I didn't get here in time to do right by his maw, but I can by him. I'd be obliged, with your permission, if you'd change his marker to read Samuel Tanahill instead of Samuel Higgins."

Maw walks over and puts her arm around Sam. "I know they would both like that."

They stand there in silence, lost in their memories and grief.

Sam knows it's time to leave. "Before I go, I..."

Maw turns to Sam with tears in her eyes. "No need, son. You're a good man, Sam Tanahill, and your coming here shows it." She points to the cemetery gate. "But your life is out there. And she'd want you to go on and live it."

Sam nods his head in agreement. He looks over at Dancy and Samuel one last time before he turns and walks to his horse. When he steps up, he turns to Maw and touches the brim of his hat in respect before riding off.

That same day, a cool northwesterly breeze gently ripples through the gray-bearded oaks that ring Shannon Hill. The noonday beams of radiant sunlight have done little to warm a breeze bent on holding its allegiance to a winter that has command of the season. Petal walks through the canyons of laden clotheslines, pulling her fingertip across the chilled linens, searching for a place to hang her next basket of fresh wash. When she reaches the end of a line, she happens to glance across the fields to the idle mill. There, standing tied to a wagon parked at the office door, are Blue Rock and a saddle horse. When she shades her eyes, she sees someone sitting on the wagon seat. She shrugs off her concern and heads on to the house.

The tattered sleeves of Helen's old denim shirt are as unruly as the long frayed shirttail that hangs down below the pockets of her threadbare pants. Her scuffed up Sunday shoes are exposed to the world by a pair of baggy pants that once reached past the heel of her shoes. Helen rolls up her sleeves for the hundredth time and resumes scrubbing dirty laundry with the house girls on the back porch. When Petal walks up and sets the basket of wet clothes on the edge of the porch, Helen stands up straight, wipes her hands on the tail of the shirt, and arches her back trying to find some relief for her tired muscles.

She looks over at Petal. "They're still not dry?"

"No ma'am. But dat breezy wind is helpin'. Just a bit mo and some of 'em be ready."

Helen puts her hands on her hips and arches her back again. This past week of "being Bell" has left her with a humbling soreness born of four o'clock mornings and of days filled with endless drudgery. She resumes vigorously scrubbing a half-washed shirt she had already started.

"Probably won't happen, girls. But I'd like to get this wash done and put up before everyone gets home tomorrow."

"No need to fret on dat, 'cause Mr. Cordell done back."

Helen stops scrubbing. "He's home?"

Petal points toward the mill. "I ain't seen him, but dat gray hoss of his be tied to a wagon over at the mill."

Helen dries her hands on her shirttail and walks off of the porch so she can see down to the mill. When she sees Cordell's saddle horse tied next to Blue Rock, she instantly knows something is dreadfully wrong, because he would never allow another horse anywhere near his prized stallion. Helen's gut reflex sends her sprinting across the cotton field at a breakneck pace. Her breath is rising in clouds of swirling gray steam as she slams into the office door. She shoulders past the door and bursts into Cordell's room.

Jolene is sitting on the edge of his bed. She stands up immediately, moving out of Helen's way. "Ma'am."

Helen has never seen her father sick a day in her life, and her mind is fixated on his sudden infirmity. She loses herself in worry for a moment, and doesn't come back to reality until Cordell smiles and reaches out to her.

"From the look on your face," he says, "I'd say I may be dead."

Helen doesn't see the humor. "What's the matter?"

Cordell continues to smile. "Just feeling a mite down. It'll pass."

"I'd say more than a mite." She points toward the wagon outside.

"There's a bed in the back of that wagon! So what's wrong with you?"

Newella, Rabbit, and Jolene all stand around avoiding any kind of eye contact with Helen. Her concern has dispensed with all of her patience, and she presses her father intensely for answers.

"Are you going to answer me?"

Cordell looks to Jolene. "Y'all give us a minute."

When the room has cleared, Helen looks at her father and asks again, "Well?"

"It's just a minor inconvenience. Like I told you. It'll pass."

"What'll pass? Please answer me."

Cordell looks off. "At times... I can't... pee, and it hurts like hell to ride a horse."

"Have you discussed this with the doctor?"

"Yeah. He says it's just part of a man getting old. Nothing he can do."

Cordell's smile does little to console Helen. "Okay. Let's uh... let's get you back in the wagon and up to the house."

Cordell knew this was coming when she burst into his room.

"There's no need. I'll be fit and upright come morning. So let's just stop all the fuss, and everyone go back about their business."

Helen is entirely displeased. "Don't be so difficult. You know it's the best thing."

"Maybe it is, but I am okay here. If I have any problems, I'll send Jolene for you. I promise."

Helen knows she'll not change his mind, so she grudgingly nods her head.

"Okay, but on one condition."

Cordell looks over at the wall and pauses. "What?"

"No more drinking until you're well."

Cordell reaches out to Helen. She takes his hand and leans down, kissing him on the forehead. Helen stands up, still holding his hand, and smiles.

"Okay. Now send Jolene in here when you leave."

"I'll be here early in the morning to check on you."

"I don't doubt it."

Helen walks back outside with an entirely new perspective on the uncertainty of life and the passing of time. In the span of just a few short weeks, two cataclysmic events have struck Helen's life, shaking not only her world, but her whole universe. The first being Sam Tanahill coming into her life, a fact that quickly changed her from a dreamy young girl with vague aspirations into a woman with a considered and specific vision for her future. And now, this second event, which has left her with the heart breaking reality that her father is not an immortal god sent from heaven. He is but a man.

When Helen steps into the hallway, Newella, Jolene, and Rabbit all have their heads hung down as if there's a burial about to take place.

"He wants to stay down here, and I agreed. But I want y'all to do this. If he has any problems, one of y'all come and get me."

Newella speaks first. "We will."

Helen reaches out to Jolene and Newella, grabbing each of their hands in hers. "Thank you." She turns to Jolene and says, "He wants to see you."

"Yes ma'am."

Helen walks by Newella and Jolene. "Rabbit, I am going to ride the saddle horse back to the house. When you finish putting Blue Rock up, come back and get him. Oh, and what's Willie T doing here?"

Helen's snappy orders cause Rabbit to stutter. "He's uh. Mister uh..."

Helen walks by him. "He's riding Blue Rock in the match?"

Rabbit smiles as he follows Helen out the door. "Yes ma'am. Mr. Sherm lent 'im, uh... lent Willie T to uh... Mr. Cordell."

Helen walks on out to the wagon, unties Cordell's horse, and steps up. "Willie, you go on and stay with Rabbit."

"Yes ma'am."

Rabbit climbs up on the wagon, mumbling under his breath.

"And Rabbit, quit that God awful fretting and get on."

Rabbit picks up the lines and clucks to the mules. "Yes ma'am."

Helen wheels the horse around and strikes a lope out across the cotton fields, headed for home. She's barely into the field when the knot in her stomach doubles in size at the sight of her mother's carriage turning into the back driveway. Helen reins the horse up to an easy walk. She has no desire to stumble into another hate-driven conflict between her parents. Their relationship is an abyss that hasn't one single emotional bridge left to cross after so many years of escalating bitterness and animosity.

When Sorrel reins the team up, Jessica stands up to get out but stumbles over an empty wine bottle. She cusses and angrily kicks at the bottle, causing her to stagger forward and fall headlong out of the carriage door. Her scream is cut short when a force stops her body in midair. It takes her several seconds to regain her bearings and realize that the force is Sorrel's massive arms. The fright fades, but embarrassment consumes her when she looks up to see that the girls on the back porch are all ducking their heads and going back to work. She shoves her way out of Sorrel's arms, and he is only too glad to set her down. Jessica, straightening her dress, just happens to look around when Rabbit drives by with Blue Rock.

Jessica turns back to the girls. "Where is Mr. Meyers?"

"He be..."

Helen rides around the corner of the house. "He's down at the mill."

"That's not a surprise." Sorrel walks by her balancing an armload of packages. "Hattie! You girls get down here and help Sorrel."

"Yes ma'am."

Helen rides up to the hitching post, steps off of the horse, and ties him up.

Jessica shakes her head as Helen approaches. "Why on God's Earth do you persist in wearing those horrible clothes?"

"Just so you know, he's sick and in bed."

"As in how sick? Too sick to go to Camden?"

"I don't really know."

"What do you mean, you don't know?"

"Mother! I don't know."

"Well! What's the matter with him? Do you know that?"

Sorrel and the girls are finished, and are waiting on Jessica's next orders.

"Hattie, y'all get back to the wash. We need to get finished."

"Yes ma'am."

Helen turns back to her mother. "He borrowed Willie T. from Sherm Palmore to ride Blue Rock. So it'd be my guess that he's still going, Mother."

"That's good to know. Because I didn't buy "us" all those new dresses to just wear them to church."

Helen walks up onto the back porch and rolls her sleeves up. "Well, when you go check on him, ask him yourself just to make sure."

"Why didn't he come to the house, if he's that sick?"

"That's another question for him."

"What did I miss here? Why the attitude?"

"Mother, I have work to do. If you say I have an attitude... then I apologize."

"You know what, I am going down there." Jessica walks over and gets back into the carriage. "Sorrel."

Sorrel hustles back up on the driver's seat and picks up the reins. "Yes ma'am."

Sorrel swings the team around the circle drive and heads for the mill.

Jolene is coming out of the kitchen at the far end of the hall with a glass of water when Jessica walks through the front door of the mill. The unexpected encounter stops both women dead still. The pause is short-lived, and the neutral space between the two begins to flood rapidly like angry seawater rushing into a sinking ship. The two women glare at each other with complete disrespect. Each would rather perish than retreat to neutral corners. They advance, closing the distance between them until they stand face-to-face at Cordell's door. When Jessica notices the leather string around Jolene's neck, the silver cross flashes to her mind. She reaches down and slowly pulls on the thong until the cross rises above the neckline of Jolene's dress. Jessica looks into Jolene's eyes, stunned and searching for a reaction of some sort.

Jolene speaks without ever breaking eye contact with Jessica. "If you take it, I won't lie to 'im."

Jessica turns the thong loose. "I want you to understand something. You're not getting off of this place alive. When he's gone, I am giving you to the overseers, right before I have you peeled to death under the whip."

Jolene opens the door, steps in front of Jessica, and walks over to Cordell. She places the glass of water on his bedside table and steps back.

"Will there be anything else?"

"Not right now. Thank you, Jolene."

Jolene turns around and exchanges one more caustic look with Jessica before walking out.

Jessica directs her, "Be sure to close the door on your way out. He's been exposed to enough filth."

Jolene walks out and leaves the door standing wide open. Seething with an anger that crushes all reason, Jessica walks over and closes the door.

"I guess complaining about that bitch is useless."

"I am feeling better. Thanks for asking."

"I don't deserve that sarcasm."

"Then what do you deserve?"

"I would think the respect of every nigger on this place. Even the ones you're fucking!"

"You know, the best crop we've raised around here lately is sin. So don't act like you don't have any dirt under your fingernails."

"Cordell, are we going to Camden or not?"

"Why wouldn't we? This little flare up doesn't change anything."

"Being down in bed isn't a little flare up. And Doc Wilson warned you."

"Careful with that touch of concern. Folks may get the wrong idea about you."

"Given all of the circumstances, I am trying."

"From what I heard outside of that door earlier, I'd say she's taken on a high priority with you."

Jessica points to the glass of water. "Well, that's an improvement over sour mash."

"If anything happens to her. I'll do worse than peel you with a whip."

Jessica pauses, then says, "It's just hard to ignore it when you make no effort to be discrete."

"You think a cabin in the woods and hotel rooms in the city are being discrete?"

Jessica hesitates. "Then you know?"

Cordell snaps. "Of course I do! Every place! Every time!"

Jessica takes a deep breath. "Then what do you want me to do?"

"I want you to go home and start packing."

"Packing? As in moving?"

"As in we're leaving for Camden in four days. I'll be home tomorrow when I am up and around."

"Cordell, I..."

Cordell cuts her off again. "Jessica. We went our separate ways a long time ago. Let's quit trying to get even with each other for it."

"I am not sure where this leaves us. But it does change things."

"You think mere facts change people? Don't be a fool. Needs drive people, and that includes the both of us."

"Honestly, Cordell, deep down I don't think I owe you an apology, given all the circumstances."

"There's that damn word again, 'circumstances'. Well let me tell you about those circumstances. They are like a bastard child that shows up on your doorstep. You better get used to it, because it's not going away."

Jessica walks to the door and opens it. "A bastard child. That's one of the circumstances I am referring to."

Jessica walks out of the door and Cordell reaches for his glass of water. He takes one drink and spits it out into the spittoon beside his bed.

"Jolene!" He spits again. "Goddamn water! Jolene, bring me a drink of sour mash!"

He lays back in the bed with nothing on his mind except winning the coming match between Blue Rock and Journey.

In the early hours of the next morning Jessica softly walks down the hall at the main house that leads to Petal and Switch's room. Upon reaching their door Jessica turns the doorknob one click at a time until the noisy latch comes free. When she gently pushes on the door, the dry hinges unleash a range of deafening creaks. With one hand keeping a chokehold on the doorknob and the other raising a flickering candle, Jessica methodically inches the door open enough for her to turn sideways and step into the room.

The foyer clock is announcing the arrival of the three a.m. hour when she steps by the traitorous door and raises the candle above her head, sending a spray of light across the small room. Both beds are freshly disturbed, but the windowless room stands silent and empty with no hint as to why. Jessica walks up to one of the rumpled beds and stands there for a moment, thinking. When she turns around to walk away, a noise down around her feet sends her straight into the air. She finally catches her breath and turns around, lowering the candle light in search of the reason for her near death experience.

Petal pokes her head out from under the bed into the light. "It jest be me and Switch, Missy."

Jessica steps back. "God almighty! Y'all get out from under there NOW! Come on, get out!"

Petal and Switch are "yes ma'am-ing" like a two-girl choir when they crawl out and stand at attention in front of Jessica, holding hands and on the verge of tears. Their fear of Jessica surpasses all of the ghosts that nightly roam Shannon Hill combined, at least in their minds.

Jessica pauses for a minute trying to collect her thoughts. "What the hell are you girls doing under the bed?"

"We was..."

Jessica holds up her hand. "That's a foolish question. I know what you were doing. You were hiding... and it's okay."

"We didn't mean no fright, ma'am!"

Petal chimes in. "No, we didn't! No ma'am! None! None at all!"

"Girls! I know! Now listen to me."

Jessica pulls a note out of her pocket and hands it to Petal. "I want this note delivered to Mr. Ike."

Petal's eyes get big. "When, Missy?"

"Right now. Before it gets light."

Petal starts to cry. "Oh Missy! In the dark, right now?"

"Okay. Switch you go with her."

Switch is just as scared as Petal, and says, "Oh ma'am. My eyes has a fright of darkness."

"If y'all don't get gone, I'll give you some fright. Now get dressed!"

The yes ma'am choir repeats their refrain as they scramble to get out of their nightshirts and into their clothes.

"Don't give that note to anyone but Mr. Ike. If he's not home, bring it back to me. Understand?"

The girls sing one last chorus of yes ma'ams before Jessica walks out of the room.

Later that same morning, the legions of Shannon Hill roosters are serving notice that the coming sunrise will arrive within the hour. Newella is sitting on the back porch of the mill kitchen, rocking and listening to the crowing contest, when Jolene, still wearing her nightgown, busts out of the back door on a dead run. She continues on to the far end of the porch and breaks over the railing, throwing up. When she finishes, she looks around to see Newella sitting at the other end of the porch, smiling.

Jolene wipes her mouth with the corner of her nightgown and says, "It ain't funny, Newella."

"I know it's not. Fact is, I just finished throwing up myself."

Jolene straightens up and rubs her stomach. "You with child, too?"

"I am." She points to a bucket of water with a dipper in it. "That water is fresh and cool. It'll settle your stomach."

Jolene walks over, picks up the dipper, and takes a sip. "Who's your baby's daddy?"

"Well it's not your baby's daddy, that's for sure."

"Not tellin', are you?"

Newella puts her hands on her stomach. "No, I'm not. It's my baby to keep and raise because the daddy never offered marriage and never will. But I'm happy, Jolene. Just as happy as a bride in white, standing before a preacher."

"I'll tell you, I'm not. I don't need Mr. Cordell's young'un in me, now or ever."

"Strange as this sounds, I think the man loves you, Jolene. So don't get crazy with your frettin' just yet."

"What he thinks or feels ain't gonna matter. Cause when that woman finds out, my ass may disappear like lots of black folks do in South Carolina."

"After you told me what you heard Mr. Meyers tell Jessica, I don't think you have a worry."

"Easy for you to say don't worry. White folks don't disappear."

Newella is speaking more to herself than to Jolene now. "White don't matter if you're poor. Money is the only thing that keeps you safe."

"I know you ain't talkin' to me, so I am goin' in. He'll be up soon."

"Go on and tend to him. I'll be in directly to start breakfast."

Jolene walks into the kitchen and leaves Newella sitting on the porch. She rocks easy, thinking about her baby and how it changes her life, but not her plans for the future. Her working days are done sooner than expected, but Rita's never was more than a minor stop on Newella's ambitious road to wealth. With nothing left for her to do at the brothel but tend bar and clean up, Newella sits and figures on how to get to her next stop: New Orleans.

CHAPTER NINETEEN

THE CHURCH BELLS OF CHARLOTTE ARE RINGING AN INVITAtion to all the locals interested in hearing the Word of God and cleansing their souls of sin. Sam rides into the barn at home and sits there thinking of Dancy and Samuel. He bows his head and silently repeats the same prayer he's petitioned God with for the last three days. His request is simple: that Dancy and little Samuel be welcomed into the Kingdom of heaven and that he be held accountable, either in this life or the next, for all his trespasses against God's Word.

"You feelin' poorly, boss?"

Sam turns around in the saddle to see Little Jim standing behind him.

He steps down from the horse and loosens the saddle. "Naw, just thinking."

Little Jim walks up and stops him from unsaddling the horse. "Here, let me do that. You look plum done in."

"Not bad." He pauses. "Where are my folks? Church?"

Little Jim drags the saddle off of the horse and starts for the tack room with it.

"You know your maw and the Lord. I played busy, or I'd be there with 'em."

Little Jim puts the saddle on a rack and waits with pure dread for the question he knows Sam will ask next.

"How's Journey?"

Little Jim walks back to the tack room door and has a hard time looking Sam in the eye. "Well boss, I've been livin' in sickness over that hoss... He's cripple."

Sam's petition to God flashes through his mind like a heaven-to-ground lightning bolt splitting the face of a towering summer storm.

A moody tone blunts Sam's question. "Crippled as in how?"

Little Jim is nervous but steady. "Hot nails, boss."

"More than one?"

"Yes sir. And they all be in his front end."

A darkness is riding over Sam. "Go get him."

When Little Jim leads Journey out of the stall, Sam gets a nauseous roll in the pit of his stomach that rises into his throat and blocks his ability to speak. The big horse steps gingerly on the soft dirt of the barn's hallway with a pained look in his eyes. The roll in Sam's stomach intensifies with each step that Little Jim forces Journey to take.

Sam holds his hand up and walks toward Journey. "That's enough. Don't make him walk anymore."

Little Jim moves out of Sam's way. "When he came up crippled yesterday mornin', me and your paw pulled his front shoes."

Sam picks up one of Journey's front feet and brushes the dirt off, feeling for heat. He is relieved to find that the lameness looks worse than it really is. Sam sets the foot down and runs his hands down the horse's leg, feeling for other injuries that may have gotten missed. He repeats the examination on the other foot and leg and is pleased when he arrives at the same conclusion. Sam's mood is a little lighter than when he saw Journey take that first step.

"He's not that lame, Little Jim. Saddle a horse and go get Old Man Felix."

"Your paw went yesterday. Mr. Felix won't be home till later today. His wife said she'd send him as soon as he's back."

Sam stands looking at Journey, confident that the old man will have him sound and ready in just a matter of days. "Alright, put him up. We'll wait on Mr. Felix."

Little Jim coaxes Journey back to his stall, one slow step at a time.

Sam turns and walks toward the barn door. "Look after my saddle horse, Little Jim. I am going to the house."

Sam has eight days before the match, and he intends on doing everything possible to get Journey ready to run, but not to the point of sacrificing the horse's health. If Journey isn't a hundred percent sound come race day, then he'll forfeit and live with the consequences. The loss of five thousand dollars gives Sam pause, but having to go west without Helen is a bet that he will never honor, no matter the consequences.

Several hours later, Sam is sitting at the kitchen table, staring into a cup of coffee and waiting on his parents to come home. He's endlessly searched his mind for a way to come to terms with Dancy and Samuel, but the punishing guilt overrides all reason. He knows he could never reverse God's will, but he wishes with all his heart that he could have held their hands until God's angels came to take them away. Sam's love for Helen only adds to the sadness he feels in his heart for Dancy. She was a good woman, and she deserved a man who loved her unconditionally. Sam takes a deep breath and grits his teeth when he hears his mother and father walk up on the back porch. There is a stiff tension in the room that everyone feels when they walk into the kitchen. Mary Beth quietly hangs her coat and scarf up on the rack next to the kitchen door and places her Bible on the corner of the table.

Owen can see the pain in his son's eyes when Sam stands up and shakes his hand. "You make it home okay?"

"Yes sir. It was cold, but not much snow."

Mary Beth comes around the table and gives Sam a big hug. "We're sorry, son, about Dancy and the baby. I know it's a cross to bear."

Sam looks off and holds tight to his emotions. "How did you know?"

Owen answers, "Rider came by evening before last. Said he was staying at the Higgins House that Saturday when she lost the baby and died."

Sam looks off again. "I appreciate you getting Old Man Felix to come look at my horse."

Mary Beth takes Sam by the hand. "Come sit back down, son, and let me get you something to eat. You look worn to the bone."

Sam shakes his head. "I don't think so, Maw. Not until Old Man Felix looks at Journey."

Owen continues to try to get Sam to stay. "He may not be here till late, son. Why don't you just sit a spell and rest?"

Mary Beth turns Sam around and aims him at the fireplace. "That's a good idea. Punch that fire up, and you and your paw go visit."

Sam tries to protest, "Maw..."

"Don't Maw me. Go on. I'll have something hot on the table directly."

In short order, Mary Beth has her apron on, and the Franklin stove getting hot. The chopping board is out, and a meal begins to come to life as if by magic. She smiles, watching Owen and Sam.

Owen hands Sam one last piece of firewood. "That's plenty. It don't take much."

Owen walks over, sits down in his rocker, and props one boot up on the hearth. Sam sits down on the hearth and stirs the hot coals with a poker.

Owen asks, "That bay you left on better than Old Slick?"

Sam smiles. "No sir. He's not near as tough as Old Slick."

"Horses are no different than people. Some are just plain tougher than others. I 'spect that's the reason you and Old Slick get along. Y'all are a matched set."

"I've faced up on some hardships, Paw. But when Maw Higgins said she buried my son with his mother, that's a hardship I can't come to terms with."

"I can understand that. But you're trying to come to terms with something you didn't have control over. If Dancy and the baby were alive, you'd be at a fork in the road. Then you would have something to come to terms with, because it would all be under your control."

"Well then, it's a burden I just can't lay down."

"You can't lay it down because it's anger that you're carrying. And be my guess it's anger toward God. You see son, carrying feelings of loss and love are all healthy. But carrying ill feelings toward God about your loss… that only rots a man. You know yourself that no man is a match for God's will."

"You're right, Paw. I've prayed long and hard, but it's been prayers set in anger."

"Son, prayers set in anger never give a man relief. And surely not for the loss of a child."

Sam sits staring into the fire. "He has a name."

"Who? The baby?"

"Yes sir. She named him Samuel. I had the marker changed to Tanahill. Samuel Tanahill."

Sam looks up at his father. "I owed him that, Paw. A man has a right to carry the name of his blood. It's the right thing."

Owen smiles easy. "It is. A man needs to carry his rightful name."

Mary Beth tells the men, "Y'all get washed up. It's near ready."

Owen gets up and says to Sam, "Come on. She'll get moody waiting on us."

Sam stands up and hesitates. "Paw... I appreciate your advice about Dancy and the baby. I know every word you spoke to be the truth—all the way around."

Owen smiles and puts his arm around Sam's shoulders. "Come on. Your maw's cooking always makes a body feel better."

They walk out the back door to wash up.

Later that night, Sam stands next to Journey, holding a lantern at eye level and looking over Old Man Felix's shoulder as Little Jim holds tight to the horse's halter. Felix's hunched over, shuffling walk gives the impression of a slow mind, which is anything but the truth. His lively brown eyes can scan a horse in a casual glance and call the best of horse traders to task for more half-truths than they care to hear. He finally steps back from Journey and stands there about a minute past Sam's patience, mumbling under his breath.

Sam can hold silent no longer. "What do you think, Mr. Felix?"

"Well, son, I've seen worse. That's for certain."

"Sir, I have a match in eight days with Cordell Meyers in Camden."

"Everybody knows that, son."

One of the main reasons Old Man Felix has over sixty years behind him is his total disregard for the word "hurry." People only tolerate his lack of urgency because of his ability of knowing what to do, when to do it, and how much to do to make a crippled horse sound again. The main requirement for dealing with him is something Sam has none of: patience.

"Mr. Felix, do you think he'll be sound for the race?"

To Sam's dismay, the old man walks out of the barn unexpectedly, rambling on about a soaking pan and a poultice wrap. When he returns with a metal pan and a foul smelling bucket of something, Sam is consumed by a nagging need for a definitive answer to his question.

"Mr. Felix, my intent is not to be rude here, but I need an answer. Is he going to be ready?"

Without the slightest change in his bent posture, the old man looks up at Sam and smiles with a mischievous twinkle. "I've money bet on this match myself, son. I'll have him breathing fire on race day."

"You placed a bet? Which way?"

The old man kneels down, places Journey's hoof in the pan, and pours in turpentine until it nears the hairline.

Felix ignores Sam's question and says, "Hold 'im still, Little Jim. I don't want him to move."

"Mr. Felix?"

"I heard you, son." Felix stands up, wiping his hands, and nods toward Journey. "On this here horse, right here. He's the best I've ever seen, and I've seen a powerful lot of horses in my day."

Sam is confused. "I share that opinion, sir, but most folks don't."

"And most folks don't know squat about horses, son."

Sam continues, "But he's already lost to Blue Rock, and lost badly. So what changes things with you?"

"You do, Sam, that's what. I've watched you train this horse, and you never hit him. I tried to tell Spence that, but he wouldn't listen. A horse has a mind like everything else on Earth, and a whip never brings out the best in a horse or a man."

Sam feels a weight lifted off of his shoulders by the old man's validation of his approach to training Journey.

"Sam, you get around Blue Rock and just look into his eyes. Whatever he gives Cordell, it's because of fear. Don't get me wrong; Blue Rock is a great horse. With a peaceful mind, he would be even better."

"Better than Journey?"

Felix turns to Sam and says, "Son, this here horse is special. I don't know that God has made another one like him in my lifetime. I believe Journey is better. By how much?" The old man smiles his mischievous twinkle and answers, "We'll see on race day, won't we."

The old man goes about soaking Journey's feet in the turpentine and begins a rambling narrative about horses, directed at no one in particular.

The next morning early, Ike and Paxton ride, hunched over, into a razor's edge north wind that's laden with swirling swarms of icy sleet. The men have their hats pulled down in an attempt to block the stinging sleet from finding bare flesh. Ike raises his head up just enough to see the mill lights, then lowers his hat brim back down and stares at the horn of his saddle, wondering how long Cordell has known about his affair with Jessica.

Before her note, Ike could look Cordell in the eye. But now that rumor and suspicion have become proven facts, he finds himself in a rough place–all because he allowed his passion to overrule his good thinking.

Ike and Paxton ride up to the hitching rail at the front porch of the mill and dismount. They shake the sleet off of their slickers and walk into the mill. When Ike raises his hand to knock on Cordell's office door, he has a sudden tremble in his fist that he and Paxton both note. Ike finally drops his scarred knuckles on the door and braces for the storm that waits within.

"Come in."

When the two men walk into the office, hats in their hands, the warmth in Cordell's smile only intensifies Ike's coiled caution.

Cordell stands up and reaches across his desk, shaking hands with both men. "Morning, gentlemen. It's a tough day to be out."

Ike's nerves are twisting tighter with the passing of each second. "Yes sir, it is."

He reaches into the inside pocket of his coat and pulls out a handful of documents that he hands to Cordell. Before Cordell takes the papers, he looks over to Paxton.

"Mr. Henry, the girls have some fresh coffee made. Why don't you step out and get a cup."

"Oh, yes sir."

When the door closes behind Paxton, Ike tries to look at Cordell, but struggles to maintain his gaze. He has played out this meeting in his mind all night long, and now, here in the moment, his anxiety leaves him unable to match Cordell's piercing stare.

Cordell reaches out for the papers and says, "Mr. Murphy, the documents?"

"Yes sir." Ike snaps back to life and hands the papers over.

Cordell sits down behind his desk and motions toward a chair. "Have a seat, Mr. Murphy."

Ike sits down, and as Cordell begins to sort through the documents, a small piece of folded paper falls out on Cordell's desk. Cordell instantly recognizes Jessica's pale pink stationary, and stops his hand short of picking it up. He sits there for a brief moment, staring at it, until a slight twitch of a smile crosses his face. Ike's hand slides down to the handle of his pistol as Cordell picks up the folded note and hands it to Ike without reading it.

"I believe this is yours, sir."

Ike summons his courage and replies, "I assure you, that was unintentional."

"I've taken issue with your character at times, Mr. Murphy. But a liar, you're not."

Ike puts the note back in his pocket. "I make no excuses for my actions sir. Every encounter has been at my insistence."

"That I believe. But my wife has encouraged that insistence in numerous ways."

Ike stands up and speaks to Cordell directly. "You'll have my resignation today, sir."

Cordell rocks back in his chair and responds. "It's not required. Unless you feel so inclined."

"I don't understand. Why not?"

"When you came here, Mr. Murphy, plantations were being sold on the block every day. Your family's being one of them. Shannon Hill has not only survived, but under your management, has made more money than ever. So what are you going to do here? Quit or stay?"

Ike stands there for moment, trying to process this strange turn of events.

"I would prefer to retain my position, sir."

"That's my preference as well, Mr. Murphy." Cordell points to the chair. "Have a seat, and let's clear the air."

Ike sits back down. "Yes sir."

"Mr. Murphy. The responsibility for my wife's personal needs, I've relinquished some time ago. So let's put something out in the open. You're not my wife's first, and assuredly not her last. The only discomfort for me this time is that she's encouraged and yielded to my manager. The fact that I know of your relationship doesn't grant you a free rein. I caution you, sir, action will be taken if there are any private encounters with my wife conducted on these premises. Is that rule clear?"

"Somewhat remarkable, but yes sir, it is clear."

Cordell starts going back through the papers. "Now, with that out of the way, let's get to the business at hand."

Ike points to a sealed packet. "That packet is from your banker. He said to tell you the brokerage house paid you in full for all of your bales. The money is in your account, and it balances against your contract price to the penny."

Cordell opens it and begins to review the ledger sheet payments.

"Those other papers there are the actual tally sheets from the brokers. I crosschecked theirs against ours, and they all matched."

Ike sits across from Cordell, trying to be patient until Cordell finishes his slow scrutiny of the documents. From the opening of Jessica's note to his cavalier discussion with Cordell, Ike has suffered a firestorm of emotions that has left him mentally scorched. When Cordell prolongs his methodical review of the tally sheets, it only adds to Ike's difficulty.

Cordell and Ike are both jarred from their thoughts when a man's loud voice erupts somewhere outside of the office door. Ike knows the problem and the cause instantly.

Cordell gives Ike a cold look. "Go see to him. Now!"

"Yes sir." Ike bolts from the chair and is out of the office in two quick steps.

Ike bumps into Paxton at the kitchen door and both men pause, Ike looking at Paxton in confusion. He peers around Paxton at Jolene and Newella, who are cleaning up a plate of food that's scattered across the floor.

Ike looks back at Paxton and says, "Were you not listening to me before we walked in here?"

Paxton's rage is on the verge of violence. "Smart mouth niggers and whores, I won't tolerate! For you or anyone else!"

Paxton crashes out the front door, rattling the walls. Ike turns back to the two women and his demented stare sends a vicious warning that doesn't require the assistance of a single spoken word. He stands there for the longest of moments before walking back to Cordell's office. When Ike walks back in, Cordell has an edge to his demeanor that wasn't there before. Ike remains standing, nervously feeling the brim of the hat in his hands. Cordell leans across his desk so that Ike can feel the gravity of his next statement.

"Make no mistake, Mr. Murphy. To whomever my attention is given, there better be shown the utmost of respect."

Ike nods his head. "And there will be, sir."

Cordell leans back and catches his breath. "I want you to ride up to the Moore place and take Paxton with you. I want that place cleaned up by spring, Mr. Murphy. No excuses."

"I understand. The fields are near complete, and the repairs to the house and barns are finished. Everything done per your instructions, sir."

"Just to make sure, you and I are riding up there after I get home from the races."

"Yes sir. About the races, sir...some of us would like to ride over, with your permission."

"As long as the work gets done, Mr. Murphy. That's all I care about."

"Thank you, sir."

Cordell makes a slight hand motion, dismissing Ike. "Go about your day, Mr. Murphy."

Ike looks away to keep his eyes from speaking louder than his words. "Yes sir."

When Ike walks out, Cordell listens for the front door to close and then calls out, "Jolene!"

Cordell reaches for the edge of his desk and pulls himself up, grimacing in pain—the laudanum he consumed this morning is already losing the upper hand to his affliction. Jolene rushes in and comes to his aid, putting an arm around his side to steady his balance.

"You shoulda stayed in bed. All this served no purpose."

"When I get to bed, fetch me a drink, and not water."

Jolene helps Cordell navigate his steps. "Cordell, you need to rest your body. And that means no sour mash. None!"

"What did you say?"

"I meant... you just don't need to drink, sir."

You said my name. Say it again."

"Mister..."

Cordell sharply cuts her off. "No mister. Just Cordell. Say it."

"I don't want the comfort that brings. It may not always be there."

"You're carrying my child. So at least address me by my name in private."

"You're mistaken. There's no child. And I don't know where you got that from anyway."

"Where did I get it from? Why, watching you get up to go pee in the morning. Usually you're half asleep, but here lately you're running for the back door. I'd say that's morning sickness."

Jolene stops Cordell by his bed. "Here, take that coat off and sit down on the bed. I'll pull your boots off so's you can rest."

Cordell lays back in the bed. "I guess I should've let you tell me."

"Them two that just left here are plum mean. Mean to the point of a hateful sickness."

"You just don't care to discuss the baby, do you?"

"I care about staying alive. So if nothing else, I'm going back to the quarters and stay with my mama."

"No you're not! You're damn sure not!"

Jolene wakes her courage up and turns on him with tears in her eyes.

"Cordell! Do you care anything at all about me?" She holds up both hands for him to be silent. "If you do, then you better make arrangements for me and this baby to go somewhere. Cause I won't live to have it if I stay around here, and you know it!"

After a long silence Cordell answers her. "I'll make arrangements to send you north when I get home. I'll hire Newella to travel with you."

Cordell's promise to send her north to freedom gives Jolene little comfort until she is actually there. Southern justice is always tilted to fit the needs of white planters when they have issues with black folks, or anyone else that gets in their way. Cordell is her shield for now, but that is in serious jeopardy because of his declining health.

"I'm sorry for speaking to you in that fashion."

Cordell reaches for her hand "Don't be. That baby makes me love you even more. Come here and lie down beside me."

Jolene lays down beside Cordell with a fear in her heart, knowing that time is not on her or her baby's side.

Paxton stands with his arms folded across his chest and a livid look of betrayal on his face when Ike walks out on the porch. Paxton is a man whose racial hatred abides by no rule of law, neither man's nor God's. His bigotry toward blacks is part of an ingrained belief structure that has been generationally woven into southern society. When a black person crosses the boundaries of that social structure, there isn't a shortage of men like Paxton to deal out cruel punishment for the infraction.

Seething with anger, Paxton points his finger at Ike. "That bitch..."

Ike cuts him off. "Get your horse, and let's walk down to the barn."

When they walk into the barn, Paxton's temper breaks way, and he rips into a fanatical tirade about Jolene and Newella and their disrespectful behavior. As his racial rant builds, his volume rises to the pitch of a delusional madman losing his grip on reality. Paxton's maniacal mood swings are becoming instant eruptions that carry a terrifying degree of viciousness.

Ike has finally had enough and steps up, getting into Paxton's face. "Enough, goddammit! Enough!"

Paxton falls silent, but his anger continues to show through, pulsating in the bulging veins of his neck. His unhinged volatility makes Ike cautious about trying to bring him down to a level of civil behavior. Ike worries that Paxton's vocal outbursts will one day have disastrous consequences for both of them.

Ike speaks to him in an even, friendly tone. "Listen to me, partner. We have too good a deal here to let a comfort girl and a dollar whore get us run off. So let's just back off and let it go."

The short end of the stick always seems to be Paxton's in all of his dealings with Ike. His constant reminder of this is the pain that gnaws at his left knee twenty-four hours a day. Jolene's smart mouth is a driving issue with Paxton, but the real irritation is Ike's unwillingness to stop it. He's tired of being used when it is convenient and then ignored when his needs don't directly benefit Ike.

"Paxton, did you hear what I said?"

"I did. Did you hear what I said at that kitchen door?"

"I told you to stay away from those two. And you went right on in there anyway."

"So now I have to walk around niggers and whores? Is that what you're telling me?"

"I'm telling you to do what I tell you to do. And don't give me any shit about it."

"There's my fuckin' problem with you, right there! For two years, I've covered your ass. Two goddamn years, and that's the answer I get?"

"Don't act like you haven't made plenty of money covering my ass. But if you don't leave that slut alone, we're both gonna lose a sweet deal. One that can't be replaced."

"You've asked me for a lot, Ike. So tell me one time when I didn't make something happen for you? One time! Tell me!"

"You got paid, Paxton. Paid in full. Now I'm telling you, let this go!"

Paxton points his finger in Ike's face. "No. I won't. I'm goddamn sure not letting it go! Not anymore!"

Ike is losing his patience with Paxton's lunacy. "Can't you understand? There's a lot to lose here!"

Paxton walks away a few steps and turns on Ike with an irrational glare of pure madness. "You bring that bitch under control, or me and my bunch are riding out. Then see how sweet your deal is without us."

"The point you're making here is not worth it. Simply not worth it!"

"It is to me! Everything you've stolen off this place I've sold— cotton, livestock, everything. Now this is under your hand. You make it happen, or I ride out."

"Just like that! You're going to ride off?"

"I've told you time and again about this. I won't tolerate a nigger getting in my face. Ever!"

Ike stands there for a moment, then nods his head. "I'll tend to it when we get back. Now get on your horse, and let's go."

The two men mount up and ride out into the cold north wind. When they're gone for the better part of a half an hour, Sorrel cautiously steps out from behind a wagon in the very back of the barn.

Early the next morning, the faint sound of a galloping horse can be heard from somewhere deep within a gray bank of fog. Sam and Old Man Felix are standing side-by-side, straining their vision against the fog that hangs like a curtain across the dirt road. The oncoming horse is splitting the ground cloud with a speed that makes the damp morning air sting Little Jim's face like rain in a gale force wind. He ducks his head and prays that nothing walks out into the path of the hard running stallion. When Journey flashes by Sam and the old man, Sam whistles in a high pitch for Little Jim to pull up.

Sam smiles and looks over at the old man. "Unbelievable. Two days ago he couldn't walk."

"Just because he can run doesn't mean he can beat Blue Rock, son."

Sam smiles and says," I thought you said he was the best you've ever seen."

"He is. But Blue Rock has bested several horses that were far better than himself."

"How can that be?" Sam asks.

"Easy. Cordell knows how to run him. The fastest horse doesn't always win. The smartest trainer does."

"You mean Journey could lose again?"

"Well, son, that has a lot to do with you."

"Then why did you bet your money?"

"I like the combination of you and the horse. You're both winners that nobody believes in."

"You've seen Blue Rock run a lot, haven't you?"

"What I've seen doesn't matter son. Doesn't matter at all."

"I think it does. So why don't you protect your bet and come to Camden with me? Plus I'll pay you a hundred dollars and expenses."

"That's a fair offer, son. But I don't know that I want back in the game."

Sam extends his hand to Mr. Felix and says, "Well, I'm leaving come sun up, sir. If you've a mind, I could use your help. Besides, be nice to be part of horse racing history, wouldn't it?"

The old man's smile reveals an envy of Sam's conquering bravado. He shakes Sam's hand and follows Journey into the barn.

That same morning, Sorrel's mind is mired in a bog of anxiety that is smothering all reason out of his every thought. He goes back and forth over whether to tell Cordell or to have someone else tell him the Ike and Paxton story. Sorrel has, after much mental turmoil, decided that the safest thing is to tell Cordell himself… but when, and how? That's the next project for his overtaxed mind. There has never been a word spoken between them about their common blood, but Sorrel prays that the blood speaks louder to Cordell than their color. There is seldom a case where the truth matters, when one side is black and the other white, in South Carolina. Color is always the guiding force in the administration of justice where slavery holds sway.

Cordell is sitting on the edge of his bed, pulling on his boots, when Newella walks by the bedroom door.

"Newella," he calls out.

She stops and walks back to the door. "Yes sir?"

"Go to the barn and have Sorrel hitch up a Buckboard. I need to go check on Blue Rock."

"Uh, Jolene said..."

"I know what she said, goddammit, but I'm getting up. So get on down to the barn and get Sorrel for me."

Newella doesn't hesitate this time. "Yes sir."

Cordell stands up, and for the first time in days, he's anxious to be outside. When Jolene left early to check on her mother, Cordell got up and sat on the back porch, breathing in the cool, clean morning air. He's surely not a hundred percent, but more time closed up in that room is not the answer. With one day left until they leave for Camden, there's a thousand things that require his personal attention.

When he walks out of the mill, he sees Jolene some distance down the road, walking toward him. Her thin frame is bent into the north wind, and she holds her old coat shut with her arms folded across her chest. The wind sweeps her wavy black mane of hair around her face, hiding one side, and then the other, in a way that arouses Cordell for the first time in days. Her flawless beauty and caring spirit are a trap for any man's heart and soul. For Cordell, she's been a sanctuary of peace, her love strengthening his heart and touching the depths of his soul. When she walks up, the tenderness of her smile affirms the Creators' intentional design of a love that bonds a man and woman. She stands there for a moment looking into his eyes, and then she begins to button up his coat.

Cordell speaks first. "I'm surprised."

"About what?"

"The smile."

Jolene finishes buttoning his coat, folds her arms back across her chest, and steps back. "If this baby kicks me half as hard as you did last night, I'll never get any rest."

Cordell smiles and reaches for her, but she steps back again. "Sorry," he says, "I couldn't sleep. A crazy dream kept waking me up all night."

Jolene looks toward the barn when she hears a wagon coming. "I'm thinking Sorrel's, uh, coming for you."

Cordell steps toward her and says, "And I think you need to stand still."

Jolene moves away again. "Tell me. Was I in your dream?"

Cordell's mood turns to a melancholy reflection of what can never be. "There was a bright haze at the foot of our bed, and you were standing there with your arms outstretched."

Jolene brushes her windblown hair from her face and smiles. "Was I naked?"

Cordell's reflexive laugh brings him back to the present. "That you were. Exquisitely naked."

Jolene's coy smile and her seductive silence accelerate a fantasy that Cordell's mind started spinning the moment she touched the buttons on his coat.

"So what's so crazy about me being naked?"

"Well for one thing, I couldn't get you to come to bed. You stood there just out of my reach trying to hand me something over and over and over and over."

"What was it?"

"That's the crazy part. It was your silver cross."

Jolene feels a rush of goose bumps that chills her in a way that nature could never duplicate. She slides one hand inside of the old coat and brushes the cross through her dress with trembling fingertips. Her playful demeanor is suddenly slain by the remembrance of Jessica's oath of retribution. Her fading smile gives Cordell cause for concern.

"Are you okay?" he asks.

Jolene bends over a little. "Just a touch of nausea."

He reaches for her, but she raises her hand and starts for the front door of the mill.

"Go check on your horse. I'm fine. It's just the baby sickness."

Jolene walks in the mill and shuts the door behind her. She stands there for a moment sending a solemn vow to the heavens that her and her baby will live in freedom no matter how many Jessicas get in her way.

The foreboding moan of a sharp north wind chases away Cordell's momentary youthful longings. His realization of present time and pressing needs robs him of the merriment Jolene brings to his life. Every morning with a solar punctuality, her smile lights his world, giving him the confidence to conquer all that he lays his hand to.

When Sorrel pulls up in the wagon, Cordell steps up on the wheel and sits down next to Sorrel on the wagon seat.

Cordell nods. "Sorrel."

"Mornin', boss. Where to?"

"The stable."

"Yes sir."

With a flick of the lines, Sorrel puts the team of mules in motion and the wagon lurches forward.

"Everything ready to go in the morning?"

Sorrel is near the point of losing control of his nerves. "Yes sir. Me and Benjie put the top up on the carriage and spit polished it to a shine, boss."

Sorrel's sleepless night was nothing compared to the enormity of the unexpected conversation facing Cordell this morning. Sorrel's retreating resolve is giving ground to the assault of a thousand reasons why he should remain silent. The battle lines between his senses of fear and duty sway one way, then the other, until Sorrel finds himself on the same high ground as before. He has to tell Cordell.

Cordell looks out across the cold landscape with an uneasiness that he makes no effort to hide.

"That's good you put the top up on the carriage."

"You still a mite poorly, boss?"

"No, not at all. Why?"

Sorrel smiles. "Just makin' sure, boss. I don't need me no Jolene trouble today."

Cordell laughs under his breath and shakes his head. "Jolene trouble? And how do you avoid that, Sorrel? By doing what?"

"By doing what she say 'do.' That's how."

"Which is? What?"

"Boss, I done been spoke out of turn here. Plum out. All that was foolishness. Just rattling foolishness."

"Sorrel, we've never lied to each other, have we?"

Sorrel swallows hard. "No sir, we haven't."

"Never. Right?"

"Yes sir."

"I want to ask you something, and I want the truth, just like all the times before. Okay?"

"Yes sir. But Jolene just wants you to stay well, boss."

"It's not about Jolene. Well it is, but not what you're thinking."

Sorrel is relieved for a change of subject.

"What's the bad blood between Paxton and Newella? And how does Jolene fit in all of that?"

Sorrel thinks for a minute. "Well, boss, Paxton never cared that Newella worked at Rita's until he heard she was givin' her favors to a nigger on occasion. He brought it to her straight, but she didn't answer him. So, he took it for truth. Said he couldn't do anything about it cause of her stayin' with Jolene. But he promised her a bad whippin' one day. A real bad whippin'."

"Are you that nigger, Sorrel?"

"Yes sir, I'm him."

"Thought so. Now tell me about Jolene. What's his rub with her?"

"It's more her rub with him, boss. Course he's come to hate her pretty hard for it."

"Why?"

"He's been downright harsh to Newella and Jolene don't allow it no more."

"What do you mean, she 'don't allow it'? How?"

"Jolene don't tolerate his foul mouth. When he starts on Newella, Jolene runs him out of the kitchen."

"You every hear him threaten Jolene like he has Newella?"

"Before I answer that boss, I gots to confess. I lied to you."

Cordell reaches over and stops the team of mules. "About what?"

"I ain't seen him threaten her, but I sure heard 'im talkin' to Mr. Ike about it."

"How is that lying? I just asked you the question, and you haven't even answered yet."

"Boss, I figure if a man knows about harm that's been done or harm that's a comin', and he don't speak up, that's as good as lyin'."

"I don't think that's the correct definition for lying, but it sure should be."

"Well boss, it's lyin' to me, and it's been killin' me holdin' on to the truth."

"Tell me what you heard, Sorrel."

"Two mornin' ago they walked into the barn. It was that mornin' they stopped to see you."

"Ike and Paxton?"

"Yes sir."

"They know you were in there?"

"Oh, no sir. I was sittin' behind a wagon, cleanin' harnesses. Lord, I'd be a dead nigger, boss, if'n they'd seen me. Not after what they said."

"Paxton threatened to kill Jolene?"

"Didn't say it boss. But he threatened Mr. Ike rightly hard if he didn't do somethin' about Jolene's sass."

"Threatened him how?"

"Boss, you know a nigger's word don't hold no store against a white man. And what I'm 'bout to say probably goin' to come at me."

"Enough of the frettin', Sorrel. Nothing is going to happen to you. Now tell me what you know."

"Jolene's sass was the cause of it. Mr. Paxton said if Mr. Ike didn't do somethin' about Jolene's mouth, him and his bunch were ridin' out. Mr. Ike went to tellin' him they had a sweet deal and to leave Jolene and Newella alone before it all come to ruin."

"What kind of sweet deal?"

"Well, boss, they been stealin' from you. Mr. Ike makes the deals and Mr. Paxton and his bunch does the deliverin'. I heard 'em say cotton and livestock. What else I don't know."

Cordell looks away down the road toward the big house. "How did it end?"

"Mr. Ike said he would put a stop to Jolene's mouth."

"How?"

"Didn't say. Just said he'd take care of it."

"You tell anyone else about this?"

"No sir."

"Then don't. I'll take care of both of them, and you won't be in it. Understand me?"

"Yes sir."

"I won't forget this, Sorrel. I won't forget what you've done." Cordell nods toward the road. "Let's go."

Sorrel clucks to the mules and rattles the lines. "Yes sir."

CHAPTER TWENTY

When Sorrel and Cordell approach the back of the main house, the tantalizing aroma of breakfast, mixed with the scent of a hickory fire, is born by a cool north breeze across the path of the oncoming wagon. The aromatic smells of frying bacon and coffee unleash an appetite in Cordell that pain has held hostage for days. His returning hunger pales in comparison to a surging hunger he feels for the life force of his Shannon Hill. Cordell would rather God take him from the Earth than to ever see another man's hand come to rule Shannon Hill.

"Turn into the back driveway Sorrel. Let's warm up with some coffee."

"Yes sir."

When Sorrel pulls the team up at the hitching post, Cordell steps down and walks toward the back porch. He turns back to Sorrel who's still sitting on the wagon.

"Tie them mules up and come in."

Cordell turns and walks on toward the back porch. When he walks into the kitchen, he finds Helen sitting at the kitchen table in his favorite chair, reading his paper. Not expecting her father, Helen puts the paper down and starts to get up.

"Father."

Cordell smiles and reaches out to her. "Keep your seat. Fact is, I've always thought you were a natural fit for that chair."

Cordell leans over and kisses her on the forehead. "Where is everybody?"

"Bell just took a tray up to Mother. The rest of the girls are cleaning the house."

He pours himself a cup of coffee just as Sorrel comes to the back door.

"Come in, Sorrel."

Sorrel steps just inside of the door with his hat in his hand. Cordell hands him his cup of coffee.

"Thank you, sir. I'll be right out here on the porch."

He turns and walks out the door. Cordell pours another cup of coffee and sits down across from Helen.

Cordell blows on the hot coffee. "Your mother crawl off in a bottle last night?"

"More than one. Things got a little out of hand last night trying on dresses. She had Petal up till two o'clock this morning, packing and repacking."

Cordell sips his coffee. "Not surprising."

Helen looks across the table at her father with an admiration that no man, not even Sam Tanahill, will ever be able to match. She hopes and prays that her quest for a place in this world doesn't destroy his. He is the first love of her life and a man who towers in her mind, taller than all the mountains of the world stacked one upon the other.

"There's something I want you to know."

Cordell smiles and looks into his coffee cup. "You'd think I'm a priest considering how many confessions I am hearing this morning. Let's hear yours."

"Well it's not a confession of sin. But I guess it is."

Cordell looks up from his coffee cup. "You guess it is? Like what kind of guess?"

"I placed a bet on the match."

Cordell looks relieved then smiles. "On whose horse?"

"Not yours."

"Well I'm real curious to know. What did you have to wager?"

"Myself."

"Yourself? And who did you place that bet with?"

"With my mother."

"I'm listening."

"The bet is simple. If your horse wins, I'll marry any man she chooses, no matter whom."

"And if Sam wins, he gets you?"

"A good possibility. But if I win, I get to choose the man I marry, no matter whom. She also agreed to stop interfering in my life completely."

"You must feel pretty sure of winning."

"I do."

"Where does this leave us? You know I'm going to do everything I possibly can to win?"

"And you should. Your honor could live with nothing less."

"Then why are you telling me all this?"

"Because when he wins," she pauses to let the word 'when' sink in, "I want you to treat him as a man worthy of calling on your daughter. He's a good man, and I know you know that. I also know he's not what you wanted for me, but he's what I want. Next to you, he's the love of my life."

Cordell wishes with all of his heart that the turn of events coming could leave everyone a winner, but he knows that life is like horse racing: there are always winners and always losers.

"I know you're in love with him, but..."

"But what?"

"You're gambling your whole life on one bet. On one bet that gives you the life you want or dooms you to a life you hate. How can you play all-in like that? I don't understand it."

"I've told you what I want. Now I'm asking you, when he wins this match, will you honor the bet I have with my mother?"

Cordell smiles. "I've raced horses and played cards against the best. But I don't think I've ever seen your degree of confidence. For whatever reason, you think you hold a pat hand. Don't you?"

"I know you're reluctant to honor her bet, but don't treat me like she has all my life. This is what I want. Win or lose."

"It is a pat hand, isn't it?"

"We'll see come race day."

"I'll honor the bet, but I feel like I'm drawing to an inside straight."

Helen reaches and touches her father's hand. "Don't you ever doubt that you're my heart."

"And you're mine, as well."

Cordell gets up, walks around the table, and kisses Helen on her forehead. "I'll see you tonight at supper."

Helen stands up and wraps her arms around her father. "Thank you."

When she turns him loose, he steps away and reaches for his hat. "I hope that's how all of this ends."

He turns and walks out the door.

The late afternoon sun strains in a futile effort to push its colored rays east through a low hanging cloud cover that stretches to all points on the compass. The clouds have held the fiery orb at bay all day, while the relentless north wind has chilled the air every hour. When Sorrel finally reins the team up in front of the mill, both he and Cordell step down from the wagon on numb feet and stiff knees.

Sorrel methodically ties the team up and follows Cordell into the mill, trying desperately to shake the chill from his bones. When they walk into the kitchen, the room is cold and the fire in the stove is burned to ashes. Cordell walks back into the hallway just as Newella comes in the back door carrying a bucket of water.

"Newella."

"Evenin' boss."

"Where's Jolene?"

Newella stands there holding the bucket. "She went to check on her mama. She'll be back directly."

Her eyes suddenly glance away, and a faint smile sweeps over the corners of her full lips when Sorrel steps out from behind Cordell.

Newella pushes the smile away and looks back to Cordell. "I was about to start supper. But I'll make a pot of coffee first."

"Don't do either one on my account." He turns and walks back by Sorrel and stops at his office door. "I'm having a drink, and then I'm going up to the house."

"Can I get you anything, sir?" Newella asks.

Cordell points to Sorrel. "Just take care of Sorrel. I'll be ready to go in about an hour."

"Yes sir."

Cordell walks into his office and shuts the door behind him, leaving Sorrel and Newella standing in the hallway looking at each other until Newella's catty smile returns.

Sorrel grins in return. "You be lookin' good today."

Newella starts toward him, carrying the water. "It's you ARE looking good today.' Not 'you BE' looking good," she corrects his grammar. "Besides, you'd say that to anything wearing a dress."

Sorrel reaches for the bucket when she walks up to him. "Only to them that makes a dress look as good as you do."

When she walks by him, Sorrel reaches and pats Newella on the ass. "My, my, what a dress it be's too."

Newella smiles, spins around, and slaps his hand. "You know that's trouble if the wrong person sees it. Besides, there's gossip enough already. Folks had proof, be some tall hell raised. So mind yourself."

Sorrel follows Newella into the kitchen with the bucket of water, his eyes firmly fixated on every move of her hips.

Cordell is halfway through a tall drink when Jolene walks into his office. When she sees the drink, she walks on toward the fireplace.

"You being in the cold all day, I'd think you would want a fire more than a drink."

Jolene picks up some wood and walks to the fireplace.

"Don't do that, I'm leaving."

She puts the wood down and stands with her back to Cordell, staring into the fireplace for a moment. She slowly folds her dress around her hips and sits down on the hearth.

Jolene looks down at her lap. "I can't lie, Cordell. I got a powerful worry on my mind and a mighty fear in my heart."

Cordell takes a drink and sits the glass back on the desk. "Fetch me Newella."

Jolene snaps a sharp look at Cordell. "Did you hear me? I'm worried scared!"

Cordell nods. "I heard you. Now go fetch Newella."

Jolene gets up, walks out, and soon returns with her. When they walk in, Jolene walks back to the hearth and sits down, leaving Newella standing in front of Cordell's desk.

"You wanted to see me, sir?"

"I did. I've another job offer for you. If you're interested?"

"I'm interested in making money sir. What is it?"

"First, I want your word, on your father's name, that what we discuss here never leaves this room. Agreed?"

"Yes sir."

"I want you to escort Jolene to New York City. I'll pay a wage, plus expenses, there and back."

It's the last thing Newella ever expected Cordell to ask her to do. Her silence and hesitation surprise both Cordell and Jolene.

Cordell sees her reluctance. "Is there a problem?"

Newella looks over at Jolene. "Well, sir, I was planning on moving on to New Orleans right after New Year's."

Cordell ponders his dilemma. "I'll tell you what. You escort Jolene north, and I'll pay your ship passage to New Orleans, plus the wages, of course. That solve your problem?"

Newella looks over to Jolene and smiles. "Yes sir. Yes sir, it does. When do we leave?"

"Let me get home from this match, and I'll make all of the arrangements."

"Yes sir. Anything else?"

"There is. I don't want either one of you here by yourself until I get home. Not for a minute. Understand?"

Both women hear the warning in his voice.

"Does this have something to do with us and Paxton?"

"Let's just say that you two are not Ike and Paxton's favorites right now. So just be careful around them. I'll see to those two when I get back."

"They're the reason for my worry. Especially Paxton. His hate for the both of us has driven him to a pure craziness."

"He may be carrying some hate, but he's not crazy. He won't do anything. But to be safe, stay together, and stay away from him all you can."

"We've tried, but here lately he's been around more than usual. Just makes a body feel a little spooked."

"Well, they're gone to the Moore Place, and then on to the match. So they shouldn't be around until I'm home."

"That's a relief."

"That's all I needed, Newella. You can go."

"If I could ask, sir? How much are you going to pay me for the trip?"

"Fifty dollars there and back plus expenses. Or there, then to New Orleans. Why?"

"Well, sir, this may not set well with you, but I wanted to ask a favor."

"Sure. What?"

"I was wondering if you could place a bet for me on the match? The fifty you'll pay me, plus two hundred more I've saved."

"I don't think I can get it covered on my horse, Newella. Not now."

Newella hesitates, then says, "I want it placed on Journey, sir. I heard they were giving two to one odds."

Cordell smiles, then breaks into a laugh of pure amusement. "I swear. There's something going on here, and I'm the only one that doesn't know what it is."

Newella's not sure what that means. "Beg your pardon, sir?"

"Never mind. Tell me, Newella, why do you want to do this? That horse ruined your family, and now you're doubling down on a proven loser. Why?"

"The bet is more on Sam Tanahill than on Journey, sir. That man is no fool. There's a reason he thinks he can win, or he wouldn't do it. Besides, I need the money to start my business in New Orleans."

"That business is not a bookstore, is it now?" Cordell asks with a chuckle.

Newella smiles, knowing Cordell is fully aware of her future business venture. "A little more entertaining than that, sir."

Cordell can't help but admire her drive and courage. "I'm sure it will be. I don't know where you got those guts from, but you got plenty of 'em. No one can deny you that. Get me your money before I leave. I'll lay it off."

"Two to one, sir?"

Cordell smiles. "Two to one, Newella."

"Thank you, sir."

Newella turns and walks out, closing the door behind her. Cordell reaches for the glass of sour mash and sits there staring off in thought.

Jolene breaks the silence between them. "I wish you wouldn't drink that."

"And I wish I didn't have to go home tonight. But I do, and I need this before I go."

When Cordell turns the glass up and drains it in one long drink, Jolene gets up and walks around to him, needing to feel his strong, tender touch. She stands there in front of him in an emotional turmoil, waiting on him to reach out to her.

"Come here," Cordell says, motioning to his lap.

She takes his hand and gently sits down. When her head comes to rest on his chest and his arms pull her close in an embrace, it calms the storm in her heart. She closes her eyes, and lets go of all the fear and anxiety she's held since her first morning of sickness. Her regimented prayers are always spoken with a trust that she and her baby live under the good Lord's design.

Those prayers also contain special thanks for the man who now holds her in his arms.

"I need to go," Cordell says, weary with the understanding of what the next several hours hold for him at home.

"Just so you know, there has never been a woman that loved a man more than I love you. I promise this baby will know that God never made a better man than its father. That's my solemn vow. I love you, Cordell."

"And I love you, Jolene. But I've got to go. Bad as I hate to, I do."

Jolene stands up and steps away from him with a comforting sense that no matter what tilts her world, he will always be there to bring it back straight. When she helps him on with his jacket, she experiences the same sensual rush of strength and peace that she encounters every time her hands touch him. When he turns around, she puts both of her hands on his chest and looks up into his eyes, smiling.

"Don't worry about me. Go win your race, I'll be here waiting."

Cordell takes her in his arms and kisses her with an unused passion that's been lingering in his heart since he saw her coming up the road that morning. She matches his unbridled passion in return. Somewhere in the kiss, they both realize for the first time that there's a parting of ways coming in the very near future. Their bittersweet kiss comes to an end, and like all of the lovers in this world before them, they find their love bound together by two parts: one part hope and one part prayers.

Cordell steps away from her and takes her by the hand as they walk into the hallway. "Sorrel, let's go."

When Cordell walks out the front door, Jolene pulls her hand from his and wraps her arms around herself, holding her old coat tightly shut against the cold. He turns around and looks into her eyes with a love that's come of age. With all of society's restrictions stripped from his mind, he reaches back for her hand. She lovingly shakes her head no, while her eyes tenderly beg for his forgiveness.

"I'll be here. Go on."

They stand apart looking at each other until Sorrel and Newella walk out of the mill. The moment broken, Cordell nods his head in agreement and walks to the wagon. Sorrel unties the team and steps up on the wagon next to Cordell in a quick order.

Cordell touches the brim of his hat and nods in respect. "Ladies."

Sorrel rattles the lines and urges the tired team forward into the failing light of the cool afternoon. The men ride in silence until Sorrel turns into the back driveway of the main house. When he reins the team up, Cordell steps down and turns back to Sorrel.

Cordell addresses Sorrel. "Be here around five in the morning. It'll take a while to get everything loaded."

"Yes sir."

Cordell turns and walks on toward the back porch. "Night, Sorrel."

"Night, boss."

Sorrel puts the team in motion in a hurried rush with one thought in mind—Newella.

Cordell hears the fight long before he ever walks up onto the back porch. When he reaches the kitchen door, he pauses and looks down the porch at the old worn out rocker. Cordell thinks to himself, why not? He walks down the porch to the old rocker and sits down easy, fully expecting it to collapse from under him. After the creaking stops, Cordell gently settles into the comfortable side of the seat and relaxes. When he closes his eyes and begins to rock, he hears the one word that he's heard enough of for one day.

"Boss?"

Cordell continues to rock.

"Boss man!"

Cordell doesn't open his eyes or quit rocking. "I heard you, Bell."

"I caught the frights when I heard that old rocker movin, boss man. Sure weren't expectin' you tonight. No sir." Bell turns to walk back in the kitchen "I'll fetch your drink right out."

"Bell, make it a light one."

Bell turns back to Cordell with a question in her eyes. Thinking better of any other answer, she shakes her head and replies," Yes sir."

When Bell turns to walk into the kitchen, she comes face-to-face with Jessica.

"Who are you talking to, Bell?"

"Mr. Cordell, ma'am. He be sittin' out on the porch."

With her drink in her hand, she all but pushes Bell out of her way and walks out onto the porch.

"How long have you been out here?"

"Long enough to know that I had rather be out here."

"Did you hear your daughter yelling at me?"

"I didn't."

"Well she was, and I want you to do something about it."

Helen walks out on the porch behind her mother. "Maybe she should tell you what she did first."

"There's no reason for either one of you to be yelling. Now what's the problem? Jessica, you first, and keep it short. I'm in no mood for this."

"I simply invited Henry Jackson's youngest son, Will, to dinner."

"As my escort. That was her invitation—as my escort."

"Did you do that, Jessica?"

"I did! But what difference does it make? I'll soon have every right, and she knows it."

"It's not your right yet!" Cordell states.

Jessica looks at Helen, then to Cordell. "She told you of our wager?"

"She did. But only for the reason that she fears you won't honor the bet."

"Sounds like she's been courting your favor. Is there something under foot here that leads her to believe that she's going to win?"

Cordell stands up and points at Jessica. "Don't make any idle insinuations that get whispered for the truth, because I'll take serious offense, Madame. Very serious offense!"

Jessica looks at her glass and says, "I think I need a drink."

Cordell walks down the porch until he comes face-to-face with her.

"You've manipulated everyone and everything all your life to fit what you've wanted. But those days are over. Starting today, you'll live by your word or there will be consequences of the severest nature. Am I clear?"

"Quite," she answers, without looking up from her empty glass.

"And you, young lady, will never, for any reason, raise your voice in this house. Especially to your mother. Is that clear?"

"Yes sir."

"Will you be coming in for dinner?"

Cordell walks back to the chair and sits down. "Maybe later. Have Bell bring me that drink. And please, leave me to some peace for the moment."

Helen and her mother walk back into the house and go their separate ways, while Cordell tries to recapture some of the peace he felt when he sat down in the old rocker. Bell walks back out with the drink and stands a step away, waiting on Cordell.

He looks around to her and tries to smile. "Take it back and pour it in the bottle, Bell. That won't solve my problems."

Bell shakes her head, confounded. "Yes sir." She turns and walks into the kitchen.

Cordell rocks and stares into the darkness until his eyes catch something moving in the shadows just off the driveway.

"Someone there?"

Newella and Jolene step into the shadowy light.

"What are y'all doing here?"

Newella extends her hand and walks forward into the light. "I brought you my money."

Jolene easies back into the shadows until there is no evidence that someone is there.

Cordell gets up, walks to the edge of the porch, and takes the money from Newella.

"Two to one on Journey, right?" she asks.

Cordell smiles. "I'll take care of it."

Jessica stands just inside of the kitchen door, listening.

"Thank you sir. And good night."

When Newella turns to walk away, Cordell speaks to Jolene standing out in the darkness. "Good night."

Cordell sees Jessica walk out of the back door from the corner of his eye. He walks back to the rocker and sits down with the money in his hand.

Jessica walks down to him. "If there's nothing going on, then why are you betting against Blue Rock with those whores? I just saw her give you some money. How do you explain that?"

"I don't have to explain anything, to you or anyone else. And I warn you again, be ever so careful with random assumptions, because if my honor comes into question for the slightest of reason, I'll show you no mercy. And my actions won't be verbal."

"Is that a threat?"

"It is. To a degree that will alter your life, should you mistake it for idle conversation."

"It seems we're coming to an impasse, sir."

"That impasse has long been in the history books, my dear. Now if you'll excuse me, I'd like a little peace and quiet."

"I think that's something we could all use." She turns and walks into the house.

Cordell closes his eyes and rocks easy. Soon he hears a soft whispered voice from somewhere in the darkness.

"Good night, my love."

The whispered words give Cordell more peace than he's ever found in a glass of sour mash. He smiles and continues to rock easy with his eyes closed.

The blistering hot forge fire radiates forcefully, forming a ring of high temperature around the two men hotter than any July day in North Carolina. Little Jim evenly pumps the forge handle, keeping the summer circle in force, while Sam's rhythmic swing of the four-pound hammer fashions a custom horseshoe from the red hot iron. He finally pauses the ringing hammer and holds the shoe up for inspection. Satisfied with its quality, Sam drops the hot shoe into a bucket of water, setting its form into a finished work of art. Owen walks into the blacksmith shop just as Sam is retrieving the cooled horseshoe from the bucket, along with the other three lying on the bottom.

"I didn't know anything needed to be shod?"

"Nothing needs shod. I just made an extra set of shoes for Journey. If he loses one, I want to be able to reset him myself."

"Well, y'all come along for dinner. Maw's puttin' it on the table."

Sam lays the shoes down on the anvil along with the hammer. "Yes sir, we're coming."

Owen turns and walks out of the blacksmith shop, closely followed by an ever-hungry Little Jim. Sam remains standing at the anvil, taking off his leather apron, lost in vivid visions of dancing with Helen on that day they first met. When she smiled and took his hand, Sam had never felt such a moment in his life. From their first shared glance until the present, his mind has an indelible memory of every time he's been in her captivating presence. He smiles, turns, and walks out of the shop, laying his apron on a bench as he leaves.

When Sam walks in, everyone is seated at the table waiting on him. The empty seat is next to his mother, who has placed her well-worn Bible between them on the table. The presence of the book is a clear indicator that the meal comes with a sermon on gambling.

Mary Beth reaches out and says, "Join hands and let us pray. Sam, if you would lead us in prayer."

"Dear heavenly Father. We ask that you lead, guide, and direct us all the days of our life. We beseech you, Father, to bless Journey and Little Jim with an inner strength that will carry them to victory. I ask for your forgiveness for all of my failings, and I pray, Father, from the humblest depths of my heart, for your blessings upon my family, and for all of those I love. I ask all these things in the glory of your name. Amen."

Mary Beth begins passing the serving bowls and says, "I don't think involving the Lord in a gambling scheme is the path a Christian should walk."

"The match is not a scheme, Maw. I've explained my reasons to the both of you, along with the Lord. I've hidden nothing."

"The Lord doesn't justify any means available to reach an end. No matter how honorable the end may be. So be careful with your justification, because it may not be his will."

"My justification is my love for Helen. That's by His design, not mine."

"On that we can agree. But His will may not be that you win this race. It could be a test of your faith in Him."

Sam has had this conversation with his mother more times than is reasonable, and it always ends the same—a mountainous logjam of strong personalities.

"I respect your objections to the match, Maw, but I've given my word. And if I do lose, I'll find another way to be with her."

"You should've done that in the first place."

Owen has had enough of the point/counterpoint at the table and lays his fork down.

"I don't want you to take this wrong, Mary Beth, but Sam's given his word, and he's bound by it. I'm bound by it, and we're going to see this to the end."

Mary Beth takes stern offense and places her hand on her worn Bible. "I'll ask both of you this, then I'm finished. What's more important? Keeping your word to man or keeping your covenant with God?"

Sam and his father are neither angry nor aggravated with Mary Beth's scalding question to which they have never had an answer. The tense silence is finally broken by Little Jim's voracious appetite.

Little Jim, seemingly oblivious to the seriousness of the moment, looks at Mary Beth and says, “Ma’am, could I have a pair of them there biscuits to go?”

Mary Beth doesn’t take her hand off of the book when she answers, “Sure, Little Jim, help yourself.”

Little Jim retrieves two of the biscuits from the nearby basket and gets up from the table. “Thank you, ma’am.” He looks over to Sam and says, “I’m goin’ to finish loadin’ the wagon, boss.”

“I’ll be there in a bit. Go on.”

Little Jim backs toward the door. “Thank you for the meal, ma’am. You got a true gift with them there pots.”

“Glad you liked it, Little Jim.”

Sam and his mother’s conversation has traveled the same well-worn path and arrived at the same impenetrable impasse as every time before. When Little Jim walks out of the room, the only sound left is a silence that re-enforces the unbending philosophies of mother and son. Sam stands up and goes to say something, but his mother’s hand on her Bible gives him pause.

“I’ll have breakfast ready at four in the morning, Sam, so you can be hooked up and gone by daylight.”

Sam walks around and kisses his mother on the top of her head. “I love you, Maw.”

“I love you, son, and I go to the Lord every day for you. So you just make sure He hears from you also.”

“I do, Maw. Every day.” Sam turns and walks out.

"He's a good man, Mary Beth, you've seen to that. But he's become his own man."

"I know he has. But this past year he's changed in ways I never dreamed of. He's just not my Sam anymore."

"Yes he is. But he's grown, and there's a terrible hunger in him now. The kind that drives a man hard and won't let him rest until he's found his place."

"I've seen the look, and that's what scares me. I just pray he doesn't lose the Lord trying to find it."

"The raising is done, Mary Beth. He is who he is. If it was me, I'd be careful with the sermons that sit in judgment. A grown man don't take kindly to it, not even from his maw."

Mary Beth gets up and starts cleaning off the table. "I've asked the Lord to help me with that, but sometimes my tongue has a mind of its own."

Owen smiles, gets up, and gives Mary Beth a hug. "I'm going to help them finish up. Don't fret on what you don't have a say in."

Owen turns her loose and walks out.

CHAPTER TWENTY-ONE

THE EARLY MORNING DARKNESS IS BEING PUSHED ON WEST-ward by the sunrise as it cracks the eastern horizon. The ragged wind that has dogged the beginning and end of two full days is finally still, denying the chilled air its ability to hold the landscape in frigid misery. The sun breaks out from behind a scattering of clouds to deliver the promise of welcome warmth that feels long overdue to both man and animal. The promise of a semi-warm day has put a lively step in Little Jim's gait as he finishes hitching up the lead pair of mules to the wagon. His humorous jig is cut short when Old Man Felix walks around the corner of the wagon carrying his bedroll and a burlap sack.

Out of a long-held reflex to serve, Little Jim reaches for the old man's bedroll. "Here, boss. Give me that, and I'll put it in the wagon."

"Naw, Little Jim, I got it. Go fetch me that carpetbag out of my buckboard."

Little Jim lights a shuck around the wagon, humming a catchy tune while the old man pitches his bedroll over in the back and drops the sack in the side box. Before he can close the lid, Little Jim hands him the bag. "I'll tend that mule of yours, if you've a mind."

"Better let me," Old Man Felix says matter-of-factly. "She's a little touched."

With an amusing wink, Little Jim turns around and heads for the buckboard. "I be that way myself, boss. No worry."

Felix is putting his bag over in the back of the wagon when Sam walks out of the barn, leading Journey. The sight of the old man instantly silences the last shred of doubt that's churned in Sam's gut all night long. The stud walks on a loose lead beside him, with a look in his eyes that matches the iron-willed determination of his owner.

Sam smiles and extends his hand to Old Man Felix. "Whatever the reason, I'm glad you changed your mind."

Felix shakes Sam's hand and says, "Fact is, be a lot of stories spun up about this race. I'd rather just see it with my own eyes than I had suffer a story."

Little Jim walks by, leading the old man's mule into the barn.

Sam turns and points at Journey. "Well you're already part of the story. You made the lame walk."

"He looks fit, that's for sure. Tie him up, and let's have a look at them legs."

Sam ties Journey to the back of the wagon and steps out of the old man's way. He kneels down and meticulously feels both of the horse's front legs, from the knees to the bottom of his hooves. Satisfied with the soundness of his legs, the old man stands up and rubs Journey's muzzle. The horse responds with an easy nudge, and the old man speaks to him in a low, even voice.

Felix whispers to the horse in a soothing tone. “Never had a chance to prove who you are, have you bud? Well, all that’s going to get set straight. Then they’ll all know. Won’t they?”

With an animated look in his eyes and a raspy-throated acknowledgment, Journey pushes on the old man.

Sam interrupts the moment. “The two of you sound confident. There’s no missing that.”

Felix replies, “He’s an exceptional horse, but you have to understand, he’s a tool. Use him in the wrong way, and like any tool, you get a bad result.”

Little Jim walks back out of the barn leading Old Slick and hands the reins to Sam. “He ain’t pulled tight, boss.”

Sam takes the reins, resets the saddle, and pulls it tight “With you to keep him sound, there’ll be no bad results, Mr. Felix. Of that I’m sure.”

Felix replies, “Sure and a fact don’t live on the same road, son. One is an opinion, the other is proven.”

Sam steps up onto Old Slick and gestures toward the wagon seat. “Little Jim.” Little Jim vaults up onto the wagon seat in an easy, cat-like move.

Sam looks down at the old man. “Well, it’s fact, sir. I saw it with my own eyes, up close.”

The old man climbs up on the wagon, sits down beside Little Jim, and looks over to Sam. “Now that’s a story I would like to hear.”

Little Jim whistles to the team and the wagon lurches into motion with a rattling clatter. With nothing more than bedrolls and clothes on board, the four big mules move the wagon down the road at an easy clip.

That same morning, at the identical hour, the departure of Jessica and her entourage is giving Cordell grief of a magnitude that would make the saints swear. The entire household is near exhaustion from two days and nights of Jessica's drinking, packing, unpacking, demanding, and in general, dumping buckets of hell on every living soul in her sight. Her obsession with wealth, southern etiquette, and social superiority is only eclipsed by the full-length mirror in her bedroom. With the decline of provocative glances and whispered sour mash passes, social events for Jessica are only accelerating her desire to savor every pleasure that life has to offer, especially those of a sexual nature.

Cordell paces the front porch of the main house, tapping his hat against his leg and mumbling vile profanity that periodically escapes his lips. He occasionally stops and looks at the family carriage and the two buckboards parked in the circle drive and shakes his head in disbelief. The first buckboard carries nothing but Jessica's luggage, and the second carries everyone else's luggage, clothes, and supplies. Sorrel, Willie T., Rabbit, Petal, and Switch finished loading the carriage and wagons over an hour ago, and now everyone waits as usual. When Bell walks out of the front door, Cordell immediately raises his hands in a gesture of "What the hell?"

"Where is she, Bell?"

"She be almost ready, boss. All she needs is me to button her dress up, and she be right down."

Cordell waves Bell off. "Bell, tell her to get the hell down here, or so help me I'll drag her out of that house if she's naked. Now get!"

Bell fumbles for the front door handle, all the while repeating, "Yes sir, yes sir," and praying that Cordell doesn't come upstairs after her. Bell breathlessly climbs the spiral staircase and finally comes to rest on Jessica's bedroom door.

Bell taps lightly on the door. "Ma'am? It be Bell, ma'am." Bell pushes the door open easy. "Comin' in, ma'am."

With the door barely cracked open, Bell turns sideways, slips in, and closes the door behind her. She leans back against the door and takes a deep breath. "Lordy, Lordy, Missy. You needs to get that dress on. Mr. Cordell gots an anger goin' that's plum frightful."

Jessica is standing in the middle of her three-sided, full-length mirror, naked as her first minute on God's Earth. She turns from side to side admiring her most treasured possession, which isn't the diamond necklace and earrings she's wearing. She turns sideways and gently strokes the cheeks of her ass.

"Bell. Why do you suppose southern gentlemen are so taken with a woman's ass? I would personally think that their fantasies would dwell on the opposite side."

Bell picks up Jessica's silk undergarments and walks over to her. "Lordy ma'am, I gots no idea what them gentlemen thinks about." Bell hands her the undergarments. "Here, put these on. Everybody be waitin' on you."

Jessica turns around and around looking at her body. "Are nigger men partial that way?"

Bell works to hold her aggravation in check. "I reckon they all be the same, gentlemen or nigger. God put that grunt and roll over in all of 'em." Bell takes the undergarments back from Jessica and bends over, holding them for her to step in. “Puts these on whilst we talk and come away from that mirror.”

Jessica moves away and stands perfectly still while Bell gets her dressed.

“Do you like to be naked, Bell?”

Bell ignores the question and franticly works at getting the under garments straight.

Jessica’s eyes come to rest on Bell for a reaction from her next question. “I mean with a man.”

Bell doesn’t like Jessica’s intrusiveness but she can’t totally ignore every question. “I have my times.”

“Do you ever worry about what you look like? Or what they’ll say?”

“I don’t think on it, ma’am.”

Jessica is dumbfounded. “You don’t think on it?”

Bell pulls Jessica’s dress up around her shoulders and turns her around so she can get to the buttons on her back. “No ma’am. Cause when a nigger comes to my bed, the only thing I think about is comfort. And I like that best in the dark.”

Jessica moves back to the mirror, followed by Bell, fastening the last buttons. “There’s nothing you want to see?”

Bell hooks the last button. “Nothin’. Feelin’ comfort is way better than seein’ it, ma’am. Besides, some niggers see too much, and it ruins ‘em fore they can even start.”

Bell steps away, and the mirror consumes Jessica's eyesight, but not her mind. "The comfort you speak of—is that more than once during a visit?"

Bell picks up Jessica's coat and walks toward the bedroom door. "Well, ma'am, it be like pecan pie. Some men are full on a taste and some are not."

"But what's your preference, Bell?"

"Ma'am, come put your coat on. It be's time to go."

Jessica steps up to Bell and looks her in the eye. "Not until you answer me."

Bell holds the coat up. "Well, I shore don't like bein' sore from it no more. Now please, ma'am, Mr. Cordell is near vicious with his anger."

Jessica turns around and Bell gladly helps her with the coat. She pulls it tight around herself and remains with her back to Bell. "What a novel idea. Being sore."

Bell steps over and opens the bedroom door. "The master be waitin', ma'am."

Jessica walks to the door and stops next to Bell. "I've been waiting too, Bell, but not anymore."

Jessica walks out of the bedroom door, down the spiral staircase, and through the front door with a grounded vision of her future. She walks by Cordell without so much as a sideways glance and proceeds to the carriage. Cordell jams his hat on his head and follows her down the red brick staircase. Before she ever reaches the carriage, Sorrel has the door open and his hat in his hand.

"Ma'am," he says as she passes him by.

When Jessica steps in the carriage, Cordell stops and happens to notice that Helen is gone. He turns back to Hattie, who's standing on the front porch next to Bell. "Hattie! Where the hell is Helen? She was just sitting there on the porch."

Hattie points in the direction of the stable, "She walked on over there a bit ago Master."

"What in the HELL for?"

About that time, Helen walks around from behind the carriage leading her saddled gray mare. "I decided to bring my mare. Is that okay?"

Cordell is a bright red, and pauses for a moment before he answers. "Absolutely! It is! Absolutely okay. Bring her here. Sorrel, tie the mare to the carriage. Willie T., grab her saddle and put it in Rabbit's wagon."

Cordell begins to pace up and down like a commanding general. "Rabbit, check Blue Rock before we leave. I don't want him getting loose."

"Yes sir, boss!" Rabbit hustles to the back of his wagon and makes sure that the stud is securely tied while Helen gets into the carriage and sits down across from her mother. Cordell walks up to the carriage door, stops, and looks back to make sure everyone is in their place before they pull out

He steps into the carriage and sits down next Jessica. "Sorrel, let's go."

"Yes sir." Sorrel rattles the lines and puts the team of sleek blacks in motion, followed by Willie T. and Petal on the first wagon, and Rabbit and Switch on the second.

The tension in the carriage is thick and edgy for everyone except Helen, who rides along looking out at the majestic live oaks that line the Shannon Hill road. Their long, moss-laden branches span the red cobblestone drive from either side and meld together high overhead in a massive green canopy. Helen looks up at the dense foliage and admires the strength and tenacity that it took for those interlacing branches to form a bond that has weathered the test of time. She believes in her heart that when she takes Sam's hand in hers, their bond, like the massive oak limbs, will not only survive, but flourish to the end of time. Her peaceful contentment is fractured in an instant when she hears her mother clear her throat. Jessica's hawkish stare immediately sends Helen into a state of vigilance. The two women silently square off, eye-to-eye, like enemy combatants ready for victory or death.

With a smug sweetness, Jessica switches into a passive aggressive, Southern Belle persona. "Why did you bring your mare?"

Helen slowly breaks eye contact with her mother and looks out over the side of the carriage. She's determined not to be baited into a situation where she has no chance to defend herself. The silence hangs tense and fragile between them.

Jessica spices the sweetness with a dash of sarcasm. "You running away with your lover? Or is it your loser? Maybe both."

Cordell's face shows signs of redness as he pre-empts the battle that is sure to come. "This is an all day trip. I'll have no more of that from either one of you. Now let it end!"

The seconds tick away with everyone in the carriage knowing that the clash between the two women will never have an end.

Jessica drops the sweetness and pours in pure sarcasm. "I'm certain it's both."

Cordell snaps, "I said let it..."

Helen cuts him off, "Father!"

Cordell is jolted hard by Helen's loud, abrasive tone, and momentarily stunned into silence, as is Jessica. Helen's heart shatters knowing that her misplaced anger has just hurt the love of her life. She slides upon the edge of her seat and looks at her father with a longing for forgiveness. From her earliest memories until the present, Helen can never remember a time when her dignity hasn't been under assault from this woman, who should have been a mother instead of a tyrant. Her sole refuge and champion has always been her father, and she hopes and prays it remains that way, because she will no longer tolerate her mother's cruel remarks and vile treatment.

"Father, I apologize. From the bottom of my heart, believe me. I meant no disrespect."

"Like hell, you didn't!" Jessica interjects.

Cordell snaps. "Dammit Jessica!"

Cordell sees the hurt in is daughter's eyes and feels a punishable guilt for not doing a better job of defending her against Jessica's toxic behavior. Helen slides back in a corner of the seat and looks back over the side of the carriage.

Jessica continues. "I think the lack of a denial speaks for itself."

Helen turns to her mother and speaks to her in a controlled, even tone. "And I think you should base your accusations on proof."

"Helen, that's enough. She's your mother."

Helen turns to her father. "She is that, but that doesn't make me her property. I'm a grown woman, and I will no longer tolerate her indignities."

Cordell points at Helen. "That's enough."

"I love you with all my heart. But that finger needs to be pointed at her, and you know it."

"What possesses you to speak to us that way?" Jessica asks.

"I'm only speaking to you, Mother. And you better listen!"

"Young lady, are you threating your mother?"

"I am, and she better pay attention!"

Jessica lunges forward, only to be restrained by Cordell. "Why you little bitch! I'll..."

Helen doesn't flinch. "You'll what, MOTHER? Insinuate I'm a whore because I won't let you run my life. OH! Or maybe you'll just get plain stinking drunk and be a belligerent bitch because you can!"

Cordell turns to Helen. "STOP IT, AND I MEAN NOW!"

"I will NOT!" Helen returns.

Jessica shoves Cordell away from her and turns on him. "Are you NOT going to take her in hand?"

"He's not and neither are you! You haven't been listening, mother! You will rein in your vile mouth or there will be consequences!"

Cordell's voice rises to a point that tells both women they have crossed a line. "I SAID STOP IT! Now both of you, sit back and cool off. NOW!"

Helen turns to her father and says, "She's unfairly used your authority against me all of my life. I would request that you deny her that privilege, and remain neutral."

Helen's candid statement gives Cordell pause. "Agreed, but only if it's civil. Anything other than that is unacceptable."

Helen turns to her mother and answers her original question. "I brought my mare because I'll have an escort going home, an escort I wish to spend time with."

"And I take it you believe that to be Mr. Tanahill."

"It is."

"Let's just presume you win the bet. Tell me why you would give up everything you have to marry such a man?"

"First off, because he's an honorable man who loves me."

"That's what Dancy Higgins thought, and look what it got her."

"That's clever, but we all know the story about Dancy. So let me ask you. What am I giving up?

"I don't think that requires much of an explanation, myself."

"Yes it does. It's a cross you've carried for years. Now please, explain it."

Jessica's agitation is hardly suppressible. "Your romantic daydreams are far removed from the realities of a hard world, young lady. A world you know nothing about. Nothing at all!"

"That's not an answer. I'll ask you again. What am I giving up?"

"A man like your father, or his equal, gives you security. Without it, life will show you no mercy. That's the shield you give up when you marry a man like Sam Tanahill!"

“Security. Let me explain something, Mother, and I don’t expect you to understand, much less agree. I’ll not have a man put his hands on me that isn’t a man, and most importantly a man that doesn’t love me. And you know why? Because of you. You’ve traded love for security, and it’s left you a cold, miserable person. I made a vow a long time ago that I would never become you or anything that resembled you. You broke a good man’s heart, and I hope one day that God holds you accountable for that.”

Jessica responds, “I have but one question.”

“Which is?”

“Are you prepared to honor our bet?”

Helen answers with her own question. “More importantly, are you prepared to have Sam Tanahill as your son-in-law?”

The word son-in-law slashes through Jessica’s psyche with a cutting force that leaves her numb. Helen slides back in the seat and savors a long-awaited moment in her life. She is a woman.

Two days later, Jolene walks out on the porch of her mother’s cabin and pulls her worn coat tight against the late evening chill that is settling over Shannon Hill. When she pushes her hands deep inside of the pockets of her coat, she pauses for a moment at the touch of a feathered object in the right hand pocket. She begins to smile when she realizes it’s one of her mother’s voodoo dolls that protects the carrier from evil spirits. Jolene is not a believer, but her mother is at an age where Jolene’s pretended belief gives the old woman great comfort. She wraps her hand around the doll and hurries off through the fading light. The evening shadows are dim and murky when Jolene reaches the front porch of the mill, out of breath and with darkness close on her heels. With her mind firmly focused on the reason for her trip, Jolene opens the front door of the mill and plunges down the darkened hallway to her bedroom. Just as she lights a lantern, the front door of the mill suddenly opens, followed by the sound of some all too familiar voices. Jolene quickly puts her light out and reaches in her pocket for the doll, which slips from her grasp and falls to the floor. She kneels down ever so cautiously to crawl under her bed and hide when a lantern lights the room.

The holder of the light says, "I bet you're an old hand at that position, Missy."

Jolene is startled when she gets to her feet and turns to face Ike. His filthy dress and rough persona are in sharp contrast to his usual dapper self. The lantern light clearly accentuates a rancid look in his eyes, the look of a man who holds no value of common decency toward anything in God's creation. Jolene makes an instant decision that if she has any chance to walk out of the front door alive, it will be through strength, and strength alone.

Ike reaches for Jolene's arm, but she jerks away before his hand touches her. "Don't touch me! Don't you dare!"

Ike steps to her, roughly grabs her by the arm, and jerks her to him. "I'm going to give you a piece of advice, bitch. That smart mouth of yours will earn you nothing but pain." Ike violently shoves her toward the bedroom door. "Now get your ass into that kitchen, and get us something to eat."

Jolene stumbles and catches herself on the doorframe just as Ike follows up with a slap across her ass. The vicious blow radiates pain through Jolene's body, buckling her knees and dropping her to the floor. Ike reaches down, jerks her to her feet, and shoves her on toward the kitchen. "Come on, bitch, we're hungry."

When Jolene and Ike walk into the kitchen, Paxton is sitting at a table across the room, opening a bottle of sour mash from Cordell's liquor cabinet. His demented smile is the mirrored image of a twisted mind preparing to serve up a brand of hell on Earth that the devil's own hand cannot replicate.

Ike shoves Jolene toward the kitchen again, this time a little more forcefully. "Be quick in that kitchen, or you'll feel my boot on your ass next time."

Jolene lights a fire in the stove and goes to work while Ike and Paxton pour their glasses level up of sour mash time and again. By the time she sets the plates of food on the table, Ike is pouring their fourth glass with a joking camaraderie that eases Jolene's mind. While both men assault the plates of food like a pair of rabid jackals, Jolene slowly turns and starts for the door.

Ike never looks up from the plate. "Get back here, bitch, I didn't say you could leave."

Jolene walks over to the table and stands just out of the reach of both men.

Ike looks up at Jolene with a desire fueled by sour mash and says, "If what's between her legs is as quality as his liquor, it has to be heaven. Don't you think, Pax?"

Paxton takes a drink, and then goes back to the plate with his head down. "Niggers ain't got nothin' in common with heaven. Cause ain't none of 'em up there."

Ike points at Paxton with his fork. "I'm not speaking about the hereafter. I'm speaking about what I'm after in here."

Ike laughs hard at his own joke, though Paxton never looks up and surely sees no humor in it.

Ike points at Jolene with the fork. "Come here." Jolene hesitates.

"Goddammit, I said come here!"

Jolene takes a step forward.

Ike waves the fork around. “Closer!”

Jolene steps up to the edge of the table.

“Now, that’s better.” He takes his fork and gently raises her long dress up an inch or two off of the floor. “I bet that hair under there is as soft as corn silk.”

Jolene summons her grit. “I’m carrying his child. He may let you live if I walk out of here right now. But you raise that dress up another inch, and he’ll hunt you down with a hundred riders.”

The alcohol has bolstered Ike’s courage past good sense. “What do you say, Pax? You want to get up between them long pretty tan legs for just a taste?”

Paxton reaches for his glass. “No sir, I’ll not partake. Never cared to fall from God’s favor by doin’ her kind.”

Ike raises the dress with the fork again, looking into Jolene’s eyes for permission that the sour mash has already given him. “Well, I believe the right opposite. Her kind is a favor from God, Pax. A pure pleasure that he made just for us.”

Paxton leans back in his chair and smiles. “Coupling with animals is an abomination that any preacher can speak to. My paw faithfully taught it to me like the preacher did him. So you been warned, Ike.”

Ike lays his fork down and starts pulling up her dress. “That warning is for believers, which I ain’t.”

When Ike’s hand touches her thigh, Jolene jumps and reaches to stop his hand. “You don’t have to do this. There’s plenty of whores down at Rita’s.”

Ike glares at Jolene. "Listen to me. You keep your mouth shut, and do what you're told until I'm finished. Or I'll hurt you so bad you'll beg to die. Understand?"

Ike grabs her hard on the thigh. "UNDERSTAND?"

Jolene nods her head yes, with tears running down her face.

Ike turns his chair away from the table so Jolene is standing in front of him. He raises her dress up with his left hand, and his right starts back up her thigh. When Ike's hand comes to rest between her legs, she squeezes her legs together on a panic reflex.

Ike tightens his grip, which causes a sharp pain that takes Jolene's breath away. "Open your legs, bitch, you've had this before." Ike squeezes until she steps her feet apart. "Now then, that's better."

Ike releases his brutal grip, and Jolene's horrific pain starts to ease enough for her to catch her breath. He rubs her gently while looking over at Paxton. "I can't believe a man culls pussy on color. I can't ever get enough, no matter the color."

Ike takes Jolene by complete surprise when he stands up and roughly takes her in a headlock with his left arm. He steps behind her and increases his grip on her neck and between her legs until she feels a fainting sickness. Right before she loses consciousness, Ike eases the chokehold and Jolene gulps the air, gagging with every breath.

"You know where you're going bitch. Right back where I found you, on your knees!"

"The only person on their knees will be you, when he kills you."

"He hasn't the balls. NOW ON YOUR KNEES!"

Jolene begins to wail on Ike and scream, "Like hell, I will. You limp dick son of a bitch!! Turn me loose!"

The unexpected accusation catches Ike by surprise, and he turns Jolene loose with an embarrassment that speaks the truth louder than Jolene's screams.

Paxton howls with laughter. "A limp dick son of a bitch! He's about to fuck you blind and you're hollering limp dick. Hell, that's some crazy nigger you got there, boss man." Paxton is rip roaring drunk. "Go on, boss, break her over the table and give her a good mule fucking, go on."

Jolene's anger rises, overcoming her fear, and she steps up in Ike's face. "Yeah! Drop them pants and give me a good mule fuckin'. Come on right now! Show us what you got!"

"Shut up, or I'll kill you, bitch. So help me God, I will."

Jolene points a finger in Ike's face, "That you can do, but you know what?" Jolene turns to Paxton and says, "He sure as hell can't fuck me, and everyone on this place knows that, except you bunch of rednecks that work for him."

When Jolene looks back at Ike, he open hand slaps her with a force that drops her like a rag. The lights dim in her eyes as she lies on the floor waiting on the room to quit spinning. Jolene finally shakes her head and stumbles to her feet.

Her rage has now driven her beyond any thought of survival. "You think slapping me changes anything? Well, it doesn't! So why don't you tell Paxton here about being in Miss Jessica's room down in Charleston? About her bein' buck naked and wantin' it and you couldn't get it up. Tell him, Mr. Ike, how she wouldn't suck your limp pecker, and she throwed you out. He'll love that story." Jolene stops and turns to Paxton with a vile hate in her voice. "Ask him about the fat girl at Rita's that's been trying to revive his dead dick."

Paxton has his eyes closed laughing when blood sprays all over his face and the front of his shirt. He looks at Ike, who stands holding his bloody pistol by his side. Paxton looks down and Jolene lies at his feet with the whole side of her head bashed in, blood now pooling underneath. He hears the pistol cock and looks up at Ike.

Ike has the pistol pointed at Paxton's forehead. "If that story gets repeated, you'll be out of favor. And I'll send you on. Understand me?"

Paxton doesn't hesitate. "Yes sir."

Ike puts the pistol back in his belt. "Now go find something to roll this bitch up in so we can get rid of her."

Paxton hurries out of the room. "Yes sir."

Ike sits back down in the chair and reaches for his drink. "Such a waste. But what the hell. Just another nigger bitch."

Ike turns the glass up and takes a long hard drink.

An hour later, under the cover of pitch blackness, Ike and Paxton carry Jolene out of the mill rolled up in an old quilt. They pitch her body over into the back of a parked wagon at the front door with an unhurried casualness. When they finish pulling a tarp over her, Paxton climbs up on the wagon seat and takes the reins in his hands.

He looks down at Ike and asks, "What if there ain't no boat when I get there? What do I do with her?"

"There's a boat there, trust me. You just get in that swamp and out before it gets too light. The gators will take care of the rest. Now get. I'll see you in Camden on Friday with the boys."

Paxton slaps the team with the reins. "Yes sir."

CHAPTER TWENTY-TWO

THE NEXT AFTERNOON, ON A LONELY STRETCH OF ROAD OUTside of Camden, Sam is riding Journey back toward town when he sees a rider on a gray horse approaching in the distance. He smiles to himself and speaks to Journey, "Couldn't be that lucky again, old pard. Not ever."

"Not ever" is hardly out of Sam's mouth when he makes out a burgundy dress on the left side of the gray horse. It's definitely a woman riding sidesaddle, but what would she be doing this far out without an escort? When he lowers his hat brim to block the evening sun, Sam immediately makes out the rider and reins Journey to a stop. Sam laughs under his breath and shakes his head. "Unbelievable." He sits and waits while Helen continues to lope toward him. When she rides up and stops in front of him, Sam is mesmerized, but not solely by her breathtaking beauty. Her radiant self-confidence is like no other woman he's ever known. His love for her is grounded in her boldness toward life and her strength of character to live her beliefs.

"You look surprised to see me, Mr. Tanahill."

Sam looks away then back to her with an easy smile. "It's just your boldness. It gives me pause now and again."

"That something you don't like in a woman?"

"I didn't say that. I said it gives me pause. Like your dress there, it gets a man's attention."

"If my boldness disturbs you, then perhaps I should keep it in check."

"Don't do that. I could never be married to a woman who wasn't bold."

"Is that a proposal, Mr. Tanahill? Because it sure sounded like one."

Sam points off down the road. "Let's ride. It'll be near dark before we're back to town." He pulls his coat off and hands it to her. "Here, put this on. There'll be a chill soon."

Helen takes the coat from Sam, pulls it around her shoulders, and they ride off together side-by-side.

Helen looks over at Sam. "Well, was it?"

"There is one coming, but not today."

"And when should I expect this proposal?"

"On Saturday. Right after I speak to your father."

"You know my answer. Why wait? Why not right now?"

"Because I need your father's release, and you know that. I gave him my word that I wouldn't call on you, and I won't break it."

"His release? It's contingent upon you winning the match, isn't it?"

"It is."

"And if you lose? What then?"

"I've agreed to go west and never return to the Carolinas."

Helen's smile puts Sam a little off balance. "Whose idea was that? Yours or my father's?"

"It was mine, but it doesn't matter. Journey out ran Blue Rock before, and he'll do it again."

Helen continues to smile. "I hope so, because I have a confession of my own. I made a similar wager with my mother. If you win the match, I get to choose who calls on me, plus I decide whom I marry. If you lose, then those rights go to her."

Sam looks over at Helen. "Will you live on that if I lose?"

"Only if you break my heart and leave me behind."

Sam stops his horse and turns to Helen, smiling. "A lot of things may happen in this world, but two things won't ever come to pass: I'll never break your heart, and I'm sure as hell not leaving you behind. That's my solemn vow."

Helen reaches for Sam's hand. "That's what I came to hear you say."

She pulls him to her, leans over, and kisses him with a hunger that's short on patience and long on passion. The intense passion of the kiss leaves them both with a burning need for some time together, undisturbed by the needs of the world. They ride off down the road with a commitment to each other that their life together, no matter what happens, will begin in two days.

Later that evening, with the light trailing away, Sam and Helen sit at the edge of town in silence. The agony of good decisions brings misery to their hearts, but they are resolved that this social parting is their last.

Sam turns to Helen and says, "Thanks for riding out today. I needed to see you more than you know."

When Helen is in his presence, his drive and strength of character polish her outlook on the world to a brightness that shines on every corner of her life.

"You remember our first dance?"

"I do. But why do you ask me that?"

"Because it changed my life."

Sam teases her. "Well, that would be your fault. You're the one that asked me to dance. Remember?"

Helen leans over and runs her hand through his thick black hair. "That was a little forward of me, wasn't it?"

"Personally? I liked it."

Helen tugs on his hair and says, "Then kiss me like you love me. I need to get."

Sam takes his hat off, leans over, and kisses her, his desire matching her own.

When Sam puts his hat back on, he points off toward town. “I’m going to follow you home. Go on and ride ahead of me. I want to make sure you get there okay.”

He motions for her to go on. “I’ll be right behind you. Go on.”

Helen takes off his coat and hands it back to him. “I love you, Sam.”

Sam lays the coat across the swells of his saddle. “I love you too. Now go on. They’ll be looking for you.”

When Helen rides up to the house, Cordell and Lanham Hawks are tightening the cinches on their saddles. Cordell pauses when he hears Lanham speak to him.

“Sir.” Cordell looks up to see Helen ride out of the darkness.

“I hope I’m not the reason y’all are saddled up.”

Cordell shakes his head and breathes a sigh of relief. “Are you okay?”

“Yes sir, I apologize. I just rode out farther than I thought.”

Cordell walks over and helps Helen down off of the mare. “I’ve been worried sick, young lady.”

Helen looks back to her left, out into the darkness at Sam, then back to her father. “No need to worry. I was okay.” She takes off her floppy sun hat and walks into the house.

Cordell stares out into the night until his eyes adjust, and he makes out a shadowy rider sitting far out in the darkness. There is little doubt as to his identity or why he is there. Cordell is grateful and nods his head in thanks for Sam seeing her home safely. Sam returns the nod, turns, and rides off into the night.

Sam skirts around town on the Old Wheelhouse Road until the distant timber glows like the cradle of a morning sunrise. The aromatic scent from a multitude of cook fires scattered throughout the wooded campgrounds lingers heavily in the chilled night air. The harmonica that echoes somewhere in the distance is Sam's guiding beacon to his final destination of the evening. When he rides up to his campsite, Old Man Felix is tending a pot of stew hanging over the fire, and Little Jim has finally given the harmonica a rest. The old man hands Little Jim the wooden ladle and says, "Here. And don't let it burn."

Felix wipes his hands on his cook apron and walks over to Journey, when Sam reins up at the wagon. The old man kneels down on the offside, checking Journey's front legs before Sam clears the saddle.

"How far did you breeze him, son?"

"Like we discussed. Half a mile twice at a little under half speed, and a mile at a little over."

The old man continues a meticulous examination of the horse's front legs. "On the mile breeze, how was he in the bit? In or out of it?"

"In, the whole time. The further we went, the stronger he got. He feels ready."

The old man stands up with a smile on his face. "I think he peaked on the right day. We'll rest him tomorrow, then breeze him light Saturday morning, right before the race."

Sam extends his hand to the old man. "Then we're ready. Thank you, sir!"

The old man holds both hands up. "Don't thank me just yet. A fit horse is only half the deal, and might I add, not the most important half either."

"I don't understand. What other half?"

The old man winks at Sam with a mischievous grin. "The strategy, son, it's what horse racing revolves around. Everyone's horse is fit, but it's how and when you use that horse. That's what's going to decide this race. And nothing else!"

Sam gets a profound look on his face. "Well! Then let's sit down and get to it."

The old man takes the reins from Sam. "We are. But tomorrow."

"Why tomorrow?"

"Because you and I and Little Jim there are going to walk every foot of that race track."

"And do what?"

"Figure out a way to win. That's what!"

Sam's patience with the old man is beginning to wear thin. "Listen. I ran that blue stud down on Journey like he was a fat plow horse. He..."

The old man cuts Sam off. "No, you listen to me! You ran down a loose horse with a scared girl on his back. I told you that. This time you're facing a seasoned jockey and a horse that's rested and fit. So you better get your head out of the clouds and listen to me if you want to win."

The gravity of the match finally comes to rest in Sam's mind with a crushing reality. The romantic mindset he held toward the match, up until this very moment, has had him considering it a forgone conclusion that the race would be won, and Helen would be his. Sam stands there grappling with the enormity of the life-changing event that his ego has put into motion. His anxiety is momentarily running rampant until his mind reaches out to restore order.

Sam's iron-willed determination wins the battle but it leaves him with a clear realization that there is work to be done if he intends to win the match. When he finally looks over at Old Man Felix, there's little doubt about his head being out of the clouds.

Sam reaches and takes the reins back from the old man. "What time?"

"The first race tomorrow is at ten. We need to be finished before that."

"First light, then."

The old man smiles and nods his head in agreement. "That works." Then he points at Journey and says, "Get done with your horse, then let's eat."

The old man goes back to his pot of stew and Sam begins unsaddling Journey.

Later that night, a hunched over driver in a weather-beaten hat guides a team of hogged back mules through the patchy darkness toward Shannon Hill. His old dilapidated field wagon rolls along to a jarring chorus of creaking boards and rattling noises. When he pulls up in front of the mill, he steps down, stretches the kinks from his tired frame, and yanks on the tarp that covers the sacks of grain in the back of his wagon.

Ira Paul waits for a moment, then yanks on the tarp again. "We're here; get up. Come on girl!"

The edge of the tarp folds back and Newella raises up with an old quilt wrapped snugly around her shoulders. When she pulls an arm from under the blanket and herds her shaggy mop of curls behind her head, it exposes a face that clearly shows the ravages of sadness and grief. She unwraps the quilt, and Ira Paul helps her down from the wagon along with her old tattered carpetbag.

Ira Paul looks around at the dark, lifeless mill. "Don't seem to be a soul around here, Newella."

Newella picks up her bag and extends her right hand. "I appreciate you doing this Ira Paul. I just couldn't bear another night in my mother's house."

Ira Paul shakes Newella's hand. "Truth is, neither could she. After your paw died, she just slam give up on livin', but you know that yourself."

"Well, everything is for the best. They're back together again, so that's all that matters now."

Ira Paul stammers with uncertainty about leaving. "Are you here alone?"

Newella turns and walks toward the front door of the mill. "God, I hope so." She walks into the mill and closes the door behind her.

Ira Paul mounts back up on his wagon, swings the team around, and heads back home at a plodding pace.

The early morning rays of the winter sun streak between and around the burlap curtains, covering the bedroom with an array of lighted strips. A scattering of the warm beams lay diagonally across Newella's face, gently coaxing one eye at a time to open and face the world. She arches her back and stretches, enjoying the familiar comfort of her own bed and the best night's sleep she's had in days. Newella closes her eyes, lovingly rubs the gentle ark in her stomach, and talks to her baby as she's done since the first days of her pregnancy.

"Good morning, my little one. You are in my prayers, and I love you beyond measure."

Newella smiles and sits up on the side of her bed with the best feeling she's had about the world in days. When her feet touch the floor, her stomach growls and rumbles.

Newella laughs and says, "You must be a boy. Only men complain that loudly about breakfast."

Newella is pulling her dress over her head and singing softly to her baby when she walks into the kitchen in her bare feet. The gaiety of her mood takes a sudden jolt when she steps in something sticky by the end of a table. When she bends over to look at her foot, she is stunned to a horrified silence. Newella steps back as her eyes trace the edges of what was at one time a large pool of blood.

On reflex, Newella puts her hands to her face and cries out, "Oh God, no!"

Frantically, Newella dashes back to her room, slips on her stockings and shoes, and grabs her coat and scarf. She has a sick feeling in the pit of her stomach that she will not find Jolene down at her mother's. When she opens the front door of the mill, the trail of crimson spots on the porch and out into the road brings a quiver to her lips and tears to her eyes.

Newella takes off running across the cotton fields toward the quarters, "Please, God. Please!"

When Newella reaches Jolene's mother's cabin, she races up on the porch to the open front door, frantically calling her name. "Jolene! Jolene!" Newella hears Jolene's mother, Auntie Lil, answer from back of the house. "Back here, child." "Oh thank God," Newella thinks as she hurries around to the back of the house to find Auntie Lil feeding her chickens. Jolene is nowhere in sight.

Auntie Lil walks up to her picket fence with a cold, stern look in her eyes. "She be gone, Missy. Gone for three evenin's past, now."

"Gone where, Auntie?"

"I told her I seen it in dem chicken bones, and there was blood spots on the new moon. But she wouldn't listen. She jest took off and went any way!"

Newella, near hysteria at this point, continues, "Went where?"

"Over to that mill, and it near dark for she left."

Newella wraps her arms around herself in a new wave of grief. She stomps her feet on the ground in anger and turns around mumbling under her breath, "Why would she do that? Why?"

"Went after somethin' Mr. Cordell done give her."

Newella turns to Auntie and asks, "The cross? Was it her silver cross?"

"Wouldn't say. Jest said she couldn't rest unless she had it with her."

Newella starts walking backwards away from Auntie, "If she comes back here Auntie. You tell her to stay here! Tell her I said stay here!"

Newella turns around and starts running for the stable down below the main house.

Auntie stares after her and says, "Oh, you need not worry on that, Missy. Cause she ain't comin' back. Not ever."

Newella is out of wind and near exhaustion when she runs into the stable, calling, "Rabbit! Rabbit where are you?"

Benjie walks out of a stall at the far end of the barn and answers, "Rabbit ain't here, ma'am. He be gone with Mr. Cordell to the race."

Newella gulps for air and walks on toward Benjie. "Benjie. I need a horse. Right now!"

Benjie hesitates and tries to find a way to avoid doing that without someone's permission.

"I done turned 'em all out for the day, ma'am. I'm sorry."

Newella stops within one step of Benjie's face. "Benjie! I have an important message for Mr. Cordell. Now if I don't deliver it, he's going to know why. Now fetch me that horse, or I'll send him to see you!"

Benjie does an about face in one second and walks out of the barn to catch her a horse.

Newella calls to him, "And not a nag either, Benjie!"

Within fifteen minutes, Benjie gives Newella a leg up on a big coon-tailed roan gelding that Newella puts in motion before Benjie can get out of the way. She holds the stout gelding to an easy lope, knowing it takes most of the day to reach Camden.

That same morning, but at an earlier hour, Old Man Felix stands at the finish line of the one mile track, lost to the thundering memories of a time when his horses were the feared legends of the sport of kings. Sam and Little Jim stand over on the edge of the track patiently waiting while Felix relives the best days of his life, which were always the day of a race. He finally looks over at Sam, smiles, and starts walking down the middle of the track through the morning mist, like an old soldier who's returned to the field of battle. After about a hundred yards, he kneels down and picks up a handful of dirt before he walks off of the track.

When Felix walks up, Sam points at the dirt in his hand. "That for luck or just plain superstition?"

The old man smiles and hands Sam the dirt. "Here. If done right, this is your edge tomorrow." The old man puts the dirt in Sam's hand and then cups his hands around Sam's. "Squeeze it hard before you open your hand."

Sam squeezes and when he opens his hand the dirt is a firm, round ball.

Sam looks at the ball of dirt then to the old man and says, "So? What do you want me to do with it?"

The old man answers, "I want you to remember it." He turns to Little Jim and points a finger at him. "And I especially want you to remember it."

Sam throws the dirt down, "I know you have a reason. Why not just tell us?"

Felix smiles and says, "Let's walk to the other end and start at the beginning. It'll make more sense to you."

When they've walked but a short distance, the men pass under the massive branches of an ancient live oak that stands near the track. The old man looks up into the branches and then back to the finish line without saying a word or missing a step. They walk the balance of the mile, each man lost in his own thoughts. When they reach the starting line, Old Man Felix walks out on the track and stands for a minute, looking off toward the finish line.

He walks back to the starting line and turns to Sam and Little Jim, then begins, "Lot of races are lost right here. Before the race ever starts, gentlemen. So let's make sure we get this right. Now, Little Jim, are you right-handed or left?"

"Right-handed, sir."

The old man says, "Okay. When you ride up to the start line, make sure Blue Rock is on your right." The old man looks at Sam. "No matter what. You claim that left side early, and don't turn it loose."

"Yes sir. But you know my question. Why?"

"Because when we pass Blue Rock, it's going to be fast and quick. A right-handed jockey makes fewer mistakes when judging speed and distance if it's happening on his right side. If we foul on the pass, we lose. Simple as that."

"How can he foul him on the pass? They're going to be running side-by-side."

The old man points down the track and answers, "Only to that big tree. When the pass happens." He turns to Little Jim and continues. "You're going to move Journey right in front of Blue Rock and hold him there until you reach the finish line."

Sam smiles. "I like the part about being in front at the finish. But why chance a foul moving over in front of him?"

"Son, Blue Rock is undefeated in thirty two matches. He's the intimidator, but not tomorrow. You remember the dirt and how hard it packed in your hand?"

"Yes sir," Sam answers.

"Well, when Journey is running straight in front of Blue Rock. Guess who gets intimidated then? Blue Rock!"

"Now I understand. The dirt will be flying in his face."

"It won't be just flying. That hard packed dirt coming out of Journey's shoes will be pounding Blue Rock like he's never had it."

Sam looks to Little Jim and asks, "You understand all this, and when to do it?"

"Yes sir. Start on his left, pass at the big tree, don't foul, and get in front of him. I got it, boss."

"One last thing. Willie T. is a smart jockey. Once you're in front, the only place he'll be able to move is on your left. When he does, don't move to block to him, because by then you'll be right on top of the finish line. All I want you to do then is ride Journey."

"But why not block him?" Sam asks.

"No need to chance a foul. Journey has the momentum. Besides, by the time Willie T. gets Blue Rock back in the race, it'll be over."

Sam looks over to the old man and says, "And we win."

"Well, we've done what we can. Now we give it to providence."

Sam stands staring off down the track, thinking about the old man's plan and thankful for the providence of Journey coming up lame that day at home. Listening to Old Man Felix lay out the strategy for the race puts Sam's mind at ease and his guts in a knot. If Sam has ever felt in God's care, it's at this very moment.

He is brought back to the business at hand when his eye catches sight of two riders crossing up on the far end of the track, accompanied by a man on foot. Even at this distance it's not hard to recognize the sleek blue stallion with Willie T. in the saddle, followed by Cordell on the other horse. Rabbit has a lead rope attached to the race bit, and he walks beside Blue Rock helping Willie T. keep the high-strung stallion under control.

When they turn down the side of the track, the old man looks over at Sam with a mischievous glint in his eyes. "What do you say we walk to town and get some breakfast?"

Sam looks back at Blue Rock for a moment, then back to Felix.

The old man's voice takes on a tone that's truthful and to the point. "Watching them work that horse serves no purpose. None at all."

Sam nods in agreement, and then looks over at Little Jim. "Go on back to the wagon and look after the horses. I'll bring you some biscuits."

"Yes sir." Little Jim turns and starts toward the campsite, and Sam and the old man walk up the track toward Cordell and Blue Rock.

Right before Cordell rides up to Sam and the Old Man, he speaks to Rabbit. "Y'all go on down and get started."

Rabbit leads Blue Rock on toward the warm up track. "Yes sir, boss."

When Cordell rides up to Sam and the Old Man, Sam is a little taken back by Cordell's smile and friendliness.

Cordell extends his hand to Sam. "Mr. Tanahill, it's good to see you."

"You too, sir."

Cordell turns to Felix and extends his hand. "My old friend. How are you?"

The old man smiles and shakes Cordell's hand. "Same as always. If I'm at a horse race, I'm blessed."

Cordell laughs to himself. "I feel the same, Mr. Felix. Blessed to be here."

Cordell turns to Sam and says, "Mr. Tanahill, you're a lucky man. This gentleman knows more about horses than the maker himself."

"I'm sure you'll be proven right tomorrow, sir."

Cordell smiles easy, looks off down the track, and then back to Sam. "Good luck tomorrow. And I mean that."

Sam, in a bold, honest way returns the sentiment. "And you too, sir."

"Thank you, son. I'll see you tomorrow."

Sam turns and walks off with Felix. "Yes sir. We'll be here."

Cordell has always admired Sam's rugged ways and his eye-to-eye approach to life. Cordell knows that a defeat tomorrow will not be the end of his association with Mr. Tanahill. Sam and Helen are in love, and will live according to proper social etiquette until it finally bars them from being together. Then all of the southern traditions and cultural norms will be removed by the force of an impassioned love that will not be denied.

Cordell daydreams about Jolene, and is envious of Sam's courage to risk everything for the woman he loves. For some time now, Cordell has entertained the thought of living the remainder of his life with Jolene and their children, somewhere other than at Shannon Hill. Her love has filled a dark, hollow void in his life with a warm sunlight that makes him want to live life rather than conquer it. The peacefulness he feels in his heart and soul at this very moment is founded in the knowledge that a woman walks God's Earth who loves him unconditionally. Cordell's daydream vision is suddenly replaced by the real world with the sound of one word. "Boss."

Cordell turns in the saddle just as Ike rides up beside him and extends his hand. "Good morning, sir."

Cordell forces a smile. "Mr. Murphy. What brings you out here so early?"

"Thought I would catch up with you before your day got too busy."

"Everything getting taken care of on the Moore place and at home?"

"Yes sir, it is. We should be finished on the Moore place in a month, easy."

Cordell looks over at Ike and happens to notice a pearl handled revolver in his waistband.

Cordell nods toward the pistol. "That new?"

Ike smiles with pride, pulls the pistol out, and holds it up "Yes sir. It's the latest Colt revolver. A friend of mine gave it to me for Christmas."

"Some friend. Could I see it?"

"Sure." Ike hands Cordell the pistol.

Cordell points the pistol at arm's length, feeling the balance. When he pulls the pistol back to examine it, he sees a spot of dried blood where the cham ber meets the barrel.

Cordell points the blood out to Ike. "Is that blood?"

Ike's good-natured smile fades, and he reaches for the pistol. "Must be from my finger, when I cut it."

Cordell hands Ike the pistol, and he returns it to his waistband.

"I know you didn't ride out here to show me that pistol. So, do we have a problem somewhere?"

"Oh, no sir. I wanted to see if you knew where I could get a bet covered. That's all."

"How much do you want to bet?"

"Well, me and the boys put together two thousand. I know it's late, but I thought just maybe you could help me."

"Well, just so happens I'm holding five hundred for a lady, but she wants four to one. I'd cover it, but I'm tapped out."

Ike thinks for a minute "Four to one. That's a little steep."

"It is. But my horse is thirty-two and zero, and Tanahill's horse is zero and one. Hard to find even money on that."

Ike finally shakes his head. "Okay. I'll do it."

Cordell reaches out to Ike and says, "The money, Mr. Murphy."

Ike reluctantly pulls a leather pouch from under his vest.

"Leave it in the pouch. I'll return it one way or the other."

Ike hands Cordell the pouch and smiles, but both men know it's not real.

Ike nods his head and says, "Thank you, sir."

"Glad to help, Mr. Murphy."

Ike can feel himself being dismissed in Cordell's tone. "If you don't need anything, sir, I'm going to town."

Cordell places his attention on Blue Rock over at the track. "Not a thing."

Ike turns to ride off, tips his hat, and says, "Good day sir."

Cordell stares straight ahead and doesn't reply.

CHAPTER TWENTY-THREE

LATE IN THE AFTERNOON, EVERY ROAD LEADING INTO CAMDEN has an array of travelers from every corner of southern society. From the elegantly dressed, wealthy planters, to the plain folks just looking for a little relief from a hard scrabble life. The options of entertainment in town range widely from invitation balls to come-one-come-all barn dances, plus a sordid variety of rough and tumble drinking establishments that specialize in cheap liquor and cheaper women. Sundown is still an hour away, but the rowdy noise of uncivilized men throughout the town is a clear indicator that a thirst for pleasure is about to be quenched. Some of the rougher element among the travelers already have the thirst well under control and feel a need to get on to the pleasure.

Paxton, Pate, Slack, and three other hard cases from Shannon Hill are riding up the south road to town, passing a bottle around and discussing their favorite subject: whores. The six men are carrying on and swapping stories when they ride upon a roan horse tied off the road out in the timber.

Paxton stops his crew in the middle of the road and sits looking at the roan horse. He asks, "Are my eyes bad, or does that roan have a coontail?"

Pate squints his eyes. "He's a coontail for sure, Pax."

Paxton turns to Slack. "I know that can't be Old Roanie. But go have a look."

Slack breaks off and rides out into the timber. When he rides up to the horse he turns in the saddle. "It's him, Pax." Slack points at the horse's hip and says, "He's wearing the SH. It's Old Roanie for sure."

"Somebody stole the son-of-a-bitch. Untie him, and bring him with us."

When Slack reaches down, Newella steps from behind the tree, unties Roanie, and steps away with him. "He's not stolen. I borrowed him."

Paxton, on angry reflex, spurs his horse toward Newella. "That fuckin' whore."

Paxton almost runs Newella down when he rides up. "Bitch! What are you doing with that horse?"

Newella pushes on Paxton's horse and moves out of the way. "That's none of your business!"

Paxton points a finger at her like a hellfire and brimstone preacher. "You answer me! Or I'll do God a favor and beat you to death right here! Now what are you doing?"

The sour mash rage in Paxton's eyes cools Newella's temper. "I stopped to pee. That's all."

"Don't fuck with me bitch. You know what I'm asking. So give me a straight answer."

Newella softens her tone. "I got money bet on the race tomorrow. I just came to watch."

Paxton cools off and his mind starts working. "What about your nanny job with your nigger friend? Where is she?"

Newella answers before she thinks. "I left her with her mother till I get back."

Newella can see the rage has turned to suspicion in Paxton's eyes.

Paxton decides that Ike needs to hear her story. "You're coming with us to see Ike. Slack, give her a leg up and let's go."

Slack steps down and helps Newella up onto the roan gelding. Before she's barely in the saddle, Paxton reaches out and brutally grabs her by the arm.

"Bitch, you ride along with us, and be real quiet like. If you say one word, or make one bad move, I'll slit your fuckin' throat. Understand me?"

"I got no reason to do otherwise, Paxton. I just came to watch the race."

Paxton turns to ride off. "Ride next to me, and do like I told you."

Newella rides along, all too aware of what her fate will be once it's dark and Ike gets his hands on her. If the issue with Paxton were about her riding a Shannon Hill horse, they would be going to see Cordell instead of Ike. But Newella could clearly see the change in Paxton's body language the moment she told the lie about Jolene being at her mother's.

Paxton doesn't know how or what Newella knows about Jolene, but he does know that she just lied to him, and for that, he's going to make sure she doesn't get a chance to talk to Cordell, or anyone else. Besides, to his way of thinking, killing Newella has been sanctioned by God because of her sinful ways. When they reach the fork at the Old Wheelhouse Road, Paxton pulls up and sits there thinking.

He turns to his men and says, "Pate, you stay with me and the woman. The rest of you scatter out through town and find Ike. Tell him we need to meet somewhere out of town. We'll wait here. Now get!"

When the men ride off, Newella is visibly shaken by the knowledge that Paxton finally has the chance to make good on his threat of giving her a beating she won't survive. Newella places her hand on her stomach and tears well up in her eyes. With a trembling heart she begins to silently pray and beg God to spare her baby, who is innocent of its mother's sins. The closing darkness only adds to Newella's mounting anxiety.

Newella fidgets in the saddle and looks over at Paxton. "I need to pee."

Paxton doesn't care, or even look at her. "No!"

Newella begins to cry. "Please! Don't make me pee on myself. Please."

Paxton sits there for the longest, then looks over at Newella. "Okay. But mind yourself, bitch." Paxton looks at Pate. "You get a holt of the hair on her head and don't turn her lose. You walk her out there and walk her back. Now get down."

Pate and Newella get off of their horses and hand Paxton their reins.

Pate reaches and grabs a handful of Newella's hair. "What about when she's peeing?"

"I don't care what goes on out there, but you better not turn her loose."

Newella stops and looks at Paxton, then says, "That's not decent."

"You're a whore. You're not used to decent." Paxton looks at Pate and says, "Take her on, and do like I told you."

Pate pulls Newella into the brush by her hair. "Come on, bitch, and don't give me any trouble."

Paxton is sitting there with his own brand of anxiety rolling in the pit of his stomach when he happens to look up and gets a surprise that feels more like a curse from the devil himself. There walking up the middle of the road is Sam Tanahill, his half-breed nigger, and an old man. Before anybody says a word, Pate comes dragging Newella by the hair of her head out of the brush and into plain sight. Sam looks at Newella, then back to Paxton. "What's going on here, Paxton?"

"That's none of your fuckin' business, Tanahill. Now move on."

"I think I'm going to make it my business. Now tell him to turn her loose."

Paxton sits there staring holes in Sam.

"Tell him. Or I'll make him."

"Tanahill. You take a hand in this, and you'll get more than you bargained for. Hear me?"

"Tell him, or it's going to get ugly. Your choice."

Paxton sits there for the eternity of a few seconds and then looks over to Pate. "Turn her loose."

When Pate turns her loose, he hurries around and gets on his horse.

"Come on over here with me, Newella."

Newella walks over to Sam with tears in her eyes, ever so thankful that God has answered her prayers and protected her baby.

"You okay?" Sam asks.

Newella shakes her head yes, unable to speak.

Paxton points at Sam. "You're going to be dealt with this time, Tanahill. You and your jumpy nigger there, in a real harsh way. So get ready."

Paxton spurs his horse forward, followed by Pate leading the roan.

Everyone stands there for a moment in silence, letting the adrenaline ease off.

Sam finally turns to Newella and asks, "What are you doing up here with them?"

"I wasn't with them, I was by myself. They came up on me and accused me of stealing the horse I was riding."

"Did you?"

"No, of course not. I came to see Mr. Cordell. I just borrowed it."

"What's so important that you took the chance of riding all this way by yourself?"

"Jolene's gone. I went home to bury my maw, and when I got back she was gone. I rode up here to tell Mr. Cordell."

Sam offers his condolences. "I'm sure sorry about your maw. She was a good woman."

"Thanks. But she's at peace now. It wasn't about the horse, Sam. Paxton figured I somehow knew what happened to Jolene, so they were going to kill me."

"So what do you think happened to her?"

"I think one or both of 'em killed her. And I think, given the chance, Paxton will kill me too."

"Well that's not going to happen. I'll send for Mr. Cordell." Sam looks over at Little Jim. "Go fetch him, Little Jim, but don't tell him about what went on here. Just tell him I need to talk to him. And be careful."

"Yes sir."

Sam tries to lighten the mood. "Come on now, you can stay with us. Mr. Felix there makes a mean stew."

The old man smiles and points at her belly. "If I'm reading that dress right, I'd say you're eating for two."

Newella finally smiles and places her hands on her stomach. "I am."

The old man puts his arm around Newella's shoulder like a grandfather, and they all three turn and walk off toward their campsite.

The chilled December night offers up a star-dotted dome that covers the night sky from edge to edge. The crisp darkness magnifies the star cover until it settles into the treetops that surround the campgrounds like a heavenly blanket. Newella sits by the roaring campfire, wrapped in a quilt, with her gaze fixed on the starry heavens as she tries to deal with the gripping sadness of losing both her best friend and her mother within the span of a few days. She turns to the old man, who's also sitting by the fire, smoking his pipe, and holding a rifle across his lap.

"Mr. Felix, do you think God passes out good luck to some folks and bad to others?"

The old man answers with a question of his own. "And why do you have that on your mind?"

"Because of today. If y'all hadn't come by... me and my baby would be dead right now. Just like my friend, Jolene, and her baby."

"Well, I reckon I can't speak to that, Missy. I'm a stout believer, but I don't know the Book well enough to say one way or the other."

"But why would you suppose I'd be saved and she wouldn't?"

"I got no answer for you on that either. But I will tell you this. Luck can jump from good to bad with no reason toward right or wrong. So I'd be real careful around Paxton and his bunch."

Sam walks out of the dark carrying a rifle, and sits down by the fire across from Newella. He cradles the rifle in his lap and warms his hands at the fire.

The old man asks, "Journey okay?"

"He's a little nervous, like he knows tomorrow is the day."

The old man smiles and says, "I don't know how, but a lot of horses sense it."

Sam looks across at Newella. "I didn't hear it all, but the advice about Paxton and his bunch, you best heed that."

Newella pulls the quilt up around her shoulders like it's a shield against more than the cold night air. "He's promised me a beating for a while now. I just never put no store in it, not until today."

"Well it's not near over in his mind. Especially after what happened today."

From out in the darkness, Little Jim calls to Sam. "Boss!"

In a quick motion, Sam stands up with the rifle at ready, and the old man follows suit. Sam strains his eyes over the barrel of the rifle trying to see if anyone is with Little Jim.

Sam relaxes when he hears Cordell's voice. "Sam, its Cordell. I've got Lanham with me, and we're coming in."

Sam lowers the rifle and relief washes over him.

Old Man Felix steps up close to Sam and whispers, "He knows about today. That's why Lanham is with him."

Sam looks straight ahead. "I agree."

Cordell is the first one to walk into the light, followed by Lanham and Little Jim.

Cordell reaches for Sam's hand. "Evening, Sam." He turns to Felix and Newella, greeting each one in turn. "Mr. Felix. Newella."

Cordell steps toward Newella while the old man and Sam shake hands with and speak to Lanham.

Cordell smiles at Newella and points toward the fire. "Why don't we sit down and you tell me about my horse?"

"Paxton tell you I stole your horse? I guess he did, or Mr. Hawks wouldn't be here. Would he?"

"Well, he said they came up on you riding my horse and you refused to come see me about it. He said you kept trying to run off, and that's what Mr. Tanahill here saw."

The tears well up in Newella's eyes and her heart breaks with sadness for Cordell. She knows that when he hears the truth, it will tear him apart. She wipes the tears from her cheeks and avoids looking him in the eye.

Cordell speaks to Newella in an easy tone. "Just tell me the truth. There's no great harm in you borrowing one of my horses. Besides, I don't blame you for wanting to come up here. You've got money bet."

Newella sits silent with her head down, unable to look at Cordell.

Sam speaks to her. "Newella." She looks up at Sam, and he says, "Tell him why you came up here."

With a broken heart and tears in her eyes, Newella can barely get the words out. "I came up here to tell you, Jolene is gone."

"Gone? Where to?"

Newella shakes her head and says, "Nobody knows. I went home to bury my mother, and when I got back she'd been gone three days."

"I'm sorry about your mother."

"Thank you, but she's resting peacefully now."

Cordell walks away a few steps and stands thinking with his back to everyone. When he turns around there's a chilling look of revenge in his eyes.

Cordell looks at Newella, "Tell me why you're crying like she's dead?"

Newella gathers up her strength and continues. "Last night, when I got to the mill, I went straight in and went to bed. When Jolene wasn't there, I wasn't worried, because she'd promised me she'd stay at her mother's until I got back. But then this morning when I walked into the kitchen, I found a huge bloodstain on the floor that was still sticky. It hadn't been wiped up very good, plus there were blood spots down the hall, across the porch, and out into the road. So I took off running down to her mother's, but she hadn't seen Jolene in three days. She said Jolene had forgotten something you'd given her at the mill, and she went back to get it just at dark. And that was the last anybody saw of her."

"Tell me how you came about being with Paxton, and where he was taking you."

"Well, it was just plain bad luck. I tied Old Roanie up and went to pee in the woods. But when I walked back out, there sits Paxton and his whole crew. At first he was mad about the horse, but all that changed when he asked me about Jolene."

"What did he ask you?"

"He wanted to know where she was and why I wasn't at home with her."

"What did you tell him?"

"I lied and said I left her at her mother's until I got home. I told him I borrowed the horse to come watch the race, because I had money bet. Even being stone drunk he didn't believe a word I said, so he sent his crew to find Ike."

"Why do you think he sent for Ike?"

"Because Ike was the ramrod in whatever happened to Jolene. If Paxton had killed her by himself, he would have ridden me out in the woods and slit my throat for lying, but he didn't."

"Makes sense. He thought you knew something, and you were coming to tell me."

Cordell won't let himself even consider the possibility of Jolene being dead until he hears Lanham say it. Everyone remains quiet knowing that Cordell's vengeance will only be quenched by blood if Jolene has been murdered.

Cordell turns and speaks to Lanham. "Mr. Hawks, I want her found. Hire the best trackers and as many riders as you need, but find her." He turns to Sam next. "We run the race tomorrow like nothing has happened. And I ask all of you to please not say a word about this just yet. I need to know what happened first."

Lanham looks over at Cordell. "I'll leave tonight."

"Thank you," Cordell says.

Lanham walks off and Cordell sits down by Newella, putting his arm around her.

"You risked your life trying to help her, and I won't ever forget that."

Newella lays her head over on Cordell's shoulder and begins to weep softly.

Later that evening, an assortment of lulling dance music drifts in from town, settling the campgrounds down for the night. The campers are saying their goodnights, but the revelers over in town are just starting their rowdy night of adult entertainment. Sam and the old man are sitting by the campfire talking when Little Jim walks up with a clean shirt on and a dapper tilt to the brim of his hat. Sam has seen the musical itch on Little Jim all day and only smiles when he plays a few catchy notes on his harmonica.

Sam points his finger at Little Jim in a friendly way. "Tomorrow is race day. So just remember those fifty whole dollars."

"I got it, boss. It be music and women tonight, and hoss racin' and money tomorrow." Little Jim makes a quick pass across his lips with the harmonica and touches the brim of his hat. "Gentlemen, I'll see y'all at daylight."

Sam's tone changes to business. "Stay out of trouble, Little Jim, and don't you dare get drunk tonight. You hear me?"

Little Jim does a quick dance shuffle as he walks off. "Boss, the only thang I'm layin' hands to tonight be a little music and a heavy woman."

Sam watches Little Jim saunter off into the darkness until he's out of sight. Sam pitches a stick into the fire and looks over at the old man. "Can't blame him none. That music sure has a draw on a fella."

The old man lights his pipe with a burning twig from the fire and points with it toward Little Jim. "If you're a mind to go with him, Newella is down for the night and Journey is tended to. So go on. Go see your girl. I'll look after things."

Sam stares into the fire and says, "Well, Mr. Felix. I don't have a girl tonight, but after I win the match, I will. I'll sure have one then."

The old man asks knowingly, "And by chance would that girl be Miss Helen Meyers?"

"Yes sir, it sure is."

"If you don't mind me prying, son, how did you ever get your courting of Miss Meyers tangled up in this match?"

Sam smiles and says, "I'll admit, it took a little work. That's for sure."

The old man chuckles to himself and shakes his head in disbelief. "So you got the Meyers to agree to let you court their daughter if you win the match? Is that right?"

"I got Cordell to agree, and Helen got her mother to do the same."

"So what are you going to do if you lose?"

Sam looks over at the old man and says, "Mr. Felix. I never make a plan based on losing."

The old man admires Sam's bold grit. "Mr. Tanahill, that mindset will serve you well in life. Don't let anything ever change it."

Sam stares into the fire, lost in anticipation of the coming events of tomorrow.

The old man stands up and says, "It's been a long day, and I'm going to turn in. You best try to get some sleep. Tomorrow is going to be even longer."

The old man turns and walks off, leaving Sam with his thoughts as he dreams of all of his tomorrows.

CHAPTER TWENTY-FOUR

FROM UNDER THE EASTERN HORIZON, AN ENCROACHING SUNrise is starting to fade out the gallery of stars and their silver threads of light. The jointly owned, predawn hour is under a peaceful transition which holds the promise of a day that will answer every horse trainer's prayers, though some of the trainers will not like the answer. The warmth of the early morning sunshine is breaking the grip of a stubborn frost that still holds most campers to their warm beds.

Sam sits by his campfire sipping on a cup of coffee, oblivious to the chilled dawn and everything else except one fact— Little Jim isn't back yet. Felix walks up, pours himself a cup of coffee, and sits down facing Sam on the other side of the fire. He blows across the hot coffee and looks at Sam over the rim of his cup. "Little Jim weak behind the bottle?"

Sam tries to smile and shrugs off his gut-wrenching intuition that Little Jim is laid up somewhere drunk. "He was at one time. But not here lately."

"You worried he won't be here to ride?"

Sam smiles and says, "I would be, if we were the first race this morning. But we're the last race after lunch. When his eyes open, those fifty whole dollars will send him running."

"Well, he's your man, and I'm sure you're right. Besides, we've got lots of work to do before we need him."

Sam looks over at the Old Man with a hard determination in his eyes. "Yes sir, we do. Today is the day."

The old man smiles in agreement. "Race day, my young friend. The day we've waited for. You ready?"

Sam nods his head and points toward Journey. "I am. I just hope he is."

The old man gets down to business. "We're going to make sure of that. I want you to breeze Journey a little different this morning."

"Different how?"

"I want you to breeze him up against your saddle horse this morning. It gets his head ready when he's being challenged by another horse. Just don't hold him back. Let him get in front of your horse and stay there, but don't let him pull away from you. If he does, he'll run himself out before you can catch him. So keep a tight holt."

"So all I put on him is a halter?"

"That's all."

"Pretty smart. It's just a short race where we let him win."

"A horse is no different than a man. Ninety percent of winning any battle is believin' you can win. Then we'll rub his legs, and he'll be ready."

"I'll get saddled up as soon as it warms a bit."

Sam hesitates for a moment and the old man can see he has something else on his mind.

"I need to ask a favor, Mr. Felix."

"Sure. How can I help?"

Sam points toward the wagon where Newella is sleeping. "I think Newella there could use a new dress and a hot bath. I was wondering if you would walk her to town while I breeze Journey."

The old man enjoys Sam's company, and has come to believe that he is, by far, more of a gentleman that all of the elitist pretenders in South Carolina.

Felix smiles and nods his head. "Soon as she's up. I'll take care of it."

Sam reaches in his pocket, pulls out some money, and hands it to Felix. "Here, this is for the bath and the dress. And while I'm thinking about it, no need to worry about Paxton and his bunch. They won't do anything when they're sober, or when its daylight. But just watch your back any way."

Felix looks over at Sam with a little craziness in his eyes. "Never learned to walk away from their kind before, and I'm sure too old to start now."

Sam picks up the coffee pot and pours himself and Felix each a fresh cup. "Just watch your back, that's all I ask."

"You too." Felix begins blowing on the hot cup of coffee to cool it.

At the same hour of the morning over at Aunt Mavis' horse barn, Cordell is leaning on the top rail of Blue Rock's stall, scratching his muzzle and talking in a low, steady voice. The relationship between the man and the horse is one that has spanned many years, but it's an arm's length respect that has never involved the heart of either one. Cordell has his back to the barn door when Helen steps inside and pauses. She's not sure, and has never seen it before, but her father appears to be upset to the point of tears. Helen turns as quietly as possible and starts back out of the door when he speaks to her.

"You looking for me?"

When Helen turns around, it is easy to see that her father's eyes are still glistening. She doesn't know what upset him, but it must be of great consequence.

"I'll come back later. It's not important."

"Yes it is, or you wouldn't be here. So what is it?"

Helen's heart has but one wish, and it pushes her to speak. "With your permission, I'd like to ride down and see Sam before the race. I'll not stay long, I promise. I just need to see him, Father. I'm so sorry for hurting you this way, but I just can't bear not being able to see him. I just can't bear it."

Cordell turns away from Helen and stands there staring into blank space, lost in his thoughts. He understands his daughter's heartbreak and longings because his own heart has had him up all night praying that God has not taken Jolene. He hopes with all of his heart that she is someplace where he can ride over, take her in his arms, and tell her how much he loves and cherishes her. The fear that she is gone forever overwhelms him in a way that drags his heart back down into the abysmal loneliness he thought was behind him. Cordell damns himself for being at the race instead of taking her north to safety.

Helen begins to worry. "Father?"

When Cordell turns around and faces her, there's a sadness in him like she's never seen before.

Cordell looks off in the distance, then back to her. "Go on. Go on and go."

"Are you...?"

Cordell cuts her off and says, "I'm okay. Go on."

Helen begins to walk off, stops abruptly, and turns back to her father. "I hope they find Jolene."

Cordell is taken by surprise. "How do you know about that?"

"Petal ran into Little Jim last night. He was drunk and told her."

"Well, tell everyone not to say anything to your mother. I'll have that conversation at my choosing."

Cordell lives in a place in her heart that no man will ever be able to fill. "Thank you for letting me go see him, Father."

"Go on now. Just be back here in time to go with us to the race."

Helen walks back over to her father and gives him a big hug. "I love you with all my heart."

Cordell steps back from Helen and kisses her on the forehead. "And I love you. Now go."

Helen kisses him on the cheek and hurries out of the barn.

Sam rides along the Old Wheelhouse Road in a slow, easy pace trying to get Journey to cool down and unwind before they reach the camp. The light morning breeze has been just enough to bring the stud's blood to a rolling boil. With a bow in his neck and the dancing movements of a sparring fighter, Journey tugs at the lead rope, challenging Sam and Old Slick to another race down the dirt road.

When the camp comes into view, Sam catches sight of a familiar sunhat trimmed out in locks of sun-kissed golden hair. He is thankful for the two best gifts God could ever give a man, the love of a good woman and a fast horse. He raises up in the saddle and strains to see her in the distance, but she walks out of sight.

Sam looks over at Journey and smiles. "That woman never ceases to amaze me. I hope you do the same today." The stud snorts loudly, as if he understood the challenge, and his hot breath rolls out in clouds of smoke that billow away in the cool morning air.

When Sam rides into view of the camp, Helen walks out from behind the wagon and pulls the brim of the sunhat down to shade her eyes. The sight of his tall, lean, rugged frame riding a horse arouses every fiber of her being. He is the love of her life, but that is a meek feeling compared to the sexual tension that he has awakened in her body, a tension she is aware of every minute and every hour of the day. When she is in his presence, she is enveloped in a feeling of safety, a warm assurance that all is right with her world. She has come to see Sam for one and only one reason this morning.

When Sam rides up to the wagon and steps down off of Old Slick with the easy motion of a big cat, there is no doubt at all about what he wants. He ties his horses to the wagon and walks around to her with a broad smile that she returns as she eagerly falls into his embrace. When his lips touch hers, what hesitancy she had about leaving her father's camp to be there this morning is swept away. Their kiss is a long and tender reminder of the commitment they've made to each other. If their wedding day ever comes, their vows will only be a public declaration of what they have already declared to each other and to God.

The sudden roar of a lively crowd over at the track breaks the moment and draws their attention. They stand together, arm-in-arm, listening to the rising crescendo of cheers as the race unfolds. When the cheers die away, Helen turns back to Sam, wraps her arms around him, and lays her head on his chest. "I need to go. I promised father I wouldn't stay long."

Sam steps back and looks into her eyes questioningly. "He gave his permission for you to come down here?"

Helen nods her head. "He understands I can't let you go. Even if you lose today, I just can't."

Sam's upbeat tone gets her attention. "Listen to me. We're going to win this race. Then we're going dancing tonight, and tomorrow I'll escort you home. So smile."

She reaches up and runs her fingers through his thick black hair. "You remember what I whispered in your ear on the road that day?"

Sam laughs and says, "I do."

"I meant every word of it."

"I have no doubt, Miss Meyers. But on another note, I've rented a carriage for the evening."

"Pretty sure of yourself, aren't you Mr. Tanahill? I may already have an escort to the dance."

"Do *you* remember what you whispered in my ear, Miss Meyers?"

"I do."

"Then I'm your escort."

Helen looks at Sam thinking to herself how she loves this man with all of her heart. His boldness toward life makes her feel alive when she is in his presence.

Helen takes him by the hand. "Walk me to my horse. I best be going."

When they walk around the wagon to Helen's mare, she stops and turns to face Sam.

"You really do believe you're going to win today, don't you?"

The steeled look in Sam's eyes says more to her than words ever could. He pulls her to him and kisses her with a hunger that shows her exactly what he believes.

Sam turns her loose and smiles as he says, "I'll pick you up at eight sharp." He unties her horse and helps her up into the saddle.

Helen leans down and kisses him lightly. "I'll be praying for you today."

She reaches out to touch the brim of his hat, and then rides off. Sam stands there distracted by his dreams of their future together long after Helen and the gray mare have disappeared around a bend in the road. Another sudden eruption of cheering from over at the track brings Sam back to face the cold reality that he still doesn't have a jockey. With the noon hour swiftly approaching, Sam's concern for Little Jim is growing into a gut feeling that liquor is not the cause of his absence. Adding to his mounting stress is the fact that Old Man Felix and Newella should have been back long before he finished breezing Journey.

Sam is contemplating his options when he hears voices coming from somewhere on the other side of the wagon. When he walks around to investigate, he sees the old man and Newella coming across the campgrounds from the direction of the track. Newella is all smiles, wearing a blue-flowered print dress topped off with a floppy brimmed sun hat, and carrying a brown paper package. Felix can easily see the worry on Sam's face as he and Newella approach.

Sam forces a smile and points to Newella's outfit. "I like the color," he says.

"Hope you don't mind the hat and purse. I'll pay you for them and the dress."

"No you won't. I'm still in your debt, remember?"

Newella laughs and says, "Not after yesterday, Mr. Tanahill." She holds up the package. "If you gentlemen will excuse me, I need to hang this wash out to dry."

Newella turns and walks to the front of the wagon.

Sam looks back at the old man and says, "I take it you came by the track."

"I did. And there wasn't a sign of him anywhere."

Sam doesn't have an answer to his dilemma, but race time is drawing near.

"It's not like Little Jim to just not show up."

"You're kinda up against it here, son. You can't just put anybody in the saddle."

"I know that, but maybe he'll show. For right now, let's get Journey's legs rubbed down and get him saddled. We'll need to head that way shortly."

Sam and Felix are busy working on Journey when Newella speaks up to get Sam's attention. He looks around at her, and she nods off toward the tree line south of their camp. There in the shade of the trees sit two riders, looking straight at Sam.

"I saw 'em a bit ago, and they ain't moved. Just sitting and looking."

Sam walks out into the middle of the road to make sure they can see him. He stands there staring at the two shadowy riders when he sees one of them turn in the saddle and speak to the other rider. When he does, Sam knows its Ike, and the other rider is probably Paxton. The grudge that the two carry against Sam is a score they mean to settle with blood— his blood.

Ike turns to Paxton and says, "When he loses this race today and starts home, I want you and the boys to make sure he never gets there."

"What about the whore and the old man?"

"Slit the old man's throat and use the whore up."

"And Tanahill?"

"I want you to keep him alive, Paxton. I'm going to beat him to death with my bare hands."

"And if he wins, boss? What do I do then?"

"Nothing. I'm sure he'll go back to Shannon Hill with that little split tail daughter of Cordell's. We'll kill him and the old man when they leave there headed home."

Paxton looks over at Ike and nods toward the road. "Boss!"

When Ike looks around, Sam has ridden right up in his and Paxton's face. He has two pistols in his belt, a bowie knife strapped to his thigh, and a suicidal look in his eyes that chills the scoundrels' courage.

Sam's tone is vicious. "You gentlemen looking for something? Or are you just plain nosey?"

"Now Mr. Tanahill, the last time I heard, it's a free country. A man goes where he likes."

"That you can. But you and this crippled idiot better go somewhere other than around me. Because my patience is out!"

Ike cracks a phony smile. "Oh and by the way, good luck with the race today. You'll need it."

Sam presses in on them. "One other point before I send y'all on your way. My rider is missing. If he came to harm because of you, it'll be a grudge I satisfy in blood." Sam points at Ike and promises, "And I'll start with you."

The intimidation flashes in Ike's eyes. "Well he is a jumpy nigger. Maybe he jumped into something that he just can't jump out of, like a whore's bed."

Ike and Paxton burst out laughing and ride by Sam. He sits there for a minute until his adrenaline level subsides to a point where rational thought returns to his mind. He turns Old Slick around and rides back to the camp with a gut feeling that his feud with Ike is coming to a head, and soon.

When Sam rides up to the wagon, Felix and Newella both step out carrying rifles. Sam can't push the anger back enough to smile, but he's come to respect both Newella and the old man for their dauntless courage.

He nods his head and simply says, "Thank you."

It's a moment of camaraderie shared between the three that words would only ruin. Felix's mind is firmly entrenched in the business at hand, which is the horse race that's due to start in an hour. He walks over, unties Journey, and leads him back to Sam.

The old man offers Sam the lead rope. "It's time we make history, Mr. Tanahill. That's what we came here for."

Sam finally smiles again as he takes the lead rope from the old man. "You think we'll make history, do you?"

"Hell yes, son! This race will be a storied legend." Felix points a finger at Sam and says, "You're about to do what thirty-two men and horses have failed to, beat Blue Rock. Now let's get to it."

Sam's only concern is Little Jim, and Felix can read the doubt all over his face. The old man hasn't the slightest clue what they'll do for a jockey, but he feels that winning this race is Sam's destiny.

"And a jockey? What do we do about that?" Sam asks.

Felix looks Sam in the eyes with a staunch belief that's hard to miss. "Who knows? Providence got us here, and it'll get us to the finish line." He gives Sam a cocky grin and holds up his index finger, "in first place."

About that time, Sam gets another vote of confidence when Journey bolts to the end of the lead rope, taking him by surprise. Sam and the old man share a laugh at the stud's sudden show of eagerness.

Sam nods in agreement and says, “I think he’s spoiling for a fight.”

“Damn right he is. All of the great ones crave it.”

“Well then let’s go give ‘em one.”

Sam turns and rides off toward the track, followed by Felix and Newella.

CHAPTER TWENTY-FIVE

THE DECEMBER SUN IS STANDING AT HIGH NOON, COVERING the track with a temporary blanket of warmth that helps to energize the crowd. The majority of the spectators are there to see the legendary Blue Rock easily defeat another upstart rival who has delusions of fame and glory.

The gray stallion has long been a crowd favorite, and today is no different, especially with a seasoned jockey like Willie T. in the saddle. Rabbit and Sorrel cautiously lead Blue Rock through the cheering crowd and out to the track.

Sam has ridden up to the edge of the crowd and is working to restrain Journey just as Cordell walks up on the judge's stand. The adulation shown to Cordell by the crowd would surely be an intimidating factor to most opponents, but not to Sam and Journey. Sam rides forward and the crowd begins to part and fall silent, like they are watching a condemned man walk to the gallows.

When he rides out on to the track, a heckler from somewhere in the crowd hollers out, "Hey Tanahill! You can't bring a mule to a horse race!" The crowd immediately lets out a roar of mocking laughter.

As the noise begins to subside, Helen stands up in the viewing stands where the social elite are seated, cups her hands, and hollers back at the heckler, "Hey stupid! The only mule here today is you!" The rough crowd goes wild at the stinging comeback, but more so because it was delivered by Helen Meyers. Helen is sitting with her mother among a group of wealthy women who strictly adhere to the social etiquette of the proper southern belle. Jessica feels the scorn of the disapproving looks being showered upon her for allowing her daughter to be so crass in public.

She pulls on the side of Helen's dress and speaks to her through clenched teeth. "Sit down this instant, young lady!"

Helen sits down, and Jessica leans over to speak in her ear, "Outbursts like that will severely damage your social opportunities."

"Opportunities for what?"

"Darling, you know for what. To marry well."

Helen looks over at her mother and speaks to her in a clear voice. "Mother, I want to point something out to you. You see that tall, good looking man sitting on that horse?" Jessica is confused and embarrassed. Helen points at Sam. "That man right there!"

Jessica looks at Sam then back to Helen, lost to her point. "You mean Mr. Tanahill?" she asks.

"Yes, Mr. Tanahill. That is the man I'm going to marry! In fact I'm going over to be with my father, so that when I holler out again, I won't embarrass you in front of your friends."

Helen gets up and promptly walks down from the stands, to the bewilderment of her mother, and of the crowd of socialites her mother calls "friends." She pushes her way through the crowd until she's standing out on the track next to Sam. She stands there for a moment looking up at him, until Sam smiles and nods his head in recognition.

Helen turns to Newella and reaches out to her. "Come with me."

Newella hesitates when she takes Helen's hand, knowing that all eyes are on her.

She follows Helen off of the track with her head down and whispers, "You shouldn't be doing this."

Helen smiles and looks over at Newella. "Why? Because of what people will think and say?"

"People are unforgiving. You know that."

"Well first of all, for this to matter, I would have to care what they think. And I don't. I only care about what two people think, and both of those men love me unconditionally. Besides, who am I to sit in judgment? Especially of a friend."

Newella raises her head and lightly squeezes Helen's hand. "Thank you."

Helen leans over to Newella and whispers, "If you really want to ruin their day, just smile. It drives them crazy."

The girls share a laugh and walk over by the judge's stand. They stand next to the platform, just under Cordell. In a moment, he looks down at his daughter and winks.

The head of the race officials, Judge Stillman Adler, stands up and raises his hands, motioning for the crowd to settle down.

"Alright, alright, settle down, and let's get this match under way." The Judge turns to Cordell and Sam, and says, "Gentlemen, you both know the rules. You will caution your jockeys to abide by those rules or be disqualified." The Judge looks over to Sam and asks, "Son, where's your jockey? He needs to get mounted and listen to my instructions."

"He should be right here, sir."

"Mr. Tanahill, there is a set hour for this race. You have fifteen minutes to have a jockey mounted up or forfeit. Do you understand, sir?"

"I do sir. We'll be ready."

Old Man Felix walks up to Sam and says, "I know you don't like this, but go to Cordell and ask for a postponement of the match. Ask before the time runs out and the judge calls a forfeit."

Before Sam can answer, a kid runs up to him and hands him a red bandanna.

Sam looks down at the kid and asks, "What is that kid?"

"A man paid me a nickel to give it to you. He said you'd know why."

When Sam takes it from the kid, he feels something rolled up in it. He slowly unrolls the bandanna to find Little Jim's harmonica. Sam quickly looks up just as the kid disappears into the crowd.

Sam calls out to him, "Hey kid, who..." Sam pauses for a moment, until the message of the harmonica flashes in his mind. He turns in the saddle and starts to scan the crowd until his gaze comes to rest on Ike and his bunch sitting on their horses far back behind the crowd. Ike smiles and touches the brim of his hat in a salute. The anger rolls up in Sam at the realization that they've killed Little Jim, and now they're just sitting there waiting on him to forfeit.

"Mr. Tanahill. Your time is running out. You need to get a jockey mounted up."

Sam steps down and hands the old man the reins to his horse and Journey's. "Hold on to him." He stands there for moment looking at the harmonica and then he hands it to Felix. "Here keep this for me."

The old man takes the harmonica and puts it in his pocket. "Sure. What are you going to do?"

"You'll see." He hustles around to Journey and begins to unsaddle him in a breakneck hurry. When the saddle is loose, he pitches it over on the side of the track and walks back to the old man.

Felix is totally confused. "What are you doing, son?"

Sam looks over at the Judge and says, "I'll be mounted shortly, Judge."

Sam looks straight into the old man's eyes "I'm going to ride him myself."

Felix is grief stricken. "You're giving up at least seventy pounds. There's no way you'll win. Come on now, go talk to Cordell."

Sam continues to stare at him. "You may know horse racing, but I know this horse. We'll win."

The old man stands there for a moment in disbelief and then shakes his head. "Okay, it's your call. Let's do it." He turns to Helen and Newella and says, "Come here ladies." He turns back to Sam. "We need to lighten the load. Give me those pistols, the knife, boots, coat, and that hat. Come on, now, don't just stand there; we're running out of time."

When Sam starts handing him the items, he passes them on to Helen and Newella. "Here ladies," says Felix, "hang on to all of this."

When Sam hands over his last boot, Helen steps up and whispers in his ear. "Just like on the road that day. Ride like you're saving me." She steps back and lightly kisses him on the lips.

Old Man Felix says heartily, "I think you're about to get lucky, Mr. Tanahill."

Sam looks at Felix, who is pointing toward the judge's stand. Cordell and the three judges have their heads together talking. Judge Adler looks at his watch and finally steps away from the other men.

"Mr. Tanahill, Mr. Meyers has requested a reschedule of the match until the Charleston races this spring. If you're agreeable?"

Sam swings up on Journey's back and says, "I appreciate the gentleman's offer, but I prefer today, sir."

Judge Adler looks over at Cordell.

Cordell stands up and shakes his head in disbelief. "Mr. Tanahill, you're at a severe disadvantage here, sir. I strongly urge you to reconsider your decision."

Sam looks at Helen for the longest of a moment then back to Cordell. "Your offer is indeed generous, but I still prefer today."

Cordell shrugs his shoulders. "If the gentleman prefers today. Then today it is."

Judge Adler pulls his watch back out and checks the time. "Then proceed we shall. Gentlemen, it's a one mile race. You can warm your horses up between here and the starting line, but not on the track. When the starting judge raises the white flag, you'll take your positions behind the starting line. You will not cross that line until the starting pistol fires. Are we clear?"

Willie T. raises his whip and says, "Yes sir."

Sam raises his hand and likewise says, "Yes sir."

"Then proceed."

Willie T. breaks Blue Rock off into an easy lope down the side of the track, followed by Rabbit and Sorrel.

The old man looks up at Sam and gives a few last instructions. "When he breaks a light sweat, just walk him and keep him moving until the flag goes up. Don't let him stand still. And remember, you have to get in front of him for a short distance."

Sam nods his head and rides off.

The common thread of whispered gossip among the women seated around Jessica in the stands is Helen. The hollering out rolled eyes, but her standing by Newella Rayburn has the gossip and speculation running at a fever pitch. Jessica feels like crawling in hole when Suwanee Sue Jackson sits down beside her. Suwanee Sue is a bookend match to Jessica, except her ruthless social ambitions lack Jessica's sophistication.

Suwanee Sue leans over close to Jessica and whispers, "The match we've discussed is in serious jeopardy. Wouldn't you think?"

Jessica shrugs off the insinuation and asks, "How so?"

"It is quite evident that your daughter has made a selection of her own, and a poor one at that. And I mean poor in every sense of the word."

Jessica smiles and remarks, "It's only an infatuation. Come tomorrow, things will be as we've agreed."

"I hope so. My Will has been so looking forward to his union with Helen. If his heart were to get broken, it would be something I could never forgive."

Suwanee Sue's social threat sends a rush of anger through Jessica that she endures for the moment. It's a threat that will not go unpunished.

Jessica turns to Suwanee Sue with daggers in her eyes, and with words veiled in sweetness she says, "There is nothing between us here today that is going to get broken: not our agreement nor your little Willie's heart. Now if you'll excuse me, the flag is up."

The starting judge has raised the white flag, signaling the riders to get into position for the start. Sam wrestles Journey around in a tight circle near the starting line, waiting on Blue Rock. The gray stallion is spinning around, balking and refusing to come anywhere near the starting line. Willie T. is about to lose control of the powerful stallion and motions for Sorrel to come to his aid. Sorrel approaches the horse cautiously, talking to him in a soft, soothing tone until he settles down enough for Sorrel to get a hand on him. Sorrel stands there for a moment stroking Blue Rock's face and scratching his muzzle before he turns and leads the stallion toward the starting line.

When Sorrel leads Blue Rock up to the line, Sam rides Journey up, stopping on Sorrel and Blue Rock's left. The big man is standing in between the two nervous stallions, continuing his efforts to calm Blue Rock. He gently turns him loose, and steps back to the horses' flanks with a hand still on Blue Rock's rump. Everyone's nerves are on a raw edge when the starting judge raises his pistol above his head.

"Ready!"

When the pistol fires, it unleashes a force of power that crystallizes the scene: two picturesque stallions stretching out into a run in their fight to cross the finish line first. With their nostrils flared and muscles bulging, the stallions are soon flying by the spectators in a dizzying blur. At the approach of the quarter mile mark, Blue Rock is half a length ahead of Journey, and running in an easy, rhythmic stride. Willie T. keeps looking over his left shoulder, waiting on a challenge that he knows is coming. While Journey pushes hard into the bit, wanting to give him that challenge, Sam holds him in place.

When they pass the quarter mile mark, Sam lets Journey ease up to almost even with his opponent, causing Willie T. to lay the whip to both sides of Blue Rock. Sam takes special notice that when the whip fell across Blue Rock's sides, there wasn't an explosion of speed. As the half-mile mark approaches, Sam sends Journey up alongside of Blue Rock again, and this time he feels Journey getting stronger with each stride. The second time is no different than the first. Willie T. goes right to the whip, and Sam sees the same effect on Blue Rock. He reopens the lead, gaining back up to a length, but it's a hard labor.

Sam decides to gamble on a different strategy than the old man's. He remembers back on the road that day chasing Helen, that Blue Rock fought really hard to stay one step in front of Journey. But what happens when he's a step behind? Sam feels certain that the race can be won within ten feet of the finish line if he pushes on Willie T. and keeps him whipping on Blue Rock.

Every time Willie T. makes his mount surge forward, he chips away at his endurance. Sam prays that he is correct and pushes Journey up to a nose-to-nose race with Blue Rock. Willie T. responds, and Sam counts the number of licks from the whip, double this time, that it took Blue Rock to regain the lead. When they pass the three quarter mark, Sam pushes Journey's head back up even with Willie T.'s stirrup and hangs there. With the finish line coming up, Blue Rock responds to an unseen force and begins to open a lead on Journey without the whip. Sam panics for a moment, but then he remembers Helen's words: "Ride like you're saving me."

He lies down as close as he can to the horse's neck and gives Journey a slack rein. The big bay responds to Sam's rubbing his neck and begins to close in on Blue Rock. Journey pulls even, and it becomes a nose-to-nose horse race that swings one way then another. Within ten strides of the finish line, Blue Rock's head passes Journey's, and Sam's heart sinks.

Sam closes his eyes and rubs Journey on both sides of his neck "Now, Journey. Now!"

The horses blast across the finish line, and Sam opens his eyes only when he hears a woman screaming. He prays that it's Helen screaming for joy. When he finally gets Journey stopped, he looks back to see Helen running down the track to him. Sam rides back toward her and steps down when she gets close. She is running full out when she reaches him and leaps into his arms. She looks into his eyes for a split second, and then kisses him with an intensity that brings tears to both their eyes. While they're kissing, Sam feels a tug on the reins and someone says, "Let me have him, son."

Sam turns around and Old Man Felix is standing there, swelling with pride, happiness spreading across his face. "It was the greatest race I've ever seen."

Felix extends his hand to Sam and says, "Congratulations."

Sam shakes his hand and asks, "How close?"

The old man smiles that cocky grin and answers, "Makes no difference. You won."

Sam smiles and says, "From the bottom of my heart, thank you."

"I'll cool him out and look after him." Felix points toward the judges' stand and says, "I think you have some business back there."

The old man leads Journey off as Sam and Helen walk away arm-in-arm down the middle of the track, toward the judge's stand. They're laughing and whispering back and forth while the crowd grows around them.

Jessica is standing in the front row of the stands, frozen in place, staring at Cordell and trying to process what just happened. Her friends are filing by with an assortment of social opinions that their eyes deliver in caustic glances. Suwannee Sue eases up behind Jessica and leans in close to make sure Jessica hears her.

"Regardless of today, I'm counting on you keeping your word."

Jessica doesn't make a sound in response to Suwannee Sue's veiled threat. She stands there with her stare fixated on Cordell, who was on his feet cheering when Sam's horse crossed the finish line first. Jessica finally catches Cordell's eye and they pause, with a clear understanding that a fork in the road is coming. Jessica picks up her dress, walks down out of the stands, and disappears into the crowd.

When Sam and Helen are almost back to the judge's stand, Cordell walks down the stairs and out to the middle of the track. He stands there with a mix of emotions that surpasses the way he felt at all thirty-two of his past victories. Cordell knows in his heart that what he gained today in losing will never be equaled in his lifetime.

Sam and Helen walk up to Cordell, and Sam extends his hand with a respect that speaks for itself.

Cordell smiles and shakes Sam's hand. "Congratulations, Mr. Tanahill. Your courage today was beyond rebuke, sir."

Before Sam can say thank you, Judge Adler calls the crowd to order once more.

Judge Adler holds his arms outstretched as usual, and commands the crowd. "Alright, settle down a minute folks. As race officials, we have one last decision before we bring the day to a close. By a unanimous vote, Mr. Tanahill is the official winner of the match."

The crowd applauds and cheers wildly.

Judge Adler waves his arms and the noise level drops enough for him to address Sam.

"Mr. Tanahill, I would like to invite you and a guest," the Judge points to Helen, "whom I presume to be Miss Meyers, to a ball at my home this evening."

Sam nods a gentlemanly nod. "Thank you, sir; we shall be glad to attend." Sam catches himself and looks at Cordell, "With your permission of course, sir."

"You've earned it. You have my release from your word."

Helen squeals and hugs her father around the neck. "Daddy, you always have been and always will be my heart."

Cordell is surprised by an unexpected request from Sam at that moment. "Sir, could I speak to you in private?"

Cordell is confused by the secrecy, but follows Sam away from the crowd like he's requested. Helen can't imagine why Sam would want to speak to her father in private. She watches as Sam is explaining something that Cordell is listening to intensely, with his head down. When Sam quits talking, the men stand there for a moment with no one saying a word.

"What do suppose that's all about?" Helen asks Newella.

Cordell finally looks at Sam and says something that puzzles Helen even more. When Sam goes back to talking, Cordell agrees to something, and then they shake hands.

When Sam and Cordell walk up, Helen looks at Sam, and then at her father. "What's that all about?"

Cordell kisses Helen on the forehead and says, "Take Mr. Tanahill here and get him dressed. You don't want him sick tonight."

Sam reaches out to Helen and assures her, "Come on. I'll tell you about it later."

Cordell walks through the crowd searching for Newella. He finally sees her walking out through the crowd to where Old Man Felix is walking and cooling Journey out.

Cordell catches up to Newella and says, "I believe we have some business, Miss Rayburn."

Newella knows what business, and shrugs her shoulders in an 'oh well' fashion. "I guess you couldn't get my money covered, could you?" she asks.

"On the contrary. I got it covered on four to one odds."

"Oh God! All of it?" she asks in disbelief.

Cordell smiles. "And then some. I loaned you an extra two fifty."

"Mr. Meyers, that's two thousand dollars. I won two thousand dollars?"

"You did. Minus my two fifty. You've got one thousand seven hundred and fifty dollars."

"Who covered that much?"

Cordell loves this part most of all. "Ike and the boys," he says with the biggest grin on his face.

The joy is rung out of Newella in an instant, and she drops her head in dismay. "God, how will I ever collect?"

Cordell reaches and touches Newella's chin, lifting her head up. He pulls the leather pouch out of his vest and says, "You don't have to. I have every penny right here."

Newella reaches for the leather pouch then pulls her hand back.

Cordell is puzzled and offers her the pouch again. "Here, it's yours. Take it."

Newella looks at the pouch and then up at Cordell. "Could you keep it until we get home? That money could get me killed if folks even think I have it."

Cordell puts the pouch back in his vest. "That's good business. When we get home, just come and see me."

Newella reaches out and shakes his hand. "Thank you sir. Thank you for everything."

Cordell smiles and Jolene comes to his mind. "You've been a good friend to Jolene. She loves you dearly."

Newella looks off and fights back the tears at the mention of Jolene's name. "We became like sisters. But at first I hated her. I despised every minute I was in her presence simply because of her color. Then after a while, I came to understand that she was just a woman. A woman like me, with all the same dreams and hopes and fears and longings that all women have. She fell in love with you because your heart never saw color. You just loved her as a woman."

Newella feels like she has overstepped with Cordell by speaking of his relationship with Jolene.

Cordell stands silent for a moment, trying to find his voice. "She is the love of my life. If I've lost her..." Cordell pauses and looks away. "I'll never forgive myself for not protecting her."

Cordell's denial has turned into heartbreaking grief. He takes a deep breath and walks off with a sadness in his eyes that breaks Newella's heart.

Ike has been sitting on his horse, out of sight, watching Cordell and Newella talk. When he saw Cordell offer Newella his money pouch, Ike couldn't help but smile.

When Cordell walks away, Ike sits there looking at Newella. "Smart move, bitch," he says to himself, "but I'm patient. I know where to find you, and I will get my money back. You can bet your sorry ass on that."

Ike turns and rides away with an anger toward the world that grows with each passing moment.

Cordell is walking across the track when he hears Helen call to him.

"Father. Father, wait please."

Cordell stops and waits while Sam pulls on his coat and shoves the pistols in his belt. When they walk up, Helen can see the pain in her father's eyes.

Cordell is impatient. "What's the matter, baby?"

Sam extends his hand to Cordell. "I didn't get a chance to thank you, sir. Your horse ran a great race, and I appreciate the opportunity you gave me today."

Cordell looks Sam in the eye and nods with satisfaction. "Son, nobody likes losing, and I sure don't. But when you do lose, it's not near as bitter when it's to a man of your character."

Sam values that compliment more than all the money he won today. "Thank you, sir."

Cordell grows tense, and Helen feels a need to say something. "I'm going for a walk with Sam, if that's okay."

Jolene is on his mind, and he struggles to conceal his sadness and worry, much less find his voice as he presses down the tears choking in his throat. "Sure. By all means." Cordell points off toward the horse barn. "If you will excuse me, I need to check on Blue Rock. Sam, I'll see you tonight."

Sam nods his head. "Yes sir."

Cordell walks off with everything in his world imploding. These last two weeks have been a strain that most men could not endure. Helen watches him walk away, and she prays with all her heart that God will grant him a measure of peace. She can see that his burdens in life are taking a toll on his mind and body to an extent that she's never seen before. Helen looks over at Sam and reaches for his hand.

Sam senses her worry. "Your father is a special man. He knows how to manage life and survive. You'll see."

Helen always finds strength in Sam's voice and thanks God that He put him in her life. They walk off hand-in-hand, for the first time able to openly enjoy what all young couples in love need—time together. Unhurried time to talk for endless hours about the life that stretches out before them. Time to share themselves in the most private of ways, in both mind and body, according to the way God designed love to foster that process. Time to fill an empty space in each other's souls that makes their relationship complete and bonds them to each other.

CHAPTER TWENTY-SIX

LATER THAT AFTERNOON, WHEN SAM WALKS INTO CAMP, HE finds Newella getting ready to start cooking dinner and Old Man Felix brushing on Journey. Sam walks over to Journey and gently rubs his muzzle and face. The stallion responds by pushing on Sam's hand and nuzzling him like he's been ignored.

Sam looks the stallion in the eyes and says, "What you did today was nothing short of a miracle, my friend. A straight up miracle."

Felix disagrees, "No miracle, Sam, just a will to win. Very few horses have it and even fewer men."

"How strong do you think that will to win is?"

"After today? He's the best I've ever seen."

"I have a proposition for you. How would you like to train Journey? Get him ready for Charleston."

"You offering me a job?"

"No. I'm offering you a business deal. You train Journey for twenty percent of the purse. And I put up the money."

The old man is almost choked up by Sam's offer. "Son, I've prayed for a horse like this all my life. Seen a few, but I've never had one." He extends his hand and says, "You have a deal, Mr. Tanahill."

Sam shakes the old man's hand and smiles. "Now we are going to make some history."

Felix reaches into his pocket and pulls out Little Jim's harmonica and hands it to Sam. "Here, I figure you'll want to keep this."

Sam takes the harmonica and stands there looking at it. "Fifty whole dollars. It was all he talked about."

"Sure no justice in it," says Old Man Felix.

Sam squeezes the harmonica in his fist. "After I walked Helen home earlier, I made the rounds looking for him. Folks saw him drunk last night but nobody knows where he went. I'd go report it, but the law don't go looking for drunks, that's for sure."

"Maybe he'll turn up. You never know."

"I wish he would, but if he doesn't, I'm not letting it go. I'll find out what happened to him sooner or later. I promise you, I will find out."

Newella, rattling the pots and pans, draws Sam's attention.

Sam looks over at her and says, "Put all that up, Newella, dinner is on me tonight."

"You ain't got to force it on me." Newella starts putting everything back up. "I get me more than enough of that cooking at the mill."

Felix walks over and puts the brush up. "Where we going tonight, boss?"

"No we. Just you and Newella." Sam pulls some money out of his pocket and hands it to the old man. "They say Martha's Place sets the best table in town. I'd try there first."

"You're not coming?" asks Felix.

"Naw. I need a shave, and worse than that, I need a bath."

Newella has finished her rattling around and walks up. "Well, we'll bring you something. What do you like?"

Sam shakes his head. "I don't want anything. Really. I just don't have an appetite."

"That's understandable after today. But if you change your mind, we'd enjoy the company."

Sam walks over and grabs some clean clothes out of the wagon.

"Thanks Mr. Felix, but I'll see y'all back here."

Sam walks off toward town.

Cordell is sitting on the back porch at Aunt Mavis', having a drink of sour mash and staring into space. The unseasonable midday warmth is losing its grip to a chilled afternoon that's dropping the temperature down to a winter's norm. An afternoon of Jolene memories has started Cordell back drinking, against his better judgment, but better judgment is no match for the despair that rules his heart. Cordell's mind is lost in a barren land of regret when he realizes that Jessica has walked out and sat down on the porch. The silent tension between them is like a smoldering fire waiting for one spoken word to fuel the inevitable explosion.

Cordell braces for the onslaught. "I know you didn't come out here to hold hands. So what's on your mind?"

"You know what's on my mind. The race."

"Listen, I'm in no mood for a cat and mouse game. Explain your indictment in detail, all at once, and spare me the endless back and forth."

"You fixed that race today so Mr. Tanahill could court Helen. The fix was blatantly obvious when Willie T. didn't use the whip at the finish line. You've had jockeys whip that horse's ass to the finish line for thirty-two straight races. So why not today?"

"I read that message on you today loud and clear. Look, you're mad because you lost. You lost a fair and square straight up bet. This fix accusation is just your way of angling to get out of the bet. Now the race is over, and you lost. So learn to live with it."

"That, I'm not ever going to live with. Now explain the whip."

"The whip was a decision by Willie T. I asked him about it after the race. He said that Blue Rock had been sluggish under the whip all day, and he thought he had the race won. And to be perfectly honest, so did I. Who would have dreamed that horse had enough left in him to win? Nobody in their right mind except Tanahill and that horse believed they could actually win. But that's what winners are made of. And let me make one other point. This is important. That's what Mr. Tanahill is, a winner!"

"That's a matter of conjecture."

"Not with me."

Jessica rocks easy and silently stares off into space. Cordell knows all too well that her silence is just a temporary lull in the fighting.

Jessica turns to Cordell and says, "I want you to know I had nothing to do with Jolene's disappearance. Whatever happened, it was without my knowledge or consent."

Cordell detected a conspicuous tone of fear in Jessica's disclaimer of involvement.

"How do you know about Jolene?"

"I overheard Petal and Switch talking night before last. Petal got the story from Little Jim when he was drunk down in the quarters. And that's all I know."

"I hope that's the truth. Because I have Lanham and a lot of other people looking into it. If she came to harm, I will find those responsible and when I do, there'll be no mercy shown. Now if you'll excuse me, I would like to finish this drink in peace and quiet."

When Jessica gets up to walk inside the house, Cordell speaks to her before she gets to the door.

"Oh yes. On that fixing accusation, I better never hear that again. That's my honor and I will defend it, even against you."

Jessica walks on into the house in silence. She smiles to herself in satisfaction and doesn't particularly care if the nigger bitch came to harm or just plain up and ran off. The only real worry that Jessica has over the whole affair is that Jolene's found alive and Cordell puts her back in his bed at the mill. Jessica's personal problem with Jolene is not with Jolene at all, but Cordell. Her wrath is because he broke their one agreed upon rule concerning extracurricular sex. The sex was allowed, but they agreed to never take up living with a carnal interest. Cordell's moving into the mill with Jolene was bad enough, but when the sex turned to romance, Jessica swore a blood oath of revenge. It's been an oath that she's worked hard to honor, but just maybe it's gotten fulfilled without her having to raise a hand. She can certainly hope for the best.

That same night, at the precise hour of seven-thirty, Sam steps down from the wagon dressed in an immaculate black suit with a two-point maroon vest, white shirt, wide tie, black boots, overcoat, and fashionable hat. With the new clothes, shave, and a trim of his hair, he definitely looks the epitome of a young southern gentleman. Sam has never had a desire to join the ranks of the southern elite or even move in their circles, until today. The reason for that change of heart is simple: money. He doesn't so much want to move in planter circles as he does to move in the planter's horse racing circles. With Old Man Felix training Journey, Sam sees a way to improve his lot before he and Helen go west. There will be a large representation of horse racing nobility in attendance tonight, and Sam plans on being a little more sociable than he was when he attended the Meyers' cotillion.

Old Man Felix and Newella are sitting by the fire, watching Sam meticulously put his overcoat and hat on. When he turns around, they each try to hide a smile.

Sam holds his arms straight out from his sides and asks, "What?"

The old man gets his usual cocky grin going. "You look a little different from that barefooted Hoosier today. Folks probably won't put two and two together. You with a shave and all those fancy store-boughts."

Newella gets up, walks over to Sam, and gives him the once over look like only a woman can do. She straightens his collar and gives the knot in his tie a snug pull. "You'll be catching some looks tonight, Mr. Tanahill. You're the man that'll send every woman there home with a fantasy."

Sam laughs to hide his embarrassment. "Newella, that's not a thought to put in a man's mind. Not when he's headed off to a social party."

"Sam Tanahill, folks are folks. Rich or poor, that urge drives 'em all. That's the reason my business is always popping. They're all looking to scratch that itch."

"I'll remember that tonight, Newella."

About that time, Sam's carriage drives up and stops on the road.

Sam looks over to the old man, and then to Newella. "It was a good day. Thanks for everything."

Felix raises his pipe in a salute. "It was all you, son. Enjoy the night."

Newella smiles and points back toward the wagon. "Aren't you forgetting something?"

There, sitting on top of the water barrel, is a bottle of wine with a ribbon tied around it, a bundle of cigars, and a box of candy.

"That stuff won't make an impression left here."

Sam walks back over and picks up the gifts. "Miss Rayburn. Thank you."

"Relax a little and remember what my mother told you, 'Smile, Mr. Tanahill you're not going to the gallows.'"

Sam can't help but laugh. "Good night, Miss Rayburn." He turns and walks out to the road.

When he walks up to the carriage, the black driver tips his hat. "Mr. Tanahill?"

"I am."

The lanky young driver steps down and opens the door for Sam. "Amadeus, sir. I'll be your driver tonight."

Sam steps in the carriage and sits down. "Amadeus, you say?"

"Yes sir."

Amadeus puts the sleek team of grays in motion, and they start off toward town.

Sam finds it interesting that Amadeus speaks English and not the slave dialect. "I would guess the name has a story?"

"Not really, sir. My mammy's boss man liked Mozart's music. So when I was born, he named me Amadeus."

"I would say by listening to you speak, he gave you more than a name?"

"Yes sir, he did."

"Do you know by chance where you're going?"

"Yes sir. My master said, pick you up, then the lady at the Hawks' place, and take you to Judge Adler's. Then bring you home tonight. Is that correct, sir?"

"It is."

Sam rides along reflecting on Helen and how she's changed his life. His true north compass had never been steady until the second he looked into her eyes. From that moment on, his dreams of adventure and going west were brought to bay by her mesmerizing elegance. Her presence in his life has now placed his goals within easy reach instead of them being a distant mirage on the horizon. Where there was once only a dream, now with her by his side, that dream is coming to life.

Amadeus wheels the carriage up to the front of the Hawks' place and pulls the grays to an easy stop. The modest, two-story, white house with its neat picket fence is manicured on the order of a plantation mansion. The orderly rockers all lounge comfortably on a front porch that's brightly lit from end to end. Amadeus opens the door for Sam, but before he steps out, he pulls his pistols from under his coat and places them on the other seat under a blanket.

Sam looks over at Amadeus and says, "Be sure to watch those for me."

"Yes sir."

Sam takes a deep breath and prepares himself for Jessica before he steps out.

When he walks up to the front door and knocks, his mind flashes back to the cotillion. The look of never-come-back in Jessica's eyes was in stark contrast to the smile and the please-come-back look in Helen's.

The door gently opens to reveal a smiling Switch. She steps back with the door and says, "Come in, Mr. Tanahill. Missy is near ready." Switch points to the gifts in Sam's hands and asks, "Can I take those thangs for you?"

Sam hesitates, completely unsure of what he is to do. "Mr. and Mrs. Meyers home?"

"No sir. They wents to dinner a bit ago. You sure I can'ts help you wit dat?"

Sam hands her the wine and cigars and removes his hat. He nods toward the candy. "I'll keep this."

Switch places the gifts on a table there in the foyer and turns back to Sam. "The hat, sir?"

Sam hands it to her, and Switch lays it on the table with the gifts.

She turns to Sam and points toward the sitting room, "Would you like to sit down, sir?"

"I'll stand, thank you."

Switch turns and walks off. "Yes sir."

Several minutes pass, and Sam begins to pace. He is absorbed in thoughts of horse racing when he hears Helen speak his name. "Mr. Tanahill."

When he turns around, he is again struck speechless by her stunning beauty. From the ringlets of her blond hair to her off-shouldered bell dress, Helen is a vision of elegance that has no equal in Sam's eyes.

"Are we back to you being unable to speak again, Mr. Tanahill?"

"How could I not be speechless? You look incredibly beautiful."

"Why thank you, sir." Helen looks at the box in Sam's hand. "Is that for me?"

Sam hands it to her. "It's candy. Miss Martha there in town made it." He gestures toward the other gifts. "The wine there is for your mother, and the cigars for your father."

Helen is enjoying his discomfort at the moment. "That's very gracious of you, Sam. They'll enjoy that."

"My pleasure," he says. "Are you ready?"

Helen turns around and hands Switch the box of candy. "I am."

When Petal walks up with Helen's cape and shawl, Sam steps over and takes the cape from her. "Here, allow me."

When Helen turns around so Sam can place the cape over her shoulders, the anticipation of his touch sends a chill sweeping over her body. Helen has been held and kissed by a couple of her young suitors in the past, but they never aroused the deep, sensual feelings that the mere touch of Sam's hand sends through her body now. Her sexual desires have become a nagging source of turmoil that's constantly begging her for freedom. There'll come a time when she'll grant that freedom, but for now she'll continue to suffer with grace.

Petal breaks the moment when she offers Helen her shawl.

"Don't forget this, ma'am. That house will be chilled."

"Thank you, Petal." Helen takes the shawl and turns to Sam with a glow on her face. "Shall we, Mr. Tanahill?"

Sam smiles and offers her his arm. "Yes ma'am."

"Sir?"

Sam turns around and Switch hands him his hat. He puts it on and touches the brim. "Good night, ladies."

Sam and Helen walk out of the house arm-in-arm, connected by a bond that God has fashioned from their hearts and souls. Their conversation picks up where it left off from earlier in the afternoon, like they'd never been apart. There's an excitement to new love that sends two people on an emotional odyssey that weaves their lives into one fabric.

Amadeus has the carriage door open when Sam and Helen walk up. When they're seated, he shuts the door and climbs up to the driver's seat. He picks up the reins and smoothly puts the team of grays into motion.

"I have to confess, Mr. Tanahill, I was a little amused today when you told me about this carriage."

"I know. You made little effort to conceal it."

"You have to admit, it was a little bold. Were you that sure of winning?"

"I was. I don't know how I knew, but I just knew. Even when I decided to ride Journey, I just knew."

Helen teases him and says, "And what else do you just know, Mr. Tanahill?"

Sam turns to her and smiles. "You want to hear everything?"

Helen can't help but laugh. "There's a list?"

Sam pauses for a moment and looks into her eyes. "No, there's a future. Ours."

His words, coupled with the tone of his voice, reassure her that she has placed her heart and soul in good keeping. With a tender longing in his eyes, Sam takes her in his arms and kisses her with intense desire. The passionate kiss adds an eternal strength to the fabric of life that they are weaving together. As their lips part, Helen takes a deep breath and smiles. She turns around in the seat and leans back against Sam.

"Tell me everything, and don't leave anything out. I want to hear all of your hopes and dreams."

Sam wraps his arms around Helen and pulls her close. His narration of their life together in the far reaches of the West fills her with a sense of purpose and belonging. He describes in detail his dreams of a large ranch with lots of sons and daughters, and a horse herd filled with Journey's offspring. Their conversation is light-hearted and filled with great excitement about their life together. When Amadeus pulls up in front of the Adler mansion and stops, they're still talking.

Sam leans up and whispers in Helen's ear, "I'll finish this story on the way home."

Helen turns and looks at Sam and says, "You promise?"

"Promise."

Amadeus lets the step down and holds the door open while Helen and Sam get out.

"Thank you, Amadeus. I'll send for you when we're ready to leave."

"Yes sir."

Amadeus closes the carriage door and steps up onto the driver's seat. He swings the team around the circle drive and parks the carriage down by the stables with the other carriages and teams.

The Adler mansion is a sprawling structure whose ornate design and gardens are reminiscent of Roman decadence. The only difference between Judge Adler's guests and the patricians of Rome is their wardrobe. Judge Adler is a true Roman statesman, amassing great personal gain from political service. His political skill set has earned him one of the few fortunes in the South not derived from slave labor. The vanity that drives him is the only thing that exceeds the enormity of his Roman palace. The crowning jewel for his showcase of wealth is a twenty-year-old wife who's thirty years his junior. Her beauty is like that of his palace, flawless.

When Helen and Sam reach the front door, a young man in white gloves and tails opens the door with his eyes cast down to the marble floor. One step inside the door, they are met by two identically dressed maids in the foyer. They take Sam's overcoat and Helen's cape. When the maids step away, Helen and Sam are left standing there looking at each other.

"Are you ready?" Sam asks Helen.

Helen is looking at something on the side of Sam's head. "No, not yet." She walks around to his side and begins to comb his hair down with her hand. "That hat gave you a wing over your ear. It makes you look disheveled." She steps back and inspects her efforts. "Now. That's better."

Sam smiles. "I sure don't want to look disheveled. Of all things, not that."

"Stop it, Sam. Now what about my hair? You didn't mess it up when you kissed me, did you?"

Sam motions for her to turn around, trying to hold his smile in check. "It's perfect. Now can we walk in?"

Helen adjusts her shawl around her shoulders and takes Sam by the arm. "Mr. Tanahill."

They walk around the corner of the foyer into a reception hall whose opulence and size are a marvel that leaves one with an indelible impression. From across the room, Judge Alder's young wife, Danila, or "Dee" as she's known in social circles, walks over to greet Sam and Helen. Dee is a free-spirited young woman of Scottish descent with a mane of mahogany red hair and an ambition to match the judge. She tirelessly works and entertains with one goal in mind at all times: the advancement of Judge Stillman Adler's political career. Her desire to become the first lady of South Carolina is no secret.

When Cordell sees Helen and Sam talking to Dee, he turns and searches the room for Jessica. She's talking to a group of ladies when Cordell politely takes her by the arm and graciously interrupts their conversation. "Ladies, if you would excuse me. I need Mrs. Meyers' council for a brief moment."

Cordell leads Jessica away by the arm.

"What is this about?"

Cordell stops and looks Jessica in the eye. "We are going over and speak to our daughter and her escort, Mr. Tanahill."

Jessica steps back "Like hell I am."

Cordell smiles and takes her by her arm gently, but firmly, and says sternly, "Come with me. And be mindful of your mouth tonight, lest I forget you're a lady."

Cordell walks on toward Helen and Sam, leading Jessica by the arm.

Jessica's tone is scalding. "You know, all of this is your fault."

"I'm sure it is."

"I told you he'd come back, but you wouldn't listen. Now the son-of-a-bitch is here with my daughter."

Cordell stops and turns Jessica to him by her arm. "I'm glad he came back, and I'm thankful for her that he did. And I won't caution you about that mouth again. Now smile; you're a southern belle."

Helen and Sam walk up just as Cordell finishes scolding Jessica. Cordell and Jessica turn around smiling like a couple held together as marital hostages by the requirements of society.

Cordell reaches out and shakes Sam's hand. "Mr. Tanahill, it's a pleasure to see you."

"Thank you, sir."

Jessica nods her head and chokes on speaking to Sam. "Mr. Tanahill."

Sam nods an acknowledgment in return. "Ma'am."

Sam sees her disdain for him has increased exponentially.

Cordell turns to his daughter and stands there for a moment admiring her grace and beauty.

He then leans over and kisses her on the cheek. "God has created nothing of your equal."

Jessica takes Helen by the hand and says, "Gentlemen, we'll leave you to your horse racing."

Helen is put off by her mother's rudeness. "Mother?"

"Come along, dear."

Jessica leads Helen through the guests until Helen realizes she is looking for someone. When Helen stops and pulls her hand from Jessica's, she immediately turns and faces Helen. The two women stand there for a moment, each entrenched in their goals.

“What are you doing?”

“Why darling, Will Jackson is here. And I just thought you should go over and speak to him.”

The anger rips through Helen, and she trembles, trying to maintain a civil tone. “Let me remind you, mother! You lost that bet today, and I full well expect you to honor that loss. So as of this minute, you will never meddle in my affairs again. Ever!”

Sam walks up and can clearly feel the tension between the two women.

He looks over to Jessica. “If you will excuse me, ma’am, your daughter has promised me this dance.”

Jessica continues to stare at Helen. “If it’s a promise, then by all means, sir.”

Jessica turns to Sam and says, “If you’ll excuse me.”

Jessica walks off, and Helen’s penetrating stare follows after her.

Sam reaches out to her and smiles. “Come dance with me.”

Helen is visibly shaken, and the excitement of their evening together feels tarnished by her mother’s rude behavior. At Sam’s coaxing, she reluctantly follows him to the edge of the dance floor.

He turns to Helen and says, “She only ruins the evening if you let her. So please, smile.”

Sam reaches out to her and stands there waiting for the briefest moment. She steps up to him and forces a piece of a smile. Sam takes her in his arms, and in one easy motion they join the dance. The selections of the orchestra make the dance floor a popular destination for a sizeable portion of the guests. The orchestra is the same group of talented musicians, led by Mr. Arthur Milinski, who played the Meyers' cotillion last spring.

When Sam and Helen walk off of the dance floor, Cordell is talking to a group of men, and he motions for Sam to come over.

Helen sees her father beckoning Sam to join them. "Go on. He thinks the world of you. I'm going to talk to some of my friends."

"You sure?"

"I'm sure. Go on."

Sam walks over to the sour mash-drinking, horseracing crowd, and Cordell introduces him around. The sour mash draws out hilariously funny horseracing stories from this group of men who have won and lost to each other for years. Sam looks over at Helen, who is repeatedly turning down dance offers from the young and old alike. She glances at Sam every now and then with a smile that makes him more impatient by the minute.

After an hour of turning down offers of sour mash and listening to stories, Sam excuses himself, despite the group's insistence that he stay. When Sam steps away, Helen gives him a look that says, "Please come and save me."

When Sam walks up to the group of young women, he nods in respect. "Ladies, I don't mean to interrupt, but Miss Meyers has promised me a dance." Sam offers her his arm. "Shall we?"

Helen gladly takes his arm, and they walk off toward the dance floor.

Sam looks down at Helen and asks, "Would a walk in the gardens interest you, Miss?"

Helen smiles at Sam's offer and says, "I would prefer it."

When Helen and Sam walk out of the side door to the gardens, Suwannee Sue walks over to Jessica. Her voice is trimmed in a displeasure that's easy to detect. "Alberta Swenson is very interested in my offer, if you're not. She has two daughters, and both have Will's attention. And he can have his pick."

Jessica's anger is hard for her to hold in check. "First off, tell your little Willie to keep his pants on. And second, you best watch your step before we become enemies."

"Well I didn't mean to..."

Jessica snaps at her. "Like hell you didn't. Now just be patient. I'll work all of this out."

"It's your loss if you don't, and Alberta Swenson's gain."

Jessica turns and walks away, muttering under her breath, "Fuck Alberta Swenson and her pig daughters."

Jessica walks over to the bar and orders a glass of wine, then another, and another, until Cordell walks up.

"Ease up a little on that stuff, it's not water."

"I don't tell you how much to drink. So don't fuck with me."

"Don't you dare make a scene. You hear me?"

"Then don't give me a reason."

Cordell glares, his voice a low threat. "Remember what I said."

Suwannee Sue's busybody ways send her out the side door to the gardens. She is sipping a glass of wine, casually walking through the gardens, pretending to be looking at the different plants and shrubs. The gardens are lit by lanterns, with some lighted areas and some shadowy areas that are dappled with light. She is walking in the shadows when she happens to see Helen standing in a well lit gazebo by herself. Suwannee Sue is perplexed, because Helen has her hands to her face, looking down at something the hedges have blocked from her view.

Just as Suwannee Sue starts to hope for the best, Helen starts shaking her head yes and crying. The smile on Suwannee Sue's face falls off as if she'd dropped dead when Sam Tanahill stands up, takes Helen in his arms, and kisses her with a fervor that sends Suwannee Sue scurrying. When she walks back into the party, she goes straight to Jessica, who's still lingering at the bar.

Jessica flags the bartender down for a refill when she sees Suwannee Sue marching across the dance floor. As she walks up, Jessica holds her hand up and shakes her head. "Whatever you're back for, save it. I'm in no mood."

"I'm not either. You've been lying to me all along, and I want to know why."

"Spare me the drama. What have I lied about?"

"You've known all along that Helen was marrying Sam Tanahill. Why did you lead me to believe we still had a deal?"

"Where did you get that shit from? She's not marrying Sam Tanahill. You're drunker than I am."

"I wish I were drunk. Because I just saw Mr. Tanahill down on one knee proposing to your daughter, and I saw her say yes. Why did you do this to me and my son?"

Jessica starts to look for Cordell. When she sees him, she turns back to Suwannee Sue. "Listen to me. She's not going to marry Sam Tanahill. Not ever! Now just be patient, and I'll make sure the right man is at the altar."

Jessica abruptly turns around and walks toward Cordell. He's been watching the heated conversation between her and Suwannee Sue with little doubt about the topic. Suwannee Sue and Jessica have worked on a match between Will and Helen for some time, and now Sam Tanahill has derailed their plans. Cordell excuses himself and walks to meet Jessica out of earshot of the other guests. When they come face-to-face, Jessica's alcohol-enhanced anger is near a tipping point.

"I was told Mr. Tanahill just proposed to our daughter. Do you know anything about that?"

"I do."

Jessica struggles with her rage. "Did he ask your permission?"

"He did."

"And why wasn't I consulted about this?"

"Well my dear, you haven't exactly ingratiated yourself to our daughter of late. Besides that, you lost the bet. She has control from here on in."

Cordell sees Sam and Helen walk in from the garden and stand by the side door. He nods to the Judge, and he starts walking toward the orchestra. Cordell reaches down and takes Jessica by the hand. "I'm telling you now. So come along, we're going to announce it."

Judge Adler walks up in front of the orchestra and holds his arms out. "Ladies and gentlemen, if you would please give me your attention. Folks, your attention please." The Judge gestures toward Cordell and Jessica. "Mr. and Mrs. Meyers would like a brief moment of your time to make an announcement. Mr. Meyers, if y'all would come up."

Cordell leads Jessica up onto the stage with him and stands there for a moment, looking out at all of his friends. He feels a deeper sense of pride over his loss today than a conquering legion marching home victorious.

Cordell clears his throat. "First off, I would like to congratulate Mr. Tanahill and his horse, Journey, on their amazing win today. It was a spectacular display of grit and guts, the likes of which I've never seen. I knew that someday Blue Rock and I would lose. I just never figured it would be at the hand of this man and that horse. But when I got to know the man and saw the will to win they both had, I knew I had lost to the best. I was glad it was them, because what I gained today by losing this race is worth more to me than winning a thousand races. Which brings me to our announcement. We are honored to announce the engagement of our daughter, Miss Helen Simpson Meyers, to Mr. Samuel William Tanahill of Charlotte, North Carolina."

The volume of the sudden clapping takes Sam by complete surprise. Cordell motions for Sam and Helen to come forward, and the applause substantially increases when they walk through the crowd. The guests on either side of Sam and Helen are reaching out and warmly shaking their hands as they pass by.

Jessica is humiliated beyond all measure by Cordell's announcement. Her anger at Cordell for allowing their daughter to become entangled with such a backwoods nobody is a sin she'll never forgive. She swears a silent oath to herself that Sam Tanahill will never become the father of her grandchildren.

Jessica has prayed with earnest sincerity that if this marriage comes to pass, she will be struck dead beforehand and spared the social embarrassment. But for the moment, as social etiquette requires of southern belles, she puts on a glowing smile and suffers with a dignity that is being strained like never before.

Cordell gets the crowd to finally settle down with the help of Judge Adler.

"One moment please." The crowd becomes quiet, but the hushed whispers of gossip continue. Judge Adler continues, "Mr. Meyers has one other item."

"Mr. Tanahill. I believe the first night you met our daughter, you danced together to Strauss's "Little Doves Waltz." In honor of your engagement, the orchestra will now play that same waltz for your pleasure."

Cordell turns and nods to Mr. Milinski. The music starts and Helen stands there waiting on Sam to take her into his arms.

Sam leans in and whispers, "I think this is where you ask me to dance. If I remember correctly."

Helen smiles and steps up close to Sam and says, "Mr. Tanahill, would you care to dance?"

THE TANAHILL STORY CONTINUES